D0402515

"With David Cowan's book, *Navigating the Collapse of Time*, we get a fascinating picture of the transition period that is approaching for the human race. What kind of a transition it will be, and what nature and direction the illusory dream of time and space will take, is up to us, depending on how we choose our thoughts. I highly recommend this enjoyable page turner."

—GARY RENARD, bestselling author of *The Disappearance of the Universe*

"David Cowan has an innate ability to make the complex and confusing easier to read and understand. *Navigating the Collapse of Time* is quite a remarkable beautifully-crafted textbook for learning about our true history and preparing humanity to move into the next chapter of human existence. What David shares with us has a ring of truth that resides in our inner being—a truth that speaks to our heart."

—DR. JOHN GILBERT, Presiding Archbishop of the Universal Gnostic Fellowship

"*Navigating the Collapse of Time* stands apart from the other metaphysical works about this timeframe transition. Simply put: David Cowan lives from a dimensional place of synergizing all theories and academics around this galactic transition. A treat awaits the reader. While experiencing the beauty of David's word pictures that warmly download the reader with energy, it's as if a catapulting occurs into self discovery as it relates to past, present, and future time and planetary evolution, with humor and fun."

—CAROL CALVERT, Share the Light Community

"I have known Dave for many years, and think highly of his work, both as an educator and an author. *Navigating the Collapse of Time* is no exception. Dave provides an educated and insightful look at what is transpiring in the world at this time. He has done a masterful job of pulling together so many possibilities and making sense of them all, helping us to navigate an uncertain but exciting future. Solid information coupled with wit and humor makes this book a 'must read.'"

—BONNIE BOGNER, Spiritual Teacher and Facilitator

"*Navigating the Collapse of Time* has codified a tremendous amount of information and insight with a clarity that is also extraordinary. Dave is a tremendous teacher, a weaver of the mysterious threads of consciousness that frequently escape capture. I highly recommend this unifying piece of work."

—KEVIN JOHNSON, Shamanic Teacher

"David Cowan has brought the question of extra dimensional contact down to earth, with a style that cuts straight through to the heart—like a metaphorical sword of truth. It is refreshing to find an author who can create new perspectives on this age of transition, when the wisdom from higher dimensional beings speaks to our souls of all that lies before us."

—PATRICIA CORI, author/channel of the Sirian Revelations

"This hitch-hiker's guide to the here and now presents difficult truths and very practical advice."

—LINDA LAKE, Astrologer

NAVIGATING
THE COLLAPSE
OF TIME

A Peaceful Path Through
the End of Illusions

DAVID IAN COWAN

WEISER BOOKS
San Francisco, CA / Newburyport, MA

First published in 2011 by
Red Wheel/Weiser, llc

With offices at:
665 Third Street, Suite 400
San Francisco, CA 94107
www.redwheelweiser.com

ISBN: 978-1-57863-496-5

LIBRARY OF CONGRESS CATALOGING-IN-PUBLICATION DATA
Cowan, David Ian, 1951-
  Navigating the collapse of time : a peaceful path through the end of illusions / David Ian Cowan.
    p. cm.
  Includes bibliographical references.
  ISBN 978-1-57863-496-5 (alk. paper)
  1. New Thought. 2. Life. I. Title.
  BF639.C783 2011
  131—dc22
                                        2011006888

Cover Design by Jim Warner

Text Design by Maureen Forys, Happenstance Type-O-Rama

Printed in the United States of America

TS

10 9 8 7 6 5 4 3 2

CONTENTS

ACKNOWLEDGMENTS

I must acknowledge the influence of many mentors as I worked to understand this time in history. While they are too numerous to mention them all, I am particularly indebted to the work of Barbara Hand Clow, Ken Carey, Barbara Marciniak, Zecharia Sitchin, Carl Calleman, Gary Renard, Ken Wapnick, Brent Haskell, Tom Carpenter, and the author of *A Course in Miracles*.

I thank all those who sat through many hours hearing these topics discussed in our classes as I was "working them out" for myself. I thank Gary Leon Hill, editor, and Jan Johnson, publisher, for their faith in this work and in me as a writer.

I acknowledge my Teacher, who spoke to me so many years ago and whose Voice I am only beginning to truly recognize. I embrace my wife, life partner, and twin flame, Erina Carey Cowan, for her undying example of True Love and for handing me the "key." I celebrate my children and grandchildren, who inspire me and encourage me that there is a wonderful future for this planet.

Thank you all. May the Spirit of your love and intent breathe through this work.

Approaching the end of the mysterious Mayan Calendar, we live in troubling and exciting times. In 1995, I received a series of messages from the Pleiades that I channeled and then published in *The Pleiadian Agenda*. In 2004, I offered a scientific analysis of the Pleiadian messages, *Alchemy of Nine Dimensions*. These compelling intelligences from the stars insist that our species is on the verge of accessing nine dimensions of consciousness, and to survive beyond the end of the Mayan Calendar, we all must become multidimensional. Now we have this wonderful and enlightening book by David Cowan, which teaches us how to surf in nine dimensions, which David calls *living in vertical time.*

Living in nine dimensions puts us in touch with the pulse of our planet, grounded in 3D while we navigate the complex world of the collective mind, the 4D zone of our thoughts and feelings. Then our hearts open, we are flooded with visions of sacred geometry, we hear the sounds of spirit, and we are inspired to co-create with divine consciousness. The completion of the Mayan Calendar is gathering us together in a new experience of Oneness, the highest calling of our species. This book is a simple and direct guide through this accelerating process as more and more people attain enlightenment.

Dave notes that the intense period of our awakening began during Harmonic Convergence in August 1987, when we began a twenty-five-year countdown to our awakening. During this period of time, many memorable spiritual teachers have brought us critical information that has been challenging us to wake up. David describes many of these new views of ancient wisdom in a clear and thoughtful manner. As we begin to complete this cycle, we've achieved a *synthesis*, and this book illuminates the actual process of becoming nine-dimensional beings. In David's description of my model directly from the Pleiades, I find refreshing new perspectives on things I've struggled to understand. He suggests the dimensions rising on the vertical axis of consciousness are like children's stacking toys. I loved my stacking toy as a child, and I give them to all the children I am blessed to enjoy.

I've said that when we shift into the higher frequency fields during the end of the Calendar, misplaced 2D elementals (such as oil and microbes) will return to their rightful home, which for them is beneath Earth's crust. David's response to this idea is to wonder if maybe anybody who is wearing non-natural fabrics will undergo an embarrassing exposure! I had a good laugh about this idea, and then I wondered if the scanners at the airport are already beginning to disrobe us all anyway?

As I write this, I'm on the verge of going to India to teach Indians about the Mayan Calendar. The cosmic joke is that *maya* in their language, Sanskrit, means the illusion of time. So, I will be lecturing about a great big illusion! I'm diving into deep waters because the Pleiadians insist that 9D is the highest dimension, which they say is time itself, the deepest mystery. Considering 9D as a dimension that is even higher than the divine, Dave comments, "we see time as part and parcel of the imaginary projection of the universe by One Mind." He notes that the "end of time" that we are experiencing right now is regarded with dread and foreboding by our time-bound, egoic perspective. Yet, as we diminish our egos, we find we can surrender a lot of things that we've outgrown, such as the illusion of time.

Considering what time might become in the future, David suggests that the nine-dimensional vertical axis is the image to use. I never thought of that, so, as I let that idea sink in, I found I *could* grasp this sense of time being vertical, not horizontal. I visualized myself moving out of feeling like we exist in horizontal zones with the past to the left and the future to the right and me somewhere in the middle. Suddenly I popped right into the Now and felt all my boundaries melting! Many talk about being in the Now, yet few people seem to spend much time in it. We're still afraid we won't make it to the car repair shop or the dentist if we just let go. My moment in the Now is free, creatively stimulating, and blissful. Thank you for this moment, David, and I hope all of you are transported by this wonderful book.

—Barbara Hand Clow
September 1, 2010
Vancouver, British Columbia

This is a simple book. It is not intended as an academic work. Rather, it is intended to give you just enough information to feel at peace with all the tremendous changes taking place on planet Earth and within each of us here and now. Chaos Theory proposes that "Out of every apparently chaotic event a pattern emerges and a higher order is revealed, *given enough perspective.*" This book is intended to do just that and to stretch the horizons of your mind—to give you enough perspective to see beyond the immediate issues and concerns of a world about to re-create itself in the image of a transformed humanity. You are in the process now; you may as well become an informed traveler.

What I present here is a synthesis of thoughts that others have already brought forward combined in such a way as to create a panoramic overview of the Shift of Ages, which will bring about nothing less than the birthing of a New World and a new humanity—*homo luminous.* One of the key outcomes of this Shift will be a re-definition of time and an appreciation of the role of the mind and its decisions in literally creating the future. You may want to follow up on some of the information presented here or you may find that you really don't need more "data" to live and thrive in the moment. My overview is intended to help you appreciate that a Grand Harmonic Plan is unfolding on Earth right now.

One of the ways we will be looking at this Shift is through the lens of the Mayan calendar as an allegory for how life has evolved from very rudimentary stages to higher and higher levels of organization and sophistication. We will explore the Mayan "roadmap to eternity," ask what it implies from a dimensional perspective, examine the potential in our own DNA for radical evolutionary change, and consider a "revised" history of humanity that helps to explain how we got to our current state of genetic and social limitation. Then we will discuss what we can expect as events continue to unfold toward their prescribed conclusion and propose practical steps you can take to help navigate these changes.

THE BIG PICTURE

Why would you want to become informed about the topics in this book? First, because the changes everyone is talking about are real. Measurable and dramatic changes have been taking place on our Sun, particularly a massive weakening of the Sun's magnetic field that began in 1999, the year *El Nino* hit the headlines and kicked off a series of global weather events. Since then earthquakes, polar ice-cap melting, crop losses, brutal winters, killer hurricanes, droughts, floods, and fires have all captured the attention of the media and triggered speculation about catastrophic End Times.

These changes affect us as individuals and as families, and as communities and nations. They force us to realize that we *must* work together at a higher level of cooperation with Nature and each other or be overwhelmed by forces seemingly beyond our control. But in the sufficiently large perspective suggested by Chaos Theory—the Big Picture— I think these changes present a momentous opportunity to reinvent ourselves and our world, an opportunity to live in a "post-Shift" world where the damaging beliefs of thousands of years of control and limitation are overcome and the parameters of living expanded.

In everything that Nature does there is a plan. At one point we did well to know that we existed as individual organisms. Then came our awareness of ourselves as part of something bigger—a family, a tribe, a nation, a planet. Each shift or expansion in the progression has required a change in our frame of self-reference. An essential aspect of this growth throughout history has been the willingness to toss out the old paradigm and allow the new one to manifest unrestricted—without really knowing what that new paradigm will bring. We as a species have had to figuratively jump off the cliff into thin air many times before. It's time for another leap.

Now we must become aware of ourselves as citizens not only of this planet but of the galaxy and the universe. We have to reinvent ourselves to fit a more comprehensive and cooperative whole. We have to achieve a sufficiently large perspective, enter the Big Picture, meet the challenge of the Shift of Ages, and join the galactic neighborhood. Our galactic neighbors have actually been very patient, waiting for us to get over our dysfunctional dualism and egoic obsessions and join the greater community. Now is the time.

The Big Picture is fantastic beyond anything you or I can imagine. The temporary chaos we perceive or experience in our time-bound lives is giving way to a whole new way of Life. Once you know more about the Big Picture you will have the perspective to make informed choices about how you will experience this change—for change there will be. You can choose to appreciate, cooperate with, and celebrate what Nature is going to accomplish here or you can resist and deny the impending change by continuing to rely on entrenched psychological defenses. The change is assured, as is your freedom to choose. Choosing "not to choose" is also a choice. What is not assured and what rests on you is the role you will play in this historic transition and how you will experience it.

THE EGO AND THE WORLD OF SEPARATION

Al Gore appeared in the documentary film *An Inconvenient Truth*. I liked it. It was well done and had the ring of sincerity about it. But when I looked more closely at the data presented, its message began to ring hollow. Human contribution notwithstanding, what is happening on Earth is also happening across our entire solar system because these changes are primarily reflecting changes in our Sun. Ancient cultures knew about these potentially disruptive but completely natural cycles. The difference is that they didn't try to control or deny them. They took a longer view. They saw the Big Picture.

"Control" is the operative word here. Our exclusive focus on the human contribution to global warming is a prime example of classic egoic reasoning—reasoning based on the assumption that "I" have an existence unique and individual to "me," as separate from the Big Picture.

Traditional cultures did not institutionalize the ego to the degree that modern Western culture has. Most pre-industrialized cultures were intimately tied to the natural world—at least until they were discovered by modern civilized cultures. Before the recent tsunami in Indonesia, one small aboriginal tribe simply got up and moved to higher ground. How did they know to do this? They listened to the voices of Nature (or their own inner voices), undistracted by iPods, cell phones, and cable news.

Many ancient societies recognized the Sun as the captain of Nature. We now know that the light coming to us from the Sun is the primary nutrient of all life on Earth. Certain yogic practices involve staring at the rising and setting Sun and receiving all nutrition in this primordial form. As humans, we are all a part of—and not apart from—Nature. The very distribution and proportion of chemicals in our bodies is a holographic representation of the same elements and compounds found in the Earth. The air we breathe is a gift from the plant kingdom. Space scientists have discovered that astronauts cannot survive without replicating Earth's gravity and electro-magnetic signature in their artificial environments. How did we in the West get so out of touch with Nature?

Our divorce from Nature is, in fact, a relatively modern phenomenon associated with the rise of patriarchal societies based in the wounded-male archetype. In these cultures, Mother Nature became a force to subdue and dominate. Most early civilizations (9500 BC and earlier) were matriarchal in structure and lived in cooperation with the rhythms of Nature. They worshipped the Divine Mother or Goddess, who represented the fertile and life-sustaining—and sometimes destructive—forces of Nature. In a way, these matriarchal societies made more sense biologically. Females represent the original blueprint of the human form and are basically protective of their offspring, thus they are less likely to send their sons to war. In fact, geneticists tell us that human males are an altered form of the basic (female) genetic plan; a "second opinion" of Nature to ensure procreation.

With the rise of patriarchies emerging out of hunter-gatherer societies came cultures of domination, conquest, and separation—all based on a limited egoic orientation toward conflict and control. The ego, which I believe is the root cause of the world's collective insanity, is programmed to survive and to tame hostile environments, even at the cost of those environments. Modern Western societies have epitomized this culture of separation in their "war on Nature," played out in the thoughtless "harvesting" of natural resources and the mindless pollution of our Earthly home. They have lost all sense of the Big Picture.

Most of the people I talk to already have a sense of the impending planetary shift, betrayed by statements like "I can't believe how fast things are changing in my life" or "Even issues I thought were done with are coming up again on deeper levels." And of course, there's a growing awareness that decisions supporting war, environmental abuse, and the ignoring of basic human rights—decisions that seem hell-bent on destroying us all—are based on an antiquated mind-set rooted in the lowest aspects of human nature. This mind-set, motivated by fear, greed, and the need to control, is now being exposed as never before, particularly with the recent public disclosures of institutional and political abuses on a scale unprecedented. Once this process is complete, I believe we will all agree to agree to create a different world based on the equality of all.

Now is the time to put new principles to work—or perish. Too many vectors are now converging, with too much change imminent, for us to revert to "business as usual." We have global crises in economics, shortages of world resources, pollution, food degradation, pharmaceutical and medical abuses, terrorism, media madness, nuclear arms and unsafe nuclear power, and an out-of-control "world management system" operating on an obsolete and self-destructive course. In other words, *something's got to give!* This is something we can all agree upon. And the joyful life force within me believes that *something's going to give.* And that change will bring something wonderful, because it will be an expression of unconditional, creative, and benevolent Love—the only True Reality.

ENDING THE TYRANNY OF FEAR

This book is in no way intended to stir up survivalist paranoia or apocalyptic images of an End Time. It is a discussion of planetary changes—not only physical changes to our planet, but also changes within our personal and social realities. I am well aware that there is a tendency for this kind of discussion to foster fear. But fear is not an option if we wish to manifest the optimal outcome of the Shift of Ages. We must see fear for what it is, understand where it comes from, and then go beyond it.

The fears stirred up by discussions of planetary change and fundamental shifts in time and space are rooted in our physical bodies' ego-based survivalist programming. Some anthropologists say the ego evolved primarily out of our need to survive in a hostile environment, and it still operates largely in this mode. The ego actually wants you to think you *are* your body, and that the preservation of that body should be your primary concern. There are also deeper fears that discussions of sudden and fundamental Earth changes can trigger—fears linked to memories of war and seemingly endless human conflict. We all have different associations with the insecurity and trauma that human cruelty has unleashed.

Barbara Hand Clow wrote of another even deeper fear that plagues the modern psyche—what she calls "catastrophobia." In her book, *Catastrophobia: The Truth behind Earth Changes and the Coming Age of Light* (Bear & Co., 2001), Clow posits a deep cellular memory that we all carry of prior global catastrophes, probably occurring at many different times, but more specifically just before the beginning of recorded history around 9500 BC. Free-thinking researchers like Graham Hancock (*Heaven's Mirror: Quest for the Lost Civilization*, Doubleday Canada, 1998) have brought forth clear evidence of an advanced global civilization that was wiped out by natural events around this time.

Mainstream science recognizes this period as the end of the last major Ice Age, which brought a significant rise in global ocean levels. In fact, there are myths common to almost all cultures of a global deluge occurring back in the mists of pre-history. Memories of Atlantis' demise echo clearly through many world mythologies.

Clow tells us that catastrophobia is not a conscious memory, but one buried deep in the data banks of our DNA. Indeed, DNA is not a static blueprint or simply the plan for physical procreation. It is a highly sophisticated memory storage and transfer system that operates on quantum principles—literally, a cosmic library of all of Life's experiences from the very beginning of time held in every living cell. Apparently, we are all characters in the same Book of Life. Cellular memories of past traumatic conditions and dramatic change can emerge as an unconscious reaction triggered by present-day events. Knowing this is the case, we can be alert to these feelings as they emerge, and entertain the possibility of a new interpretation, based not on a fearful past, but on a hopeful future.

Accepting the ideas presented here requires a fundamental shift in the way we think about ourselves, so it is not surprising that thinking about these subjects can bring up some fears or doubts. The trouble with fear, however, is that it limits our options. It creates a kind of tunnel vision. Fear always results in some form of contraction—and contraction is not compatible with seeing the Big Picture. Contraction supports a compromised level of consciousness. When we are afraid, we tend to revert to the known, to past conditioning, cutting off our ability to think creatively. Fear dictates that the future will repeat the past. It is the "box" outside of which we must think if we are to gain sufficient perspective to comprehend the nature and scope of the changes going on around us. The cosmic joke is that fear is totally unnecessary, based as it is on the false assumptions of the ego as it navigates a shadowy dream world of illusion based on its own idea of separation.

So I encourage you to put aside your fears as you read this book and look around you with an open mind. You can do this in part by acknowledging that anything you can observe in yourself—including your fear—has already begun to shift according to the "observer effect," a proven quantum principle. Your Inner Observer—what Zen Buddhists call the Big Mind—is actually not fazed at all by any of life's events. It sits in a silent, eternal place smiling with gentle amusement at your life's personal dramas. The problem is that many of us today are disconnected from the awareness of this Big Mind, so we can't see the Big Picture. We take our first knee-jerk impression of events to be "who we are." We *re-act* based on past conditioning rather than acting in new and creative ways. But it's time for that to change. By picking up this book, you have demonstrated your willingness to consider what is possible. A path of greater understanding opens before you as soon as you take the first step. Congratulations!

SKEPTICS, CYNICS, AND THE DOUBLY BLIND

In esoteric traditions, spiritual learning typically involves the removal of "veils" of illusion, false beliefs, and assumptions to allow the natural remembering of what is hidden in our cells, hearts, and minds. Rather than learning what is true, we "unlearn" what is false. The Hindus call this process *Neti, Neti*—simply "not this; not that." The process of elimination continues until all the veils have fallen away from our spiritual eyes. The inherent wisdom and knowledge that is revealed in this "unlearning" is your birthright. The knowledge of who you are as a Divine Creation is in safe-keeping within you. Remembering and finding out is the great adventure.

Some of the information in this book may seem incredible to you. Some of it may not meet the requirements of solid "scientific" validation. Some of it may simply reflect points of view. Some of it may challenge you to "unlearn" beliefs and assumptions you have previously held dear. Most of my own personal experiences and deeply held beliefs would not necessarily meet the test of scientific proof. But if we go through life with the scientist's need to test everything with "double-blind" vigor, we just may end up doubly blind, questioning everything and accepting nothing. It is curious how this modern academic orientation to knowledge passes as wisdom, yet confirms nothing but its own skeptical nature.

This book is not written for those who want to argue facts. As it turns out, "facts" always represent a choice; they are a reflection of perception, which as we will discover is an unreliable roadmap of reality. I have learned that the motivation or purpose behind a question is far more important than the question itself. A question always stems from an assumption rooted in an unexamined past perception. And perception is always partial and incomplete—and therefore not in and of itself True.

Once, as I was being grilled by a group of retired scientists as I was explaining some new applications of quantum physics in healing, I realized that the room was half-full of skeptics and half-full of cynics. The skeptics were open to my arguments. They could concede that the new information might possibly be true, and were simply waiting for sufficient evidence. The cynics, on the other hand, had their minds made up; they didn't want to consider anything that might contradict the "facts" as they already saw them. They clung emotionally to a world view in which they had invested the better part of their lives, and they weren't about to entertain any "pseudo-scientific fantasies."

To the skeptics, I say you will be rewarded for allowing the possibility of a different point of view. To the cynics, I say return the book and avoid the frustration of arguing against the expansion of your own minds. To the rest of you, I ask that you accept that mainstream culture and established science have a huge investment in their own point of view, the advantages this has brought them, and the perpetuation of "business as usual." Do not look to a dysfunctional world to explain or even understand itself. Don't ask the patient for a diagnosis. Some of the information I present may upset some of your culturally inherited and unexamined beliefs. My advice is to consider whether beliefs that can be easily shaken were all that solid and reliable to begin with. Truth needs no defense.

You may, of course, regard everything in this book as fantasy—which is fine. I will not be offended. I have absolute trust that all Truth is self-evident—eventually and inevitably. Truth stands perfectly unified and harmonized with All That Is. What is not Truth, never was.

Despite brief moments of fleeting happiness on this planet, we are all afloat in a sea of insanity. I do not mean this in a negative or judgmental way, or to imply that I am a little less insane because I perceive the insanity of the world. I am simply stating that the fundamental assumptions of this world and how we have lived our lives here are built on a false premise—an unquestioned belief in a separate self. When we adopted this belief, we fell from a graceful state of Oneness into a dualist, ego-centered, and conflicted unreality. It is through our collective recovery from this insanity that we will find our way home. Forgive us, Creator, for we are all insane here.

As the mind is made intelligent, the capacity of the Soul for pure enjoyment is proportionately increased.

—Lew Wallace

BOOK I

NAVIGATING THE
COLLAPSE OF TIME

CHAPTER 1

GETTING FROM THERE TO HERE

As I see it now, I was blessed with never quite "fitting in" here. In the phase we call growing up, it usually felt more as if I were cursed, especially as a young person desperately trying to discover myself in the actions and reactions of everyone around me. And maybe nobody ever really feels as if they fit in here, as this *is* a very strange planet operating on some very bizarre premises. It takes real effort to adapt to a dysfunctional system, and it never truly works, as there is always this underlying feeling that, "Something is terribly 'off' here. Is it just me, or does everybody else know this, and if so, why is nobody saying it?" And "Isn't that Emperor actually *naked?*"

Maybe I was more of the sensitive type growing up. Or maybe we are all the sensitive type, and some are more successful in denying this to themselves. At any rate, I remember being out of step with my peers as early as the third grade. This was a time when the prevailing wisdom in education was to "skip" students who seemed to be academically advanced for their age. My dad was a teacher and my mom a nurse, so perhaps I was blessed with being raised in an intellectually stimulating environment. I'm not sure. At times I could argue so well with my mom, she often said I should be a lawyer. Lucky for both of us, that didn't happen. I know my parents loved me and did their very best for me.

It soon became apparent to me, however, that skipping from grade three to five was like sliding down the slide in the game Chutes and Ladders—from the peak of feeling smart and cool, to being at the bottom of the social pecking order—a "runt of the pack" if you will. No longer was I the apple of the teacher's eye; I soon found myself scared to the core and out of step with kids more socialized and developed than I. Whereas in my third grade teacher's eyes I could do no wrong, I now had a brand-new, very insecure, teacher fresh out of university who seemed to find in me a good reason to exercise her disciplinary authority! The other boys in the class were bigger, more self-assured, and better at sports, but not necessarily smarter. I've had a lot of judgment around "bone-head jocks" to get over, folks! The peer-group misstep starting at this point followed me for the rest of my school years, and beyond. Having a year or a few years difference in age in adult society makes little or no difference in relationships, but in the tender growing-up school years it made all the difference in the world. This sense of not belonging basically set the template for the rest of my school years, and well into my career years for that matter.

Please do not think that in any way I am whining or blaming anyone at all for these circumstances. From where I sit now, *all* is in perfect order, and I am eternally grateful for *not* fitting in to what I now clearly see as an insane illusory world. No apologies are needed from anyone. But at the time, I definitely felt like the odd man out. Maybe, on some level, we all do.

Then of course, the whole Hippie thing happened, and I found myself instantly drawn into a lifestyle that seemed to appeal to my alienated sense of self. This was right around the time of the Vietnam War. Even as a school kid growing up in western Canada, the war had a profound effect on me.

This was likely due to the fact that it was the first truly televised war. News and entertainment blurred. We could sit around with our TV dinners and catch the body count along with the hockey scores. What the hell was that? At an age when, developmentally, most youth are expected to question the mores and wisdom of their parents' generation as a normal part of individuating, and perhaps creating a world where some "wrongs" could become "rights," here I was seeing the abject murder of innocents ("It's okay, they're not like us!") for clearly political and economic motives. Even I, as a naïve 15-year-old, could understand that. I lost all interest in "making it" in a world that could sit back and watch this happen. Clearly, we had learned nothing from all the wars in the past. Clearly, this place *was* insane.

I remember a few years later, as a first-year university student, meeting a young American man who had just gotten back from Vietnam. My roommates and I befriended him because he had a great car and some good drugs. I couldn't help but sympathize with this guy, however, as he seemed hell-bent on obliterating his mind with dope— maintaining a 24/7 high that he was using to try to numb the pain of what he had seen and likely done. It was just so tragic. My disillusionment with the world grew deeper.

It was easy for me to drop out of university, move in with a band of rock musicians, and become a non-committed gypsy, along with many from my disaffected generation. As we all know, the world continued on its dysfunctional trajectory despite the number of societal drop-outs. But at the same time, a renaissance in the arts and creativity blossomed out of this movement. For me, I was able to survive on the fringe of the global war-boom-bust economy as a musician and private music teacher. In my own way, I was keeping the faith by spreading the joy of creativity through music to my young students and appreciative audiences. Later, during the 1980s, it was even possible to make a passable income, raise a family, and not go too deeply into debt by playing music instead of "working for the man."

But let me backtrack to around 1970. By now, I was a committed Hippie and had begun to dabble in meditation, Eastern thought, vegetarianism, etc. while playing in a rock band. I was pretty much looking into everything—except disco! A couple of years prior I had an experience when a friend asked me if I would like to pray to Jesus and "have my sins forgiven." Religion and traditional Christianity in particular had always left me feeling queasy, conjuring images of dust, cobwebs, and moldy old doctrines and empty rituals. Religion still feels this way to me for the most part. There is a definite distinction between religion and spirituality. These are not necessarily mutually exclusive, but they often don't mix well either. There was an innocent sincerity in this particular invitation, however, and so I said, "Sure, why not?"

Although I don't recall what I said in the prayer, I do distinctly remember feeling all "warm and cozy" with an inner sense that somehow my prayer was heard and answered. There was a new, tangible lightness in my being, especially when I thought about the things I knew I had done that hurt others. I felt less guilt, and that's a good thing! The friend went on to follow a path of fundamentalist belief that held no appeal for me (take the "fun" out of "fundamental" and it leaves "duh...mental"), but I did start to develop a curiosity about Jesus and the Bible, which I started to read and tried to understand. Life went on, but a new understanding—a glimmer only—was beginning to form.

My girlfriend at the time, later to become the mother of our six children, invited a couple of Jesus Freaks back to our humble flat. These were Hippie Evangelists who pounded the pavement looking for lost souls to save. They were clearly sincere and committed fanatics. When I came home to this rather unusual company, one of them asked me, "Have you accepted Jesus?" I told him about my experience with prayer.

He then pointed out, rather matter-of-factly, that the next step in the process, as outlined in the Book of Acts, is to ask for the power of the Holy Spirit in order to live more in alignment with Jesus' teachings, as the disciples had. This seemed reasonable enough for me, and the guy was sincere without being obnoxious, so again I said, "Sure, why not?" I don't know how much of this was just my being courteous, but I do know I was curious and had no resistance toward the idea of Jesus somehow being real.

I have not told this story to many. What happened next was of a deeply personal nature, and so I am taking a strong leap here in writing this for publication. But, as Sgt. Friday from *Dragnet* says: "Just give us the facts." So I will. Maybe something similar has happened to you or someone you know.

As soon as I prayed and asked for the Holy Spirit to fill me, I was hit, literally, with an energy blast the likes of which I had never known. It literally "blew my mind." I found myself immediately in a state of being where, for lack of a better description, I understood everything in my experience and environment on multiple dimensions simultaneously. It was as if all the TV stations available came on together at the same time, but I could still understand each one individually. Needless to say, this was staggering. It made the best acid trip seem like a mere preview—this was the big feature!

The next few days found me stumbling around quite disoriented. Yet I was fascinated as well, like an archeologist suddenly overcome at the sight of an immense treasure. I understood this was a state of expanded awareness, but I had no roadmap or set of instructions, or anyone to share it with. All this as a result of a half-hearted prayer? Thinking back, my poor wife must have been freaked! She really did keep her cool, however, and must have had some level of trust that all would turn out okay. Either that or she was secretly planning to have me committed.

The fascination and awe of the experience, however, could just as easily slip into fear. Sometimes my own thoughts loomed so large I did not seem to have a way to shut them down. The chains of my own thoughts could easily imprison me with thoughts of catastrophe and calamity that seemed to come out of nowhere. The biggest fear was, "What if I never come down? Is this how my life will be from this time on? How can I survive being in such a state?" I truly felt that if I were voluntarily to take myself to the hospital for a check-up, I would quickly be fitted in a white coat with oversized sleeves!

The energy moving through me was so strong and palpable that when I walked into a crowded room, conversations stopped and people turned to look at me with stares saying, "What the heck just happened, and who the hell are you?" This didn't help my inner freaked-out state.

Needless to say, these changes left me for the most part confused, self-conscious, and wishing "it" would just go away. As it turned out, it was about three weeks into the experience that I recall lying on my bed saying to God: "Look, I don't even know if I believe in you or even if you exist, but whatever this thing is, please take it away. It's killing me!" I was truly afraid. Then, just as amazingly as it had come over me, the energy left at my request, feeling like a cool breeze passing from my head to my toes. That in itself was a big confirmation that whatever this was, God was part of it; the experience was part of a bigger plan somehow—and it was probably okay.

As soon as the energy left and I was feeling normal again, the quest began. What was that? Was it Divine or demonic? Who could help me understand? Who could possibly understand what I'd been through?

As a "default" response to my experience, I ended up being a devotee of the particular band of youthful fanatics who had introduced me to the experience. What else was one to do after this? Funny, however, no one in the seven years I spent immersed in that particular movement ever provided an explanation; they just accepted me as I was, and I guess that was good enough at the time. I did, however, learn first-hand what a personality cult is all about, and how human organizations, even ones centered on an altruistic or spiritual path, all eventually succumb to the same process. I call it the "cheese principle." The cream rises to the top and, because it likes the power, authority, and respect of that position, refuses to leave. It then becomes hardened, authoritarian, and fear-ridden that it will lose what it values most. And so the organization becomes a tool for ego-aggrandizement. It is simple, really. I see it all around in almost every human organization.

Yes, I did eventually leave that group. The time spent there was the time in life when most of my peers were getting locked into careers, families, and mortgages. Again, I see the perfect orchestration of events to keep me from being totally drawn into the corporate-consumer culture of our time. There was another path for me. I was not destined to "fit in."

LOOKING FOR ANSWERS

The first source of information that shed any light at all on my experience was the biography of Sri Aurobindo, an Indian sage who was one of Gandhi's big influences. (*Sri Aurobindo or the Adventure of Consciousness*, The Institute for Evolutionary Research, 1970). Sri Aurobindo was educated in England over 100 years ago, returning to India as a young man to explore the depths of his own culture and religion. He talked about spiritual awakening as a process of "descension" rather than "ascension." In ascension, we try to get out of the body and the world, escaping, as it were, into a higher more pure state of being. With descension, however, we find the power of spirit wanting to join with us here in the body, creating a more integrated and fully multi-dimensional experience.

This seemed, at least, to begin to describe what I had experienced. I had been touched by the Divine, and would never be the same. The Divine literally "descended" at my request and left me permanently altered. I now appreciate that there are many terms and descriptions that could fit my experience. The Divine is not concerned about what concept or language we use to try to describe the indescribable. In one sense, I experienced my Higher Self coming through with a sneak preview of a future potential and maybe just as a curious observer as to what is going on here in this dimension. It is said that the conscious mind operates at only 10 percent of its potential. So even if we are hit with another, say, 10 percent of our total Being, it may seem like a stupendous opening of awareness.

I also had a sneaking suspicion that what I had experienced for that brief period was a prediction or foretaste of the future and that, if I were ever to return to that state, I would (hopefully) be much better prepared to handle it without freaking out. And not just predictive of my own possible future, but the future for all of us—who we could become when we fully awaken to our real nature as Spiritual Beings having a human experience.

More recently, I read of a researcher in the San Francisco area (John Weir Perry) who was studying traditional cross-cultural Shamanic initiations. He noticed some similarities between the emergence of what the natural tribal people recognized as the marks of a new Shaman, and what we call schizophrenia. These spontaneous events seemed to occur mostly to young males. The big difference was that in our culture we pathologize this sudden onset of a different way of perceiving. In natural societies, in agreement with the ideas of pioneering psychologist Carl Jung and psychiatrist

R. D. Laing, these symptoms are recognized as the early stages of spiritual emergence, and are treated with respect, even reverence. These cultures had a specific ritualized program in place to help young initiates navigate the disorienting process. In forty days, a new Shaman emerged, confident and in calm acceptance of his power and calling. He was welcomed into the tribe and afforded the respect of the people. Of course in our world, the person with a spontaneous spiritual-emergence experience is diagnosed as sick and all efforts are made to suppress or divert the symptoms by means of toxic chemicals, with the goal of curing the "disease" and returning the "patient" to the former state. (See pp. 343–345, Geoff Stray, *Beyond 2012: Catastrophe or Awakening?* Rochester, VT: Bear & Co., 2005.)

Perry thus set up a study where for forty days he simply supported the new schizophrenics admitted to his clinic and did not try to suppress or deny the validity of their experiences. The results were the same as in the natural societies; after forty days the patients were able to negotiate their new state of consciousness and integrate back into the world—to be "in it," but no longer "of it"—adjusted, as it were, to the formerly "real" world.

The memory of this time in my life and my quest for meaning proved to be a prime motivator for the next few decades, eventually pushing me to study psychology as an adult. I also found myself in a dual career of musician/music teacher and child and family counselor. The musical side gave me an opportunity to express feelings, and to teach others to do the same. It was "safe" for a male to wail on the guitar—safe and socially acceptable. I just loved the whole British Invasion thing, and am still a fond fan of Sixties music, blues, and *avante garde* music.

I also felt myself drawn deeper into the "helping" professions. I had an inner knowing that I wanted to work on the level of the mind rather than the body. The few laboring jobs I picked up did not do it for me at all! I also knew I wanted to work with individuals, as I felt social and collective change must begin there. It is on the level of individual choices that all other human activities and experiences emerge, I felt. As a youth counselor, and eventually a counselor for the unemployed, it dawned on me that many were running their lives on dysfunctional assumptions and beliefs. Many also were woefully ignorant in areas of nutrition and the cultivation of a healthy lifestyle. No wonder their relationships sucked, or they couldn't hold down a job! Running on sugar and caffeine is no way to be a well-adjusted human!

I ended up taking a certification in Applied Nutritional Science. The information in this program was so helpful and so grounded in common sense that I often ended up turning a normal counseling session into a nutritional consultation. And the results were great in those who followed through. It was what their parents, culture, and educators had failed to teach them about the basics of being a healthy human.

At this time I was introduced to some ground-breaking technology that took the whole field of Nutrition and Natural Health full speed ahead into the 21st century! Quantum biofeedback is a computerized two-way energetic communication system that can analyze and deliver "missing" or disharmonious frequencies at biological speeds via computer software. It is so far beyond our "modern" medical paradigm in theory and practice that it makes the latter look as if it were still crawling out of the Dark Ages! For the next decade I immersed myself in this field, eventually becoming a trainer and international speaker promoting the technology and Natural Medicine. I saw many "miracles" of healing and the technology, as all technology does, drew me deeper into my own inner potential.

All along the journey I had this burning desire to understand the historical period I was in as a potential portal to this new state of Being that was possible—not just for me, but perhaps for all of us. My prayer experience was always in the back of my mind. Maybe it never actually left, but was just turned down to simmer. I was magnetically, some might say compulsively, drawn to any kind of information that could shed light on the transitional phase in evolution I/ we appeared to be in. I read voraciously any material I could find on the topic of the Great Shift of Ages—from ancient documents to science fiction and channeled materials. For the most part, all of these sources seemed to be saying pretty much the same thing. There was a common thread weaving through many sources, creating different patterns but weaving the same garment. All of the authors I quote throughout this book and many others provided steppingstones of understanding, leading me to the undeniable conclusion: Yes, there is definitely something *big* going on, and it is fascinating as well as mysterious. And it is undeniably *good*!

Slowly, a coherent body of knowledge was congealing in my mind. My studies became the basis of an evening presentation I gave after hours in my biofeedback training events. I began to touch on the topics that are expanded here. People seemed to like the talk, especially how it left them feeling confident about the future. From no matter how many angles I looked at this present time in history, I was compelled to draw the same basic conclusion—that this is a time of "birthing" something unprecedented. This means we don't have a historical record or precedent with which to view what is happening now or in the near future. I also recognized that only one perspective by itself is not sufficient, and that a narrow interpretation of events is more likely either to lock one into a limiting dogmatic mindset, or simply create fear. I see fear as the great "blinder" that is being lifted, if we want it to be. Too small a view can lead us too easily to fearful conclusions, blind allegiance, and fanaticism. But by taking a step backward and gaining perspective, the Big Picture becomes most reassuring. And as I have learned, there is *always* a Big Picture because perception is always partial, never complete.

My journey thus far has been one of puzzlement, leading to information "showing up" in one way or another, followed by a new puzzlement. I have learned to trust that I receive exactly what I need for my own understanding and to be of service at the same time. I thank the Divine for "kicking me in the pants" all those years ago with a foretaste of the new state of Being—that is, being consciously multi-dimensional. With that experience as my developmental background, there is no way I can ever "fit" into this world, for which I am eternally grateful. The alternative for me is like wanting to fit in at an insane asylum run by the inmates! I don't think so.

And I am also eternally grateful to you, my readers. Clearly you are also emerging into something other than your former ideas about yourself (ego), or you would not be reading this. I thank you for having the courage to step beyond your limitations and the old "stories." I know this courageous desire in you is reaching out and positively affecting everyone else and the world that is being birthed before our eyes. As the hero of the movie *Avatar* repeated often: "I see you!"

Understand that the picture I draw here for you is of a changing landscape. Therefore, please do not grow too attached to any of it, or make dogma out of anything here. What is coming is beyond any of our abilities to say or predict accurately, so you are getting my best guesses for today. I do ask that you commit to remaining open to what Spirit has to reveal to you. Become an empty vessel so something new can pour in. An important prerequisite to receiving Divine inspiration is the voluntary emptying of your mind—realizing that all that you have learned and believed up to now may actually be preventing, rather than assisting in, your spiritual Awakening. Do not fear the Void. It is a place of Love Forever.

CHAPTER 2

COSMOLOGICAL ALIGNMENTS— REALITY'S MIRROR

Perhaps the most concrete thing we can look to as reflective of this time of big changes is what is happening on the scale of the solar system, especially in its relationship to the galactic center. The Milky Way galaxy is a spiral-type galaxy composed of about 100 billion (100,000,000,000) stars. Of course this number only describes the ones we can see, or whose luminosity we can measure. Further, ours is one of billions of galaxies. Most of the matter in the galaxy is beyond our limited perception. Scientists know there must be a lot more matter in the galaxy and universe than we can see because the gravitational effects of this "invisible" matter can be measured. Curiously, the proportion of missing matter in the galaxy is just about the same as the proportion of the brain it is said we don't consciously use. Is there a connection between our current limit of perception "in here" and what we call reality "out there?" More on this possibility later.

THE GALACTIC CORE

The galactic core is where all the real action is. The luminescence or brightness there is 20 million times that of our Sun. This is an unimaginable amount of energy! I have a hard time imagining a place that's just 100 times as bright as the Sun. In the galactic core, stars, planets, and vast fields of space gas converge in a relatively compacted state. The rate of motion here is also highly accelerated compared to what we see in the local community of stars and planets around us. The farther out you go from the center of the Milky Way, the more the stars are separated by space and the slower the rotation rate around the galactic center. At the center of the galaxy and providing the gravitational hub of the wheel is a gigantic spinning vortex called a Black Hole. It is named thus because the gravity here is so intense that all matter in the vicinity of the Black Hole—even light, the basic building block of matter—is sucked into this vortex and disappears, transported to who knows where. Some suggest the "other side" may just be another Black Hole in this or another universe—a "White Hole." We know that matter and energy (as interchangeable, thanks Einstein!) cannot be destroyed; it can only be moved or transmuted into another form, so all this matter/ energy is going somewhere.

Things must be pretty wild and crazy near the edge of the Black Hole. I remember the Disney movie of that title in the 1980s providing a pretty graphic depiction of what it might be like to get too close to the edge. Whoa! Look out! Here we go into the great sucking vortex.

Even though the center is where all the action is in the galaxy, we can't see it from where we are. Our solar system is about two thirds out from the center between two of the arms of the galaxy. This is an advantageous position to be in for viewing, as the local star systems are not as compact as they would be if we were inside one of the arms or closer to the galactic center. We have a moderately good view of stars in the galaxy, as well as a clear view of Deep Space outside the galaxy. However, between us and the galactic center is an awful lot of matter, obscuring practically all light from the center. Astronomers can "see" the center, however, with specialized types of telescopes that measure infrared, x-ray, and other frequencies beyond visible light.

A few years ago, I toured the archeological site at Monte Alban near the city of Oaxaca in Mexico, a site erected around 660 AD by the Zapotec culture. There, I saw a five-sided building with the pointy side aimed directly at the galactic center. How did the people of this culture know this? I think I have an idea now, but we'll get to that later.

You can find the galactic center yourself if you are fortunate enough to live where the light pollution from city lights doesn't obscure the stars above. On a clear night, go out and look at the Milky Way. It will show up as a massive band of stars and grey-looking stuff stretching overhead from horizon to horizon. Binoculars make the experience so much richer. If you've never seen this, you owe yourself a camping trip outside the city. If you plan your trip near a New Moon, all the better, as a Full Moon on a clear night will obscure many stars from view. (A Full Moon puts out one seventh the luminosity of the Sun). If you have a simple star map, available at most science or hobby shops or free on the Internet, locate the constellation Sagittarius. Look at the tip of the arrow he is holding in his bow and you'll be looking right in the direction of the galactic center. Take a moment, get nice and still, and try to *feel* your connection to all the stars you see. It is an awesome sensation to feel you are *in* the galaxy sharing the same gravitational dance with every heavenly body you can see. Talk about a sense of place!

Not all of the matter spilling into the Black Hole is disappearing, however. Right at the very edge of the hole, an area known as the "event horizon," matter is torn apart right down to its fundamental state, which is light. Most of the light disappears into the hole, but a significant amount of light energy is also released from the rim of the event horizon back out into the galactic wheel. The light then radiates out into the rest of the galaxy as a thin band of extra light called the photon band. A photon is a quantum, or smallest possible particle, of light. The galactic light in the photon band is of a very high frequency, or vibration—in the gamma range and beyond. These are "higher octaves" of light beyond our ability to measure. They are thus "metaphysical" or what some may call forms of spiritual light. Gamma radiation is among the highest measurable forms of radiation, and has been linked to genetic mutations. The effect of the photon band on human life will be more apparent when we look at the nature of our DNA, and some of the potentials that lie dormant within it now.

This band of light was first noticed in modern times in the early Sixties at Lowell Observatory in Flagstaff, Arizona. It was also observed that our solar system was moving toward this band and would eventually be engulfed by it. I haven't heard any discussion from the mainstream media of this—although you'd think this would be big news, wouldn't you?

THE GREAT YEAR

Here's where the story gets a little complicated, but incredibly fascinating. It turns out that our entire solar system rotates in a 26,000-year cycle known as the Great Year in former informed cultures. The ancient Vedic culture, Sumerians, Egyptians, and Chinese knew of this cycle, as did the Mayans, Incas, and Aztecs. As it takes seventy-two years to progress only one degree through the cycle, obviously the knowledge of the ancients was not based on any individual's observation. It must have been based in the accumulated knowledge of a large number of educated generations, or on knowledge from some outside source. The complex calendars of these societies charted multiple patterns within this cycle, and they were able to be somewhat predictive of future events based on this deep knowledge of cycles.

The Great Year is responsible for what we in the West notice as the precession of the equinoxes—the gradual change in our alignment with the various constellations around us accounting for the different "ages" of the zodiac. With each age lasting around 2160 years, multiplied by the twelve signs of the zodiac, you get, voilà, 25,920 years. Most astronomers attribute the precession of these constellations to a "wobble" in the Earth's axis, but this notion is thoroughly investigated and challenged in Walter Cruttenden's recent book, *The Lost Star of Myth and Time* (St. Lynn's Press, 2006). The lost star he refers to is the "twin" of our Sun—our gravitational "dance partner" holding the center of the 26,000-year orbit responsible for the observed changes in the position of stars around us. The top candidate for this relatively fixed star is Alcyone, the great central sun in the Pleiades star group. It would actually be statistically rare for our Sun *not* to be bound gravitationally to one, two, or even more stars, as this is the norm when we look out at our stellar neighbors. Stars are like people, I guess. We would much rather dance with another than alone.

It is interesting how many ancient cultures looked at the Pleiades as (one of) humanity's ancient sources. In Barbara Clow's excellent book *The Pleiadian Agenda* (Bear & Co., 1996), she describes how the Pleiades sit in the galactic photon band all the time, anchoring and reflecting for us, as it were, the galactic light energy even when our solar system is out of the beam, which is most of the time. This may be one reason ancient cultures looked to and revered the Pleiades as it reflects to us galactic light, and thus spiritual Light, even as we traverse the galactic night outside the photon band. The Pleiades serves as our "galactic connection," reflecting spiritual Light to us at all times throughout the Great Year.

But let me backtrack here. Do you have a clear mental image of the band of light spreading out through the galaxy, like a thin wafer smack in the middle plane of the wheel? Well, at two points in our 26,000-year cycle, the entire solar system passes through the galactic photon band. Calculations indicate that it takes about 1000 years for our solar system to traverse the main body of the photon band before emerging back out into the galactic night. As you may have guessed, this is actually where we are at this point in time— at the entry gate of the galactic photon band.

The year 1986, identified by Jose Argüelles and others as the year of the Harmonic Convergence, marked the beginning of a 25-year countdown to planetary initiation into the photon band. If you do the math, that brings us to the year 2012. If you have not seen this year mentioned in some context in the past few years, I'm afraid you're just not paying attention!

In 1986, as the Sun approached the primary boundary of the photon band, the Earth itself began to dip periodically into the band. Initially, this was only for a period of a few weeks a year, with the Earth being exposed for longer periods as each year passed. You can see Nature's elegant plan for our gradual initiation into this region of intense energy. If we were to be totally immersed all at once, it might not go so well for life on Earth. The Mayans had a term for this 25-year transitional period—the Time of No Time, indicating that by the time it's over, post-2012, time as we know it or experience it may not exist at all. Or at least our relationship to time will have changed dramatically.

If you look closely at the nature of time, you will see it is no more than a construct of the mind—something we have made up to explain the unfolding of events in this dimension. We separate and tie events together by assuming a cause-and-effect relationship between them. It doesn't take much insight to appreciate that assumptions of cause and effect are seriously limiting, as they do not take into account any other factors that go into any specific experience other than what we in our own conditioning expect or assume. In a larger reality—in the Big Picture—everything that has ever happened at any time is a cause of or precursor to our current experience. The ultimate cause of everything here is the Big Bang. And what caused that? So to say A caused B is seriously flawed and limited logic.

The principle we are describing is referred to as "quantum entanglement" by quantum physicists, who say everything in time and space is connected. Thus, the beating of a butterfly's wings can "cause" a storm on the other side of the world. Here we see another good example of how perception is essentially illusory—a functional illusion in terms of our experience here perhaps, but essentially *not real*.

We all know how the experience of time can be quite variable, depending on our psychological state. Time feels completely different in a dentist's chair than when we are enjoying a good movie, for example. When we look closer at the Mayan calendar, we will see how the Maya accounted for the flexible nature of time, and even described what we are now experiencing as the "speeding up of time." Actually, the flow of time hasn't changed, but the amount of awareness or light (information) coming into the world as we move into the photon band has greatly accelerated, creating more experience in less time, which is perceived by us as compressed increments of time. This breakdown and reconstruction phase of our experience of time will continue to accelerate thus at exponential rates! If time is, however, a construct of the mind, what is implied here is that it is the mind, or consciousness itself, that is changing and evolving. This would be a more accurate picture of what is happening, I believe. Remember, it's *all* an inside job!

Actually, the Earth has been feeling the influence of the photon band for at least the last 500 years. Witness the

Renaissance, with the invention of the printing press, the rediscovery of art, music, and romantic love, and the ending of the Dark Ages. These were the early murmurings of awakening planetary consciousness. Now, however, the alarm clock has gone off, and there's no time to stay asleep. If this observation is accurate, there is likely going to be a 500-year "decompression" phase once we go through the band in 1000 years. The entire photon-band experience can thus be viewed as a 2000-year process in total—that is, 500 years pre-entry + 1000 years in the band + 500 years post-exit. Settle in folks, the ride's just beginning.

We cannot consider the impact of entering into this region of intensified light in space without considering the electro-magnetic implications for life. The electro-magnetic field of the Earth is generated by internal processes, as is that of the Sun, I presume. When the Sun entered the photon band in 1999 as predicted by the Mayan Calendar (more on this later), its magnetic field was observed by NASA to have, in their words, "collapsed," because it was no longer entirely dependent on internal nuclear processes to maintain a stable energetic output. It was receiving an outside injection of light energy from the galactic center, and thus took an energetic vacation.

An electro-magnetic field acts as a limiter on ambient frequency. So when this field drops in a system like the Sun, huge amounts of energy are released as frequencies that affect energy and matter. We witnessed this as the release of solar flares so intense that they broke and continue to break all previous records. It is these flares and the subsequent effect of solar winds on Earth that is primarily responsible for the weather extremes of the last decade— not carbon emissions or other Earth-caused factors claimed by those who prefer that we not look at the Big Picture.

Earth's magnetic field, in sympathy with Sun's massive field, is also dropping. We see as a result the measureable drifting of the magnetic poles, a process that may predict an eventual magnetic collapse and repositioning of the poles on Earth. According to geologists, this has actually occurred many times in the past, as revealed in the changes in the magnetic alignment of iron-core samples going back eons in time. We will visit the possible psychic and spiritual implications of this electro-magnetic shift in a later section. As we'll see, these solar and planetary changes play a significant part in providing an understanding of at least the physical basis for this time of monumental change.

If we are at the critical jumping off point now, and given that the solar system traverses the band twice in its 26,000-year cycle, then the last time we went through must have been around 13,000 years ago, or around 11,000 BC. Coincidentally (or not!), this time coincides with the end of the last major Ice Age, accompanied by cataclysmic changes on the Earth involving a dramatic rise in ocean levels. Some archeologists have decided that the damage to the surface of the Egyptian Sphinx could only have been caused by massive amounts of water moving as a giant torrent around this time. Moreover, it was recently discovered that the size and spatial relationship of the three main pyramids in Egypt match exactly the positions of the three main stars in Orion's belt *as they would have appeared on the horizon in 10,500 BC*. Robert Bauval and Adrian Gilbert suggest that this was an intentional "message" left to mark an important date for future generations (*The Orion Mystery: Unlocking the Secrets of The Pyramids*, Three Rivers Press, 1994).

Looking at the Grand Canyon one can imagine a huge inland sea rapidly draining into the Pacific and carving out massive amounts of earth in the process. The gradualists would have us believe the canyon was carved out over eons by a river the volume of the existing Colorado River, which is much harder to imagine!

The Vedic version of the Great Year has a unique perspective on the rise and fall of consciousness and civilizations throughout the cycle. This system of ages, referred to as *Yugas,* is described in Swami Sri Yukteswar's *The Holy Science* (Self Realization Fellowship, 1949). The Yuga system looks at how the solar system declines into ages of lower consciousness for half of the cycle as we move away from our gravitational twin and galactic influence, while we experience a rise in consciousness during the approach phase. The rising-consciousness phase culminates in a Golden Age where humanity enjoys the fruits of its highest potentials for a while. A major implication here is that there have been prior Golden Ages, perhaps many—which coincides with what survives as stories and what we assume are "myths" telling of ancient advanced societies. The dark phases of the cycle are marked by a decline of human culture into materialism and spiritual ignorance. Hmm...this sounds too familiar! According to the Yuga system, the cycle turned from the downside to the upside as recently as 500 AD. Although this time period was followed by the Dark Ages in the West, there was a gradual rising of consciousness from this point forward—perhaps just a seed that has been growing with exponential speed of late.

It is now appreciated by some that around 10,500 BC and before, the planet hosted a global society that was linked not only by shared technology and science, but by a worldwide network of sacred temples linked to coastal centers and evenly distributed over the planet in exact mathematical relationship to each other, forming an intentional geometric grid pattern. (See Graham Hancock's beautifully illustrated *Heaven's Mirror* for the evidence.)

It is obvious from this understanding of history that human progress is not a neat, linear process moving evenly from the past to the present. Of course the modern materialist ego prefers to think this, as this makes *us* the "crown of creation." The modern myth of progress has blinded us to the cyclical movement of history and in so doing, denies us the riches and insights in the form of lore and legend left to us from earlier ascended human cultures.

It is hard for many in modern academia to accept even the possibility that former generations had technologies or knowledge that is simply beyond our ability to replicate or understand today. It's hard for the modern ego to admit that it's not necessarily the finest accomplishment of Nature. The myth of progress was fueled by Darwin's assumption (circa 1850) that all current species represent the epitome of survival and adaptation—especially when it comes to us. This presumption was applied to cultures as well with, of course, Darwin's own culture of white Anglo-Saxon warrior societies representing "Nature's finest." Nazi Germany provides a good example of where this unbalanced, unidirectional, and hierarchical view of progress eventually leads. Modern institutions of education, science, and government are still largely based on this short view of history, and so cast a disdainful and dismissive glance at much of the wisdom of our ancients.

Conveniently for the short-sighted, much of the evidence for these advanced global societies was wiped out in the cataclysms of 10,000 to 9500 BC. What information did survive this period was later burned, suppressed, and denied by powers threatened by information that could be potentially liberating and empowering to the individuals living in these times. Today, the same thing is going on in the willful suppression of the work of break-through researchers like Tesla, Rife, and Wilhelm Reich. Denial is a defense against an uncomfortable truth. And the truth today is that humanity, in order to mature into a responsible species, no longer needs to be managed by dysfunctional parents inculcating the same limiting patterns of fear and control that have been held unquestioned for untold generations.

On a more esoteric level, and assuming you accept the existence of life on other worlds, the galaxy appears to be set up to accommodate a variety of dimensional life forms and expressions. Given the concordance between the Great Year (26,000 years) and the distance between us and the galactic center (roughly 26,000 light years), it appears there may be a correspondence here. If there is, then it is feasible to at least consider that the closer they are to the center of the galaxy, the faster the stars orbit in their prescribed gravitational dances. This likely means they move more quickly through their evolutionary phases and that life forms in these systems are propelled to evolve more quickly. Given our position two thirds out from the center of the galaxy, there are probably twice as many civilizations more advanced than we are—"we" being civilizations at a similar stage of development or distance from the center.

Here are some other amazingly "coincidental" numerical patterns:

The circumference of the Earth is roughly 26,000 miles.

The current human life span is approximately 26,000 days (71.2 years).

The human gestation period is 260 days.

Physical development into an adult is considered complete at 26 years.

Mass extinctions have happened on Earth roughly every 26 million years.

And, more esoterically, by using the correspondence table A=1, B=2 ... Z=26, we find that the name "God" in English yields the number 26. Is it any wonder that the Maya observed the 260-day cycle of gestation as one of the primary cycles of Nature and of their amazing calendar?

Multiple cycles are converging around the year 2012. I refer you to the excellent work by David Wilcock that explains many of these things in a scientific and grounded manner. You can view his various videos at *www.youtube.com* and tune into his website at *www.divinecosmos.com*.

We have now completed four of these 26,000-year solar-system cycles, for a total of 104,000 years. This is a sacred number referring to the Grand Arcturus cycle recognized as significant by some astrologers. We are also apparently at the end of a 225-million-year galactic day. This is the number of Earth years it takes the galactic wheel to spin around once. We are now at the same point of galactic rotation as when the dinosaurs first appeared on Earth 225 million years ago. You could say that the dinosaurs have "had their day."

This becomes more significant, perhaps, when we consider the dominance of the "lizard brain" in human affairs for as long as we can recall. The lizard brain is the psycho-physiological term for the structures of the primitive brain stem—the seat of our survival instincts and the lower, egoic emotions associated with aggression, dominance, and territoriality. We share this structure with all living mammalian and lizard species. We further share the overlying "mammalian brain" with all mammals, which facilitates higher emotions like nurturance, devotion, and loyalty. This is why we prefer to make pets of mammals rather than lizards. Mammals can return these more "human" emotions, while lizards can't. Given chance and opportunity, your lizard would just rather eat you!

Uniquely human are the neo-cortex or "new-brain" structures that allow us to experience even higher levels of consciousness, including mental states like Oneness or Unity Consciousness as described in many spiritual traditions. It is clear that we must transcend the old lizard consciousness individually and collectively—and soon! It is no longer working, if it ever did. Its functioning is simply based on fear, separation, and survival representing an obsolete way of being in the world. The lizard brain is yesterday's news. I find it fascinating that this dynamic of consciousness is being so elegantly and accurately reflected to us in these grand cycles of nature, giving credence to the notion the universe "out there" is nothing more than a projection of the universe "in here."

The Tibetan Buddhist tradition identifies 2012 as the time for the re-appearance or discovery of Shamballa, the Sacred City of Light that is currently invisible to us. Hopi predictions include the appearance of a Blue Sun in the sky after 2012. What these predictions may be indicating is that these things already exist outside our current field of perception. As we expand more into our multi-dimensional potential as awakened humans, we will begin to perceive more of the missing or "dark" matter—that 90 percent of the universe nobody has found to date. Could it be we've been looking for it in all the wrong places?

The mass extinctions that are part of the geological record imply that Earth's history involves long periods of gradual adaptation of life forms, interrupted by periods of intense change. It appears that historically, the pattern involves an almost complete extinction of earlier, simpler life forms, replaced each time by a higher order of genetic expression. In other words, life expresses through interrupted evolution. This is the same pattern we see in the Mayan calendar. Should we be surprised if the current conjunction of multiple cosmological cycles correlates well with times of dramatic change on Earth?

Cycles in and of themselves are not causes of dramatic change. I look at them rather as correlates—the physical out-picturing or projection of points of opportunity for growth in awareness. We can think of them as "hinge points" reflecting the inner conditions for quantum leaps in evolution. If we look at the phenomenal universe as the expression and expansion of Spirit or light into matter, these cyclical nodal points in time may represent a change in the quality, intensity, or "completeness" of the light. Or if we look at the universe of form as the projection of that light through human consciousness, then the cyclical nodal points may be when the film gets changed, creating a new improved movie. Whatever a cycle conjunction means is essentially up to us, and the intent or purpose we see for Life itself. As such, we have the Doomsdayers almost reveling at the prospect of Armageddon, and we have those who dare to dream of a Golden Age of peace, love, and joy. If we are indeed the movie makers, the better choice seems fairly obvious, does it not? What kind of future do you want for yourself, your children, and your fellow travelers in time and space?

You could say the cosmological alignments and cycles have come to our attention now in order to help us appreciate an expanded view of the meaning of life and human evolution—the Big Picture. There are no accidents in Creation. Everything is operating according to a Grand Design. In order to see this design in the midst of what may appear as random and chaotic events, we need a really large perspective. "Outer" space is as large as it gets! Without a mental picture of foreign shores, the discoverers of continents would not have had any reason to leave home. Without any idea of the harmonies and synchronicities in the macro-universe, we may not be motivated to venture into the inner worlds where the experience of a unifying Truth lies waiting in our minds. If these macro events are mirroring to us the inner terrain, what we are being shown at the very least is a set of some kind of highly unique intersections that may be reflecting to us a giant evolutionary leap forward. If energy follows thought as my dowsing teacher Raymon Grace states, then I prefer to entertain that possibility. By doing so, I may actually be playing a proactive role in creating a new Earth. Want to play along?

THE HOLOGRAPHIC MODEL

The holographic model, wherein each aspect reflects the whole, has provided a valuable cognitive tool to help us appreciate the essential connectedness of our universe. An inference here is that if we can positively affect our little slice of the whole, the whole benefits. Nothing here is insignificant. It seems that no matter where we look in this space-time hologram, we see reflected back to us a general pattern of expansion (the expanding universe) and the seemingly further separation of objects. Is this image reflecting back to us our state of consciousness of ourselves as allegedly separated beings, "lost in space," as it were? Or is this movie/universe showing us our Divine potential as Creators of worlds of beauty and the elegant expression of Divine intelligence? It appears we may have a choice about which universe we belong to by choosing which view we prefer.

We will now turn our attention to another way of looking at the changes going on around and within us by considering a dimensional model. The fact that we can look at this Time of Shift through various models and perspectives and see them align perfectly is encouraging to me. It helps me accept that the Big Picture is not only pointing to the inevitable nature of progress and change, but that we can choose to look at this time of change any way we prefer. No one way of seeing is either right or wrong. All points of view inevitably converge. It just takes time!

CHAPTER 3

DIMENSIONAL DANCING

The notion of dimensions of existence can be confusing, especially as we have been conditioned only from within our limited three-dimensional viewpoint. The classical use of "dimension" is to describe a quality of space—the three dimensions of physicality being height, width, and breadth. Einstein added time as a fourth dimension, as he observed objects in space only exist in time, and time and space form a single inseparable thing he identified as space-time. Thus we call these spatial dimensions, which only apply to the three-dimensional world.

Our use of the term here is somewhat different. We are using dimension to describe a specific frequency range of vibrating matter/energy/light. This view is based on the idea that the universe is made up of the same stuff all vibrating at different speeds, which again can be attributed to Einstein's discovery that E (energy) equals M (matter, mass) times C (the speed of light) squared, or $E=MC^2$. All the stuff of the universe can be called light, but not the kind of light we are used to seeing. Visible light, along with all the visible colors, only makes up 1 percent of the entire electro-magnetic spectrum of energy. I like to call visible light "physical light," as it operates within and defines the boundaries of our physical sight. Other species with different kinds of light-detection organs perceive different frequencies of light and so inhabit a completely different world, or "dimension" if you like.

Any dimensional model we use is simply an arbitrary— that is, made up—point of view. We are merely attempting to understand "all that is" through our perceptual and intellectual filters. The word "uni-verse" can be interpreted as "one song," implying a unified vibrational whole—a single system of energy with every part connected as One. In order to try to understand and navigate the idea of the One in human terms, however, we use language to describe the bits on which we are focusing. This is all the rational mind can do.

In the Biblical version of Creation, Adam is said to have fallen asleep so Eve could come forth. Nowhere does it say he woke up! His first job given by the Big Boss in his dream state was to name the animals. Is the allegory here that in our fallen state of individuality, separation, and spiritual sleep, we naturally fall into slicing up experience with the sword of language, which is inherently dualistic and divisive? Thus we dream of a world of separate forms only, and lock ourselves into the illusion of the dream through perception and language.

We carve up reality to fit our own need to understand and describe. Both perception and language represent an attempt to reduce everything that is happening at once to a focal point of attention. The caution here is not to mistake our models, words, or perceptions for reality. We do this most of the time. This is where we get into trouble, and take *our* way of seeing far too seriously. We make a linguistic model or image in our minds, and then run off and play with it as if it were real. And you thought fantasy-making was only for children! This has been done repeatedly throughout time, and so our linguistic perceptions take on a kind of pseudo-reality in our minds. We mistake the map for the territory. It's a process called "reification," or mistaking the word or concept for the thing being described. Paper money is a good example. "This note is legal tender"—and we act as if it were! Because we agree collectively on many of the same images and the meanings we give them, the dream takes on the appearance of a shared reality. This does not negate the fact that perception is essentially illusion.

You can talk about tomatoes until you are blue in the face, and even be regarded as an expert on tomatoes, but until you bite into one, you don't *know* what you are talking about. The total experience (knowledge) transcends the need for a substitute image (perception).

Any system of describing dimensions, as stated, is simply an arbitrary convenience, and does not constitute anything more real than our preference for description at the time. So there is no one "correct" system of dimensional modeling—just, perhaps, ones that are more useful for our purposes than others.

When we describe ranges of energy vibrations, we are describing dimensions of which we probably do not have any direct experience, at least on a sensory or conscious level. This is where we must rely on the wisdom and records of those who have. The Vedic culture, in particular, has kept records for untold centuries codifying the direct experience of human-potential experimenters known in ancient times as *rishis* or saints. These were/are people who have dedicated their lives to the exploration of "inner space," the vast unlimited oceans of Mind within. The Vedic tradition has described many different levels or states of consciousness connecting them with specific spiritual practices for their attainment. Tibetan Buddhism is another example of a record-keeping culture in this area, as were most Shamanic and naturalist societies.

There is throughout recorded history (which represents only a small sliver of total human history) a common thread of spiritual beliefs and experiences, described by Aldous Huxley as "the perennial philosophy" (*The Perennial Philosophy,* Harper Collins, 1944). Huxley traces a common thread of knowledge through time coming from largely isolated cultures and records. From this observation, he concluded there must be a united and common human drive and potential that transcends time and culture despite appearing in a variety of forms. This common thread is in agreement on the main points, particularly in the notion of our essential Oneness with each other, Nature, and a Divine Source or Prime Creator.

Despite our beliefs and wishes to the contrary, the human body and mind have not changed dramatically for 100,000 years. Our perceptual filters have remained the same. This is one reason we have so many degenerative health challenges today. Although we are living longer, we still inhabit Stone Age bodies built for a more natural diet and leisurely lifestyle. All of this time evolving on Earth has allowed humans to gather a great amount of experience, wisdom, and knowledge. Much of this data, rather than being learned in the classic sense, is already stored deep within our DNA and cellular memory banks, but it is inaccessible if we are looking outside ourselves for the answers to life's mysteries. If you allow your intuitive self to consider the possibilities being described here, you may trigger your own cellular memories of when knowledge of these dimensions was much more real to humans, and to you in particular.

Any dimensional model, then, is an attempt to describe "all that is" to a mind used to focusing on particulars and largely limited at this time to a narrow band of sensory data.

The dimensional model I am going to describe is the one offered by Barbara Hand Clow in *The Pleiadian Agenda* and later developed in *Alchemy of the Nine Dimensions*

(Hampton Roads, 2010). The model is both metaphorical and material in that the dimensions manifest physically from the core of the Earth and up into space, creating a "vertical axis of consciousness." Remember that this is just a model, albeit a very helpful one. Let us now look at these different aspects of "all that is," recalling that to be human (*hu-man* or "sacred man") is to be able to co-exist in all dimensions simultaneously and navigate each one consciously. This has been the goal and *modus operandi* in all Shamanic and historical spiritual traditions—to know Oneself as All That Is.

FIRST DIMENSION: THE CRYSTAL/ IRON CORE AND GRAVITY

The first dimension is the source of gravity—the anchor and glue that holds all the dimensions together. It is represented by an area 1500 miles wide in the center of the Earth composed of intensely dense iron crystals. The first dimension vibrates at 40 Hz, and resonates with the iron in your blood as well as with the root chakra (bodily energy center). You can visualize the first dimension as a rod of energy extending up through all dimensions and keeping them all aligned, like the post of a child's stacking toy. All the dimensions, physical and non-physical, rely on the stabilizing and ordering influence of the first dimension. The lower physical dimensions tend to weaken and lose integrity when removed from this stabilizing energy, as when astronauts stay too long in space. Artificial gravity is needed to support physical life in space. Even sleeping above the ground, as in a second-story building or higher, disconnects us from the Earth's gravity and electro-magnetic field. This is why some have found "grounding mats" or "earthing pads" useful to recover sound, natural sleep patterns.

Gravity is the "great attractor" that mediates the movement of all matter in space. It is calling out the dance steps as cosmic objects swirl about in space, rarely colliding. Scientists are looking for theoretical gravity waves and particles, or "gravitons." If we can imagine them, they are "there" somewhere. Consider the holographic model of the universe as representing the projection of the One Mind. Whatever any aspect of this universal mind can imagine must reflect something within its totality. Whatever you can imagine must exist in some dimension of time/space within the hologram, of which you are a complete-in-yourself part containing the Whole.

Iron carries life-giving oxygen through your blood stream to every cell in the body and connects every body to the bosom of Mother Earth through the force of gravity. Iron also connects you to the Earth's electro-magnetic field, which is generated as a result of the rotation of the core within the liquid magma surrounding it. The electro-magnetic field of the Earth affects all life forms on the planet by stabilizing and holding all frequencies, and thus all matter, in a steady state.

Grounding meditations strengthen our first-dimension (1-D) connection and can calm us and slow us down when we are over-stimulated or activated. Certain gems and stones, like hematite, can be helpful in keeping us grounded. The Earth's center also provides us with an image of absolute stillness. In most introspective spiritual practices, coming to inner Silence or stillness is a pre-requisite to receiving Divine inspiration. So even metaphysically, the first dimension is an essential element in our unfolding and spiritual evolution. If you meditate, consider visualizing a beam of gravity energy rising up from the center of Earth and passing right through the center of your body, stabilizing you as it continues to go upward to stabilize all the upper dimensions. Recall that image when you feel "ungrounded" or disconnected in any way. I like to do this whenever I'm in a jet at 30,000 feet. It even works there.

SECOND DIMENSION:
THE ELEMENTAL BIOSPHERE

This dimension includes the physical elements, viruses, bacteria, and a "hidden" biosphere extending miles within the Earth. It is thus represented by the "body" of the Earth in this model. Metaphysically, these life forms are represented by two-dimensional (2-D) beings, the Elementals, which include Nature spirits like gnomes, fairies, sylphs, and the "wee folk" of lore and legend. We call the personified forms of the elemental kingdom "devas" (day-vas), the root word for "devil." Every plant and mineral is represented by a deva. This idea is somewhat in line with the idea of morphogenic fields, which we will discuss when we describe the sixth dimension. Literally, the modern invention of "the devil" is a reference to the potential competition patriarchal religions felt coming from the Earth-based religions of prior matriarchal epochs. The "Old Boys' Club" has never done well dealing with competition. Apparently, these non-physical 2-D life forms can be seen when we attune to them in a *theta* brain-wave state. This is a lower frequency than our everyday *beta* or waking-state brain waves. For most adults, we only experience theta when going to sleep or on our way to awakening. This is when adults are most likely to encounter the Elementals or other extra-dimensional beings and forms. Young children up to age three and the elderly can be in a theta state when awake, however, which is why the existence of these and other "imaginary" (to the "better-informed" adults) beings can be experienced by them. We beta- and alpha-brainwave-bound adults just smile condescendingly and remark on what colorful imaginations they have!

The second dimension was a source of life emerging from within the Earth after surface conditions improved on the developing planet. Microbes from this dimension emerged onto the surface once conditions were tolerable. Many toxins on the surface of the Earth today are simply "misplaced" 2-D elements—elements that don't normally belong outside of that dimension. Industrialization and pollution have played a major role in displacing these otherwise harmless elements—like lead, cadmium, and mercury as well as radio-active elements. Many man-made toxins are "unholy alliances" of elements not found in Nature's blueprint. Some of these synthetic compounds we call medications, which always cause unpleasant so-called "side" effects. These are really actual effects—the response of a healthy body to a foreign toxin or poison.

The second dimension is also the realm of constantly renewing supplies of petroleum as a byproduct of microbe populations inside the Earth, according to Clow's research in *Alchemy of the Nine Dimensions*. Part of the Shift of Ages may involve the spontaneous return of misplaced 2-D elements back into the body of the Earth. If so, it appears Nature has a massive clean-up program in mind—an instantaneous and complete return to the second dimension of all the misplaced elements and compounds. This is why some say it may be wise to wear only natural fabrics these days and avoid possibly embarrassing exposure!

THIRD DIMENSION:
LINEAR SPACE AND TIME

The third dimension (3-D) is the "borderland" where physical and non-physical dimensions meet, and is represented by the Earth's surface. A distinguishing feature of 3-D is that it supports the three spatial dimensions of height, width, and depth, as well as linear time. Perhaps more distinguishing is that it supports duality.

Duality is the co-existence of opposites or polarities. Not all dimensions are dualistic. In 3-D we not only see opposites play out physically—hot and cold, up and down, right and left, day and night, north and south—but non-physically as well in our experience of joy and sorrow, health and illness, life and death, and good and evil. The third dimension is thus a very challenging one to live in as we must constantly navigate the tug and pull of these seemingly endless opposites. It is a setup for both conflict and learning. A main advantage of living in 3-D is that we are forced to exercise our will in choosing between these opposites. It is in exercising our will that we eventually discover our true identity as One with the Divine Will, which is Love. From a non-dual perspective, accessible, as it were, from the non-dual dimensions, there is *only* Divine Will. Therefore, exercising *our* will is connecting with the Divine. Divine Will awakens in you as your will. We will all leave here ultimately by learning the lesson that the apparent separation of wills, yours and the Divine's, could not and did not in fact happen.

The human mind is designed to operate in both dualistic and non-dualistic modes. You could say the split into two brain hemispheres reflects this "two channel" potential. Trouble is that our attention seems to operate on one channel only and there's little if any communication between these modes of operation, so those functioning in an entirely dualistic mode may be totally oblivious to any other way of seeing at all. This is the "forgetting" we experience when we incarnate on Earth. It is the spiritual blindness that seems to come with the territory. The challenge and opportunity of being here is that we *can* transcend duality even while living in 3-D. We do so by choosing to use our thoughts differently. We begin to choose non-dual thoughts to help us get over the idea that we need to make choices at all. True sacred writings are based in the experience of non-duality translated back into terms the dualistic mind can understand. Eventually we learn that by changing our thinking, we can change our experiences here in 3-D.

You could say the third dimension is a place to learn to choose and experience thoughts and emotions (feelings) as portals to becoming multi-dimensional, healing, as it were, the inner conflicts reflected within duality. The task in 3-D is to balance polarities and unitize dualities, thus collapsing conflict in the mind and opening to Peace and our true identity as Spirit. It helps to accept that as conflict is always between two opposing perceptions and that perceptions are partial and illusory, conflicts are always between two illusions. Accept this, and this where is the conflict? The most constructive approach to 3-D is as a "duality school" where you get to live with the consequences of your choices, and then choose again. By becoming responsible choosers, we can reduce suffering and graduate to operate from dimensions of greater stability and creativity—the non-dual dimensions. Although we often look to beings operating in "higher" dimensions with awe as somehow having higher status, they look on us with wonder and admiration, maybe even a touch of envy, as we are working in a dimension seen as the fast track to spiritual evolution where we can evolve by leaps and bounds in a relatively short time! Aren't you glad you came here? This is galactic grad school!

At this time, the rate of vibration in all the dimensions is going up, as we all go through the photon band. Earth herself is poised to leap from 3-D to 5-D status, passing through 4-D on the way. This implies a healing and coming together of the currently "split" mind (4-D) individually and collectively as we move into becoming unified in our remembrance of Spirit (5-D). I would say that is down-right exciting!

FOURTH DIMENSION: ASTRAL PLANE, WORLD OF MYTH AND ARCHETYPE, THOUGHT FORMS, AND COLLECTIVE CONSCIOUSNESS

The fourth dimension is the first non-physical dimension with a rate of energy vibration beyond the physical 3-D Earth. Of course what characterizes a physical dimension is simply energy that vibrates slowly enough to congeal into what our senses report to us as solid matter. If we had a different sensory apparatus, like the insects I mentioned earlier, we would literally live in a completely different "world." The fourth is the dimension of thought and thought forms, collective thoughts that precede our experience of them. Thought forms can be either weak or strong, depending on how many minds feed that particular energy and the emotional intensity invested in the thoughts. Some thought forms carry culturally determined images with them, such as our ideas of angels and demons, which are simply mutually agreed projections of dualistic thought. As thought experiencers we are unbound by 3-D constraints of time and space or the body and can go anywhere in space or time. Thus 4-D can be called a "non-local" or quantum dimension—characterized as a spiritual dimension by some. I hesitate to call any dimension "spiritual" as our definition of the word is "inclusive of All That Is and the Source." More accurately, we will refer to 4-D as a non-local or non-material dimension.

Thoughts are accompanied by measurable electrical impulses in the brain detected by EEG biofeedback devices. Did you notice I said "accompanied by" electrical impulses? These electrical impulses are not proof of the brain producing thoughts; they are simply an electrical byproduct of the thinking process. The classic view that the brain produces thought is up for review in light of what is now understood about brain structures. Rather than being a "producer" of thought, the brain is now understood to act more like a "transceiver" of thought. This implies that the thoughts exist outside of the brain and are attracted to or somehow picked up by a receptive brain, which can then send back to the source another thought, much like a two-way radio.

The pool of thought energy where thought forms pre-exist prior to our experience of them is the fourth dimension. As this pool is non-local and thus available to all, it is no surprise that so many of us think alike. Could it be that the notion of private thought needs review? This new view of thought as a collective energy field makes things like mind control a little easier to accept as possible, doesn't it? Notice how scientific researchers know they must rush to patent a new idea or invention immediately after their "Aha" moment of discovery. Their experience tells them that someone else on the other side of the world, usually from some competing political system, has undoubtedly discovered the same thing. More obviously, look at the motion of flocks of birds or schools of fish—how they all think exactly the same thing and respond as one at lightning speeds.

Some say that the Shift of Ages will open the way to planetary telepathy. Perhaps this is not so hard to imagine considering that all minds are already joined on the non-local level of 4-D. It is only our individual erroneous belief in ourselves as separate, primarily through body-identification, that is blocking this natural mode of communication. Of course we have those who already can do this; psychics and intuitives are simply the precursors and pioneers of the next evolutionary step in our inevitable movement back to Oneness. Consider how much more responsible we will be with our minds and the thoughts we entertain when we realize that *everyone* can "hear" us!

Our dimensional model extends the range of 4-D to include thoughts, ideas, and even movements of mass consciousness. In other words, the thought experience, whether seemingly individual or collective, is an effect of interacting with 4-D, and is not an isolated biologically generated event. Collective consciousness is simply the result of many preferring to tune into the same information at the same time. Some thought patterns are resilient over time, manifesting as entrenched inherited cultural, religious and family, or tribal beliefs and attitudes. The more of us who are resonant or "in sync" with a certain thought or belief pattern, the stronger it will grow in the 4-D field, in a kind of expanding feedback loop. This seems to explain how things like fads, trends, and tastes tend to sweep the population. If we are drinking from the same pool it's no wonder we taste the same water! Don't you think advertisers and prime-time programmers know this? What comes to mind here is naming babies. How many parents do you know who thought up a really unique baby name, just to find out there are three other kids in the daycare group with the same name? This happens in every generation.

As noted, 4-D is subject to quantum reality—that is, it is non-local, and responds to the movement of attention and intention, or the observer effect. This means that the thoughts you entertain will tend to attract more thoughts of the same quality. Many spiritual practices and traditions involve the study or memorization of "sacred" ideas. Devotees find that these ideas begin to saturate their attention and awareness to the point of literally "transporting" their minds into heavenly realms.

As 4-D is vibrationally situated between dualistic 3-D and non-dual 5-D, it carries some of the properties of both.

In other words, there are thoughts more entrenched in negative aspects of dualistic perceptions that are necessarily limiting. You can call these "lower astral" thoughts. Perception is always dualistic, as it by nature leaves out everything other than the focus of attention. This is what we paradoxically call "waking consciousness." At its worst, dualistic thinking descends into negative thoughts of divisive destruction, anger, blame, etc. There are, however, thoughts reflecting non-duality—thoughts of Oneness, you could say, or "upper astral" thoughts—in which we touch upon 5-D wherein duality collapses in on itself and leaves only a state of wholeness or unity. These could be called Holy (whole) thoughts—the ideas that have resonated throughout history and served to help lead mankind out of the blindness of his own limitations.

Just as 'positive' thoughts (upper 4-D) tend to lead us to experiences of peace and Oneness, 'negative' thinking (lower 4-D) pulls us into further separation, isolation, and suffering. If only reality as Oneness is real, however, we could say negative thinking only pulls us into further illusion. As we shall see, separation and perception (thinking) are fundamentally illusory and so is the suffering experienced in illusion. Recall the analogy of the dream. All suffering, although feeling very real, can only ever be a temporary state. Cognitive therapists have discovered that feelings can change as we consciously choose new thoughts. The causal link between thought and feeling is not unidirectional, and as such we can choose our feeling state as well as our thoughts. The ego prefers we stay victimized. You and I can choose differently.

Perhaps this is a good juncture at which to posit the basic differences between dualistic perception and non-dual reality. In duality, the observer is always outside of the experience of perception. So it is always an experience of "I and the other," "me and you," "me and my thoughts," "me and God." These never merge into wholeness, but retain "I" as an isolated self perpetually suspended in a separate universe of "my experience." This isolated position describes the state of existential angst that gripped the philosophers of early last century, especially as they threw out their own spirituality when they tossed out the traditionally prescribed version of God. This is a depressing state of being marked by loneliness and powerlessness. We now appreciate that in throwing out "God," what they intended was to throw out the mental vise grip of dualistic religion. What they really accomplished was to throw out the non-dual reality of the Self as Divine. This is why so many early 20th-century philosophers and intellectuals got so depressed and ended up as alcoholics or suicides! They mistook dualistic human-generated religion for true Spirituality. They had cut themselves off from Source and were lost in 4-D—lost in the endless permutations of a conflicted mind.

The non-dual view proposes that unified Reality cannot be carved up, or it would not be One Reality! There is either Oneness or nothing. Therefore, duality is an illusion—a trick of the mind and an ontological impossibility. More accurately, the experience of duality in the dualistic dimensions particularly is being projected by a mind split between its perceived individuality (illusion) and its deeper memory of Oneness, Truth, or Spirit. A split mind perceives a world of conflict, opinion, "positionality," and alienation—what we also call the world of the ego.

Duality assumes a separation between the inner and outer worlds of experience. We know from studies in perception and neurophysiology that "outer reality" is actually and only an inner experience involving nerve pathways and images in the brain. So the world "out there" is literally all images happening "in here," and nowhere else. One of my favorite and most liberating mantras is "I only ever experience myself." Try it for a while. You may like how you feel when it really sinks in.

The part of the brain that navigates duality "out there" is cut off from the knowing (remembering) of non-dual Reality. We know it somewhere, but have blocked this knowing out of our minds as the only way we thought we could handle the experience of 3-D duality. Denial is always the first defense of the separated ego-mind when it feels undermined. As the fourth dimension is also subject to duality, our personal and collective thought fields tend to support the illusion of separation in its endless forms. These are the thoughts and assumptions that run automatically in the form of conditioned responses and linguistic-based conceptual patterns, and as cultural norms making up 99 percent of what we like to think are our private thoughts. Deepak Chopra calls this the "hypnosis of social conditioning."

Typically, it is the left-brain structures that operate primarily in duality mode. This is the brain hemisphere that is active during linear discrimination, cause-and-effect thinking, problem solving, and language-based intelligence. You could say the left hemisphere (for most right-handed people, anyway) is wired into the lower fourth dimension, while the right hemisphere with its penchant for non-verbal intelligence (appreciation of art and beauty, intuitive awareness of patterns, and non-verbal states of consciousness, including states of Oneness) is wired into the upper fourth dimension—the realm of higher thought that is vibrationally in touch with the non-dual fifth dimension.

The fourth is thus the dimension of devils and angels. These beings are simply images the dualistic mind has projected onto the screen of consciousness in order to dissociate from the discomfort and pain of the inherent contradiction of duality within itself. The pain of individuation and separation from Oneness is too hard to bear, even if only imagined, so we attempt to put it all outside of us, thus fooling ourselves into believing that "the world happens to me and, as a helpless victim, I am not responsible for any of it." Oh the dysfunctional and disempowering dance of duality! Are you tired of the "duality two-step" yet?

One thing stands firmly between the worlds of duality and non-duality, of which only one is real—the will, the inner motivation and desire that moves us away from pain and toward peace. It seems that only when we have had our fill of suffering through duality and finally realize there is nothing outside ourselves—nothing in the world of separated forms that ever delivers inner peace but only seems to disappoint—can we make a decision to see things differently. This life shift often is triggered by a perceived loss. Yet if we truly make the shift, we find to our delight that we have lost nothing at all. We only gained the Peace that comes from the end of inner conflict and mental division. This happens when the mind finally transcends the inner split and the two minds merge into one in a sacred marriage and emerge as whole, healed, and One with All That Is. It has become fifth-dimensional. It has transcended the world "out there" by transcending the world "in here." It now becomes a beacon of light, peace, and joy enlightening other minds that have yet to make the leap. It is a mind that is "in the world, but not of the world."

What I have been describing in terms of individual awareness can also be applied to the collective awareness of humanity at this time. The entire planet has been imprisoned within the limitations of the lower 4-D thought field for so long that it almost seems normal. The insanity of war, inequality, poverty, disease, and domination can only be a projection of the basic dualistic split in the collective human mind. As we all drink from the same well of 4-D—which is a way of saying "all minds are joined"—each one of us, as we return to full awareness of non-dual Reality in our own experience, contributes exponentially to the healing of all of us, the planet, and the universe. You can think of your part in this as raising the frequency of the planet through your devotion to Truth.

As you entertain thoughts of a non-dual nature, your mind begins to attract more of the same. Lower 4-D thoughts no longer hold the same appeal, and you begin to appreciate how thoughts of separation, victimhood, and blame only serve to keep *you* in suffering. I saw this bumper sticker recently: "Holding on to resentment is like taking poison and expecting someone else to fall over." Any experience or situation offers you the choice as to how you want to perceive it. You can feed the ego with lower 4-D thinking, or switch channels and choose higher 4-D thought, which will eventually take you to the border between the fourth and the fifth dimensions. The highest-frequency thoughts available to us in 3-D and 4-D are thoughts of True Forgiveness. You will be standing at the Gates of Heaven.

So please do not be discouraged by what appears to be a hopeless situation on planet Earth. *You* are the great hope of us all. Change your mind about yourself, and *you* change! Change your mind about others, the world, and life, and everything changes.

FIFTH DIMENSION: NON-DUAL HEAVEN

Once energy accelerates to the speed of the fifth dimension, duality can no longer be sustained or supported. It's as if once the blender speeds up enough, all the separate ingredients congeal into a unified, coherent fruit smoothie! This is not to say that the collapse of duality is only the result of the increased rate of vibration, for as we will see, some higher dimensions are again dualistic. But 5-D, thank Heaven, is not! And it is not so far removed from 4-D, or 3-D for that matter.

You could say that the physical body resonates primarily in 3-D, while the mind does so in 4-D. It turns out that the Heart, in its physical and metaphysical sense, resonates in 5-D. It is from the Heart that we can touch non-dual Reality in the form of unconditional Love. Unconditional Love is an idea that gets watered down and qualified by the 4-D mind. The mind in its dualistic mode always wants to put limits, definitions, conditions, exceptions, and boundaries around experience. It always wants to slap a judgment or past-oriented assumption on experience so that it feels it's still in control.

But the Heart—ah yes, the Heart can sing and open to include all in its loving embrace without argument. The eternal bond between mother and child is a very good example of 5-D Love. This is love in its purest expression that puts no conditions, needs, or demands on the other. It comes from a memory of Oneness. It allows all in absolute freedom, wanting only what is good for the other with no fearful thought of its own needs. It is what we hope God is like—totally loving, unaware of any guilt or sin, always reliable and non-judgmental. Don't we too want to be seen in our innocence, free and whole and accepted just as we are?

As I indicated in the discussion of 4-D, it is possible for the mind to resonate itself very close to a unified 5-D state. This involves a joining and healing of the brain with the split parts of itself and the Heart. The modern world of hierarchy and division reflects an inner division between brain intelligence (4-D) and heart intelligence (5-D). Many of our inner conflicts are about whether we should follow our hearts or logic and common sense. Apparently the Chinese and classical Western meaning of "mind" was originally inclusive of the heart. Our scientists today (Valerie Hunt comes to mind) are re-affirming that the neural net of the heart (and gut, for that matter) rival that of the brain in density and complexity. The heart actually puts out an electrical field fifty times as powerful as the brain according to Hunt (*Infinite Mind*, Malibu, 1989). It appears that biologically, humans are hardwired to be heart-centered rather than brain-centered beings! While the mind reasons, the heart accepts. The mind perceives, judges, and projects. The heart yearns to forgive, see beyond opposites and duality, and extend Love.

There have been a few examples of those who have reached a state of 5-D Unity Consciousness while still in the body, and then affected many people though their presence, sayings, and legacy. Buddha, Lao-tse, and Yeshua (Jesus) come to mind. Many of these beings demonstrated what to us are super-human abilities—bi-location, raising the dead, miracles of manifestation, etc. Yet was not Christ quoted as saying that *we* would do all these and even greater things?

Eckhart Tolle, author of *The Power of Now* (Namaste Publishing, 1999) and *The New Earth* (Penguin, 2005), has described these rare individuals as the "early flowerings" of humanity. He says that now, however, the "entire field is about to bloom." What he means is that these saints and sages of ages past were not special in any way other than that they spiritually matured before the rest of us. They certainly did not come to establish dogmas, disciplines, or dualistic religions. That is what those still caught in the dream of duality preferred to do with these forerunners of *homo luminous*, rather than receive their messages and strive to model their example as beings fully reflecting non-dual Reality, which is unconditional Love.

When we look at the planetary ascension process from a dimensional perspective, we see the potential for the vibration of Earth-matter and its life forms to be lifted out of 3-D, pass through 4-D, and arrive into a 5-D state of vibration. The mechanics of this process are provided by—or perhaps more accurately, reflected in—the alignment of our Sun with the galactic photon band. What applies individually also applies collectively. In order to ascend to "heaven" (5-D), we must master our thoughts (4-D). The mental and emotional aspects of our being must come into a state of peace, acceptance, and silence through True Forgiveness. This can only be achieved when we are open to a re-definition of self. That is, a self no longer tormented by false division, but united with all beings in recognition of our Source and Oneness with each other. As we continue through these times of change, there may be many who experience mental pain and traumatic old emotional memories as they more or less are obliged to observe these things as they "vibrate out" of their fields or as they pass through the 4-D "wall." Ultimately, we will all realize that we are only hurt or limited by our own thoughts. And since those are groundless, they are not real!

Your Heart's wish to pass beyond the limits of duality is a clear signal from 5-D. This is felt as an inner yearning and longing for something better. Allow your mind to be changed and to come into alignment with your Heart's wish. Know that your Heart's desire is the same as everyone else's and the Heart of the Creator—to be happy, to be at peace, to experience joy, and to create. When you hear your inner voice screaming, "I've had enough! I can't stand it anymore! No more suffering!" be glad! Know that your Heart is demanding that you return to sanity! And the Heart knows that you can, because in reality, you are!

No matter how someone's behavior appears, whether good or bad in our judgment, it is being driven by this same inner urge emerging from the hidden memory of Love. People only "act out" from an inner frustration and anger that things are not happening as they know at some deep level they could. No matter how hard we try, we cannot completely lose the memory of our own Divinity. It burns perpetually in our infinite minds. Forgiveness of others and seeing their innocence and Divine Will in action is the most effective and available way to break down the 4-D mental prison of judgment, perception, and opinion in ourselves. This is not the ego's forgiveness, which looks at the fault and then forgives. It is quantum or non-dual forgiveness that simply sees that in truth there is nothing real to forgive. It was just a mistake, and mistakes can be corrected or repeated, as need be, until they can be recognized and forgiven.

If you start thinking like a 5-D human, you will quickly become one! Then watch in delight as those around you begin to light up in the new vibration you carry. You will discover to your relief and delight that we are all fifth-dimensional, and beyond. We've just fallen asleep here, and are dreaming a dream of suffering.

True Forgiveness, as mentioned above, is very different from forgiveness from a dualistic view. This is a very key idea to understand. Not understanding True Forgiveness keeps so many people locked into a cycle of blame, pain, and attack. Dualistic forgiveness keeps the offense alive while forgiving it from a place of moral superiority. It thus makes the offense real and fundamental to our positive view of ourselves as forgiving.

Non-dual or quantum Forgiveness comes from an appreciation that only Love is real, and all behavior stems from either an expression of or call for Love. Thus, Love is the Will behind *all* behavior, no matter how it appears or how I perceive (judge) it. The only truly appropriate response to any behavior is Love. Knowing that all else is illusion and not real, there is in fact nothing to forgive. This is a good example of a non-dual thought. Do you sense the peace that comes from its acceptance? Peace is the best evidence of healing—that your mind, which is One with the Cause of Everything, is healing and becoming whole.

At this point in history, our planet is going through a natural evolutionary cycle leading to a new 5-D version of Earth. We are in the birthing process now. You can play a proactive role by allowing 5-D to be birthed in your awareness now. Begin to process your experiences through your heart space instead of trying to figure things out in your head alone. The breath is an excellent ally in this new way of being. Use the natural pull of the in-breath to take your attention down into the center of your chest. Use the out-breath to send out the Love that lies waiting there into each situation and relationship you encounter. Listen and speak from your heart. It may surprise you and others what comes out, but it will always be uplifting and joyful. A good example of a 5-D statement is "I love you." I love you.

SIXTH DIMENSION: SACRED GEOMETRY AND MATHEMATICS

As we go up the scale, the dimensions become more abstract to our understanding. The sixth dimension is where the geometric templates for the forms of creation for the denser dimensions exist. These exist in the form of geometric shapes or patterns of energy that are highly organized and reflective of Divine creative potential. These templates also exist as mathematical constants, or what Plato called ideal forms. When you gaze at sacred geometric forms, even those as simple as a circle or triangle, there is a captivating attractive quality to them. Something in us responds positively to these organizational blueprints. This is because they are imbedded within the forms of Nature at all levels, from the atomic to the cosmic, reflecting a greater intelligent Wholeness or totality. Plato identified five geometric forms, the Platonic solids that were behind all forms of matter and life. Perhaps these forms are part of what is inherently attractive about Nature as we sense Divine Intelligence reflected everywhere we look for it.

Crop circles are an excellent example of how 6-D sacred geometry both informs and transforms mind (4-D) and matter (3-D and 2-D). See if you are not mesmerized when looking at pictures of them. By the way, the debunkers of crop circles have themselves been thoroughly debunked by the sheer size and complexity of these forms, which appear almost instantaneously. Even the words "inform" and "information" imply an organizational effect of bringing data and knowledge into material form.

Freddy Silva, author of *Secrets in the Fields* (Hampton Roads, 2002), speaks of the significance of the geographic area in England where most of the crop circles show up each year. He said in a lecture in Denver a few years ago that this area of England lies over a vast bed of limestone that makes up the world's largest fresh-water underground aquifer, or reservoir. He said all the underground fresh-water systems on the planet are affected by what happens here. The crop circles, he went on to say, are homeopathically imprinting all the water on the planet with healing energies within the coherent 6-D geometries. Are these the "signs in the earth" of the End Times predicted by scripture? Some of them are revealing new mathematical theorems that have never before been formulated. Are they 6-D math lessons?

It stands to reason that if Earth and humanity are ascending to the fifth dimension, new and advanced templates for the forms of Nature are coming in at this time from 6-D to support a higher order of life, perhaps to replace the more dysfunctional dualistic aspects of Nature in the form of poisons, venomous and vicious species, etc. with life forms more reflective of a non-dual Reality. "And the Lion shall lie down with the Lamb." This can perhaps put a positive spin on the disappearance of alarming numbers of species from the Earth at this time. Are they naturally giving way to a more evolved version of themselves, or are they transporting ahead in time in order to get out of the pressure-cooker of the birthing we seem to be in? Maybe we'll find them happily awaiting us on 5-D Earth!

English zoologist Rupert Sheldrake infers the influence of 6-D in his theory of morphogenic fields (*A New Science of Life: the Hypothesis of Morphic Resonance,* Park Street Press, 1981). Sheldrake proposes that for every life form in 3-D there is a corresponding and pre-existing universal energetic template informing and connecting, as it were, the physical manifestation of the species. Even if there were only two representatives of a given species on Earth, there would be a planetary morphogenic field to support that species. He goes so far as to say that even non-living entities and commonly held beliefs (4-D thought forms) are supported by a pre-existing non-physical template.

Sheldrake's theory is consistent with Harold Saxton Burr's L-Field theory as applied to animal life forms. This Harvard professor theorized that every life form has a corresponding energy field that acts as a template and developmental map for the physical expression of that form (*Blueprint for Immortality: the Electric Patterns of Life,* Neville Spearman, 1972). His view was later illuminated by Robert Becker in *The Body Electric* (W. Morrow & Co., 1985). Becker found he could stimulate limb regeneration in animals by electrically stimulating scar cells on a limb stump to resonate with the energetic template that was still intact and functional, not affected by amputation. As we shall see, these ideas may be in line with how 6-D works. Forms in the lower dimensions are "informed" by information from the higher. Lower and higher here do not imply hierarchy, just ranges of vibration. When we discuss the even higher dimensions of light and sound along with creative intent, we can see how 6-D acts as a defining filter whereby these amorphous and more abstract energies from the higher dimensions can eventually materialize as they descend into matter.

The sixth dimension is, however, subject to duality. It is interesting that non-dual 5-D is nestled between two dualistic dimensions—4-D and 6-D. This implies that geometric and mathematical forms can be forces of either creation or destruction. It also implies that the positive aspects of 6-D may be applied to balance the negative. What is a negative expression of 6-D? I can only guess. Perhaps the negative aspects of geopathic stress, cancer-causing energy lines, and negative Earth energy vortices are indicators of 6-D's "down side." Or perhaps some of the energetic shapes and forms used by those in the "black arts" to cast spells and hexes. When the process of creative manifestation, filtered through 6-D, becomes unbalanced, as in the case of nuclear breakdown and radiation, energetic disturbances in the land, diseases in the body, the destruction of planets, or the collision of galaxies may result. Perhaps even the unregulated growth of cells and tissue in the case of cancer has a 6-D aspect, given that even cellular biological structures are supported by a 6-D geometric and mathematical template. There are even those in military intelligence (did someone say 'oxymoron'?) who have developed horribly destructive weapons based on low frequencies of sound. Get over it, guys! There's only One of us here! Would you do this if you saw me as only an aspect of your Self?

On the plus side, there are many systems of healing based in 6-D geometry. The use of *yantras* in Hindu meditation is an excellent example. This is a yoga involving gazing at sacred visual forms that restore harmony to mind, body, and spirit. Yogic postures in general mimic sacred forms, and create a 6-D resonant field in the body that facilitates higher states of consciousness and physical well-being. This gives another meaning to "getting into shape," doesn't it?

Ancient script and languages can also carry hidden 6-D information, locked, as it were, in the forms of the letters. The languages of the ancients, including Sanskrit, Chinese, and Hebrew, have been analyzed mathematically for their numerical qualities. Even the geometries of the shapes of the letters have been examined to identify specific subtle energies that may have inherent healing properties. The Meru Foundation and Stan Tenan (*www.meru.org*) have done a lot of this work. Len Horowitz summarizes some of these and other amazing findings about language, sound, and light geometries in his *DNA: the Pirates of the Sacred Spiral* (Tetrahedron Press, 2004), where he observes that all of these ancient so-called sacred languages were found to flow in a mathematically coherent way, even in how the letters are organized into words, sentences, and paragraphs. For us, these languages seem to read awkwardly on the page, from right to left or down to up. However, by comparison, the English language, our new "global standard," runs mathematically and numerologically backward! Who would have imagined that although English is regarded as the gold standard of world culture, and of economic and technological advancement, energetically, it appears to be a seriously flawed and even "dumbed-down" language?

Much of classical architecture and art around the world is rooted in sacred geometric forms that reflect higher levels of harmony for creating sacred spaces of worship. The European cathedrals built in the Middles Ages by the Knights Templar embody copious 6-D influences, all aimed at stimulating a holy (whole) experience and resonating with Divine principles. Labyrinths are also a good example of 6-D "spiritual technology," as are many forms of art, sculpture, and architecture. Playing with geometric solids and drawing geometric forms can put you in touch with the sixth dimension. Ever wonder where those creative "doodles" come from when your mind is distracted and they seem to just pour out of you? 6-D calling!

SEVENTH DIMENSION: SOUND AND LIGHT

More refined yet is the seventh dimension, the realm of energy as sound and light. These energies are closer to the Source in that they represent even more fundamental creative impulses than the forms of 6-D. Hans Jenny coined the term "cymatics" to describe the study of geometric forms that appear in sand when it is vibrated on metal plates as specific tones and sounds are played. An interesting example of how 7-D sound can express as 6-D scared geometry is seen in his observation of the formation of the Sri yantra, a yogic shape involving nested pyramids, which appeared in sand as a result of simply playing the sound "OM." This process implies the creative aspect of sound, "in-forming" 3-D with 6-D geometric templates. You could say that 7-D is a fundamental power source behind manifestation in the physical dimensions.

It has been said by many outside orthodoxy that the medicine of the future will be primarily sound and light, as we discover the deeper levels of healing that can occur by going to this more fundamental level of causation and organization. A pioneer in the use of light in healing was Dinshah (*Let There Be Light*, Dinshah Health Society, 1985). His system has set the standard for modern light-healing practitioners. Of course he was hounded and persecuted for operating outside the established medical "box"—primarily because he got results!

The creative power of sound is described in the Bible: "In the beginning was the Word." This power is also reflected in the primordial sound meditation in the Vedic tradition as promoted by Deepak Chopra. Ayurveda, the ancient Hindu healing philosophy, places a lot of emphasis on the benefits of chanting tones or *mantras* for their specific healing and consciousness-altering properties (see Ashley-Farrand, *Healing Mantras*, Ballantine Wellspring, 1999).

The Light we are discussing as part of 7-D is not limited to the narrow range of light our eyes can see. The visible spectrum is an infinitesimal representation of the complete electro-magnetic spectrum, making up no more than 1 percent of what is here. In Einstein's day, the speed of visible light was considered the fastest that anything could go—the limit of reality. As far as what our senses can perceive, this is true. But are the universe and the works of the Divine limited to what I can see with my limited photon receptors? We must open ourselves to the possibility of octaves of light energy extending into as yet unknown realms of energy. Here we may consider the ancient notion of "spiritual Light" as perhaps describing these upper octaves.

Einstein believed that all matter vibrating up to the limit of the speed of light was subject to specific laws, including the second law of thermodynamics. This law states in part that all matter, particularly living matter, is subject to entropy—the principle that the energy of an object or life form will ultimately take on the characteristics of its environment, and ultimately just fall apart as it dissipates back to the dust from whence it came. Again, within the limits in which our senses operate, this is true. In Gerber's excellent work *Vibrational Medicine* (Bear & Co., 2001), he notes that, according to the Tiller-Einstein theory, if light could be accelerated beyond Einstein's limit it would no longer be subject to entropy, but would rather tend toward higher states of organization and intelligence.

Tiller was inadvertently describing how many believe the human aura or energy field operates to mitigate the effects of stress, aging, and trauma to the body. What is further implied here is that the more energy we have operating in this light field, the more we can slow down the aging process or limit entropy. Dare I say, we can slow down time? Inversely, damage to the energy field from a variety of possible causes will ultimately weaken the physical body and increase its vulnerability to entropy through stress, disease, and misfortune. Consider this process in light of (pun intended) our collective entry into the photon band.

Through theories like these and, of course, the proven tenets of quantum physics, we are finally beginning to see scientific validation for many ancient healing arts and beliefs previously discounted as superstition by neophyte and arrogant believers in the new religion of material or empirical science over the last two centuries.

We cannot discuss the healing benefits of sound and light without mentioning the most radiant physical influence on our planet—the Sun. The Sun has received a bad rap of late, being blamed for high counts of skin cancer in particular. We are now seeing reports, however, of the dangers of the overuse of sunscreen concoctions that not only contribute to cancers themselves, but also contribute to a general deficiency of vitamin D, a hormone that depends on at least fifteen minutes of UV exposure daily for normal production in the body. Vitamin D is necessary to metabolize calcium. Therefore, it is also most important for normal bone development. Its deficiency is believed to be associated with bone loss/density issues as well as poor immunity.

All our nutrition ultimately originates from the Sun, concentrated within the plants and animals we consume. The Sun is the energy source for all biological life on Earth. As we have seen in our discussion of the photon band, it is changes in the Sun's characteristics that are driving the dramatic physical evolutionary changes we are seeing on the planet. We can hide from, but ultimately not avoid, these changes. I am not advocating irresponsible over-exposure to sunlight, especially by those perhaps pre-disposed to certain risks. But in fearful avoidance of the Sun and its light we may hinder adaptation to a process that Nature is expressing that will ultimately help to move us to the next stage of human development.

As we move up through the dimensions the influences become more subtle and less obvious, but no less significant. There is no hierarchy of importance when we talk about "levels" of energy, just differences that we, by the act of perception, create in our own minds. This is good to keep in mind as we discuss these things, as taking our own thoughts and perceptions too seriously has gotten us all into a lot more trouble than necessary in the past.

As 7-D is a dimension of sound driven by light, it is helpful to keep in mind that the source of the Light we are discussing is the eighth dimension—Divine Creative Intelligence, the Mind or Will of God. As such, this Light may be regarded as fundamental to sound. The light and sound of 7-D provide the impetus and energy to stimulate the forms of 6-D, which again precipitate into matter via the lower, denser dimensions.

To tune into 7-D, we again turn to Nature and its sounds and energies. We open to the possibility of octaves of light beyond the physical—the Great Rays referred to by the metaphysicians of the past. And we can determine to give ourselves respite from the sounds and energies of the mechanical world on as regular a basis as we can. The grating noises and maniacal ravings of the ego-dominated media and entertainment industry do not serve your development into *homo luminous*. They are representative of the ego's fear to let go and let God be—to let you just be. Essentially the Sound of 7-D, in physical terms, is heard in Silence. Through cultivating physical and mental silence, we can learn to tune into the music of the spheres—the now faint yet ever-present tones of Creation.

Here is a simple exercise to help focus attention on 7-D and pull some Divine Light into your 3-D experience. This is best done outdoors actually facing the Sun, but you can also do it indoors facing the Sun's direction. Put your two forefingers and thumbs together to form a triangle. Hold this shape over your heart space or forehead and say out loud, "I now receive the Light from beyond the Light." Repeat until you sense a fullness or completion. This is, believe it or not, a good way to quell an appetite if you are looking to lose some weight, as you are opening to receive a higher dimensional form of nutrition. You may also want to hold an image of the Sun pulling in and reflecting to you the light emanating from the galactic center. Your mind and the decisions you make are your most powerful transformational allies. After all, you made the universe!

EIGHTH DIMENSION: THE MIND OF GOD

Here we find the primordial creative impulse sending the inspiration of life into the formative dimensions below. This is the representation of Source in the universe of form. But it is not the Source itself, or the home of God for that matter. The Divine Source of All is totally formless and abstract, and therefore cannot be confined to any single dimension of existence—or to any concept at all. That is why any discussion of God will simply devolve into a set of opinions, theories, and preferences, or all-out war. God exists in absolute abstraction beyond this and any other model, as does the Mind that is consciously One with God.

But the Divine can be known from here in perhaps two ways. First, as mirrored in its creations. You in your Divine totality and perfection as Spirit are the one and only direct creation of God. Man-made dualistic religions like to think that God created the world and universe of forms, including human bodies. But if this is so, how could a completely perfect-in-itself Being even conceive of, much less create, duality, suffering, destruction, time, death, ego, and all these other aspects of Creation that somehow bespeak a curse or fall from Grace. It is not possible. So if God is the Prime Creator but did not create the universe of separated forms, who did? Simple. We did! It goes like this: God... You...the Universe. As the universe "lives" only in your imagination of separation, only you as Spirit and God as Creator exist in reality.

In the modern non-dual perspective of *A Course in Miracles* (Foundation for Inner Peace, 3rd edition, 2005), it states that we—that is, collective humanity as we are as One, and as the only creation of the Divine (the one Son of God if you like)—dreamed up the universe of separate forms in response to a desire for something "other than" Oneness. I say "dreamed up" because in reality *nothing can truly exist outside of perfect Oneness.* If it could, there would be no "perfect Oneness." But within that Oneness, it is possible to imagine separation, as it is possible to imagine anything and everything within perfect freedom. And that is what happened. As simply an imaginary idea within the Mind of the "Son" of God, one in which we forgot to laugh at the ridiculousness of the idea, the world and universe of form came into being—sort of.

By that I mean that it came into being in our minds, and nowhere else. This is why we can honestly and truthfully say "the universe is in your mind." As the universe appearing "out there" is an out-picturing of your mind, you can go anywhere at any time and experience anything at the speed of thought. The reason this is not our experience right now is we have too many beliefs and thoughts that tell us this is not so. This is why looking anywhere outside the mind, or primary cause of the universe, for truth will ultimately fail and eventually bring you to this understanding, usually by means of elimination, frustration, and surrender, although this path is not absolutely necessary. Understanding this answered a deeply disturbing question for me, as it likely will for many who can't accept the Sunday School version of creation. The question is: How *could* a supposedly loving Creator make such a messed-up world of pain, suffering, disease and death? The answer, which seems obvious to me now, is "He/She didn't." Yet how powerful and masterfully creative we are to create such an intricate and seemingly real dream out of a mere whim! The dream bespeaks the thought of separation and all the endless permutations of separation, but is no more than a trance-inducing hallucination or illusion, as we read in ancient non-dual thought systems like the Tao, the Vedanta, and recently in *A Course in Miracles*. What makes a good illusion is its believability. Because we added time as an essential ingredient in the illusory spell of separation, the dream-illusion actually seems to have some kind of permanence, or at least continuity. Dreamers are always convinced their dreams are real until they awaken. The analogy is very apt here.

Within the pseudo-reality of the dream universe, we have the imaginary separation of All That Is into dimensions of vibrating energy. And the imaginary dimension that symbolizes our own Divine creative impulse is the eighth. You could say the eighth dimension embodies the human will to create, a will we have inherited from our Creator, but have misused—as a child picks up a real object and plays with it as if it were a mere toy. The beauty of this exercise of the will is that it is, despite its present misuse, the Divine Will expressing through us, just colored or compromised at this time by our desire to be separate egos.

Stepping back again to keep perspective, none of this is real outside of our perception of it. You could say the universe of form is a movie projected by the One Mind that is dreaming it. Remember, this is *all* an inside job. The One Mind paints images on the screen of consciousness. This implies that consciousness itself is part of the illusion. When you think of consciousness as simply the idea of a separate "I" with its unique perspective and experiences completely separate from all others and the Divine, how could "my" consciousness be anything but an illusion?

In my Divinity, I am dreaming of separation. Who I really am is unaffected by my dream. So the spark of Divine creativity emanating from 8-D is in actuality the spark of our own Divine Nature. You could say it is the domain of our collective Higher Self—the aspect of Self that remembers Oneness before the split and the dream and expresses creativity, albeit within a state of separation. Duality implies *both* illusion and truth operating in tandem. The illusory aspect projects the ego and its world of suffering. Spirit projects the memory of Oneness and Divine Love. The eighth dimension is where the One Mind expresses as Creative Spirit. It is both representative of our true home in the Mind of God, which is beyond form and duality, and the inherent creativity of the Created One (all of us) to imagine into being new worlds of experience, even one like this. Earth is the world of all possibilities where we get to play out our fantasies of being other than what we are, and then deciding when we've had enough to go home.

The second way we can know the Divine is in our personal feeling experience, particularly the experience of inner Peace and Silence. When the dualistic mind is in neutral we are flooded with true perception and we know without thinking. This is not as esoteric as it may sound, as what I am describing is also true of what is known as right-brain perception, or non-verbal intelligence. The appreciation of art, beauty, and Nature defies analysis. It just *is*. The experience of mental silence through meditation, contemplation, breathing exercises, or mindfulness practices are universal doorways into the ocean of awareness waiting in silence just beyond perception. Trance dancing, the use of mind-altering substances, and the worship of symbolic deities are common to all known natural cultures. These practices, no matter how distorted they may become, are all indicative of the need to *feel* Spirit and transcend, if only temporarily, the disparities and conflicts within duality, physicality, and perception.

The eighth dimension comes through as Divine inspiration in the form of answers that transcend our own thoughts and conditioning. These are truly original thoughts, unlike most thoughts from the 4-D collective field, and are usually ideas that operate as "win-win" solutions and always for the highest good of all. This right-thinking part of the mind lies next to the Mind of God. At best, our individuated mind becomes a bridge to the Source of the One Mind we share. Eventually, the Divine Mind will pull us entirely into its realm, where we will no longer need a body, time, or space. This transition represents the ultimate in the surrender of the ego—the end of all valuing of and attachment to illusion. We become the Divine, with no distinction. In the meantime, while we still operate here in bodies and time, we can receive directly from the Source via our 8-D connection. Only Spirit can see all of the countless ramifications of every thought and action. Spirit's answer is always right for everyone.

The eighth dimension is thus not the domain of God, but is reflective of the true nature of God's Creation, which is us. This dimension is as close as we can get to God and still remain in the universe of form. It's like

Space Camp, with all the feelings and props of the real experience—enough until you graduate and get to go into space for real.

NINTH DIMENSION: THE SOURCE OF TIME WAVES

A further indication that 8-D is not God itself is that there is a dimension vibrating beyond it, and what can be beyond God? In Clow's model, 9-D is symbolized locally by the Black Hole in the center of the Milky Way. Out of this transformational vortex emerges a template of time or a pattern of how time will be played out in the galaxy. You may think of this as an impulse or wave movement carrying the story of time as we in the galaxy are living it out. What this image implies is that one wave will be followed by another, and another, etc.

These ideas are pretty consistent with the model of time proposed by the Mayan calendar. The Maya envisioned a holographic resonant pattern in the Black Hole called the True Cross of Creation or Tree of Life responsible for generating this wave. This notion has been expanded by Calleman in his latest work, *The Purposeful Universe* (Bear & Co., 2009), where he cites the discovery of a similar structure operating on a universal level as well. His research strongly supports the notion of vibrating creative templates dictating the expression of the universe on multiple levels within the total hologram of creation from the scale of the entire universe, down through galactic, stellar, planetary, organic, and cellular scales of expression. A must read!

A time wave is simply an idea of how time can be experienced. Waxing non-dual again, we see that time is part and parcel of the imaginary projection of the universe by the One Mind. Time, a dualistic concept, is one of our prime illusions along with space and the body, as these exemplify and symbolize the idea of separation constituting an almost air-tight belief system within the dream. In reality, because of the impossibility of splitting Oneness, the dream of the universe of form was over the split-second it occurred. It simply could not happen other than in a dream. But when you are the dreamer unaware that you are dreaming *and* the main character in your dream, it seems as if the dream is undeniably real. Time marches on. And it will continue to do so until you awaken. When you awaken inside of the dream, you begin to operate lucidly—that is, with the awareness you are in a dream, but not of the dream. This is knowledge you hold in your 8-D spiritual memory.

The current time wave is about to crash on the shores of this part of the galaxy and dissolve. According to Calleman's calculations in *The Mayan Calendar* (Garev Pub. Intl., 2001 and *www.calleman.com*), this is scheduled to occur on October 28, 2011. This date corresponds to the "descent of the nine Lords of Time," completing the nine-step model as described by Calleman. A new experience of time will possibly begin, but one with much less rigidity; rather we will know time as a series of complete-in-themselves moments unfettered by a past or future. This state has been described as the paradoxical Time of No Time. As we will be ascending into a 5-D physicality, the dualistic and linear aspects of time will be greatly reduced if not gone for good—perhaps just used as a functional necessity for coordinating certain common activities, but otherwise an anachronism.

From a time-bound or egoic perspective, the End of Time is regarded with dread and foreboding. Time is a primary anchor in the false dream of separation. "Running out of time" is analogous to death in the ego's view. Death is one of the ego's biggest fear games, as it knows it is when the body dies that you discover you are not either a body or an ego! There are no unbelievers on the deathbed.

As much as we have invested in our identity as time-, space-, and body-bound beings, we will be proportionately discomfited by needing to reinterpret time. Taking a glass-half-full perspective is recommended. Rather than thinking simply of the End of Time, think "the beginning of a new interpretation of time"—one that promises to liberate me, you, and all of us from all of time's limitations. For a further discussion of the End of Time, please refer to Book II of this work.

The next chapter will take you deeper into the plan of time and its conclusion. The notion of time being part of a cyclic unfolding implies an outcome for this plan. In the meantime, we can use time constructively by using it to unlearn the belief in time as being necessary at all.

TENTH DIMENSION AND BEYOND

In our model, 10-D simply describes the totality of all nine dimensions so far described. Again, the notion of hierarchical structures is inherently dualistic, and is only a convenience we have constructed in order to navigate the dualistic dream universe. Even the totality of what we have described does not account for what may lie beyond our current perception. It is not inconceivable that there could be infinite dimensions of time and space, depending on our ability to observe them. More fundamental to an appreciation of all this is that the universe of form, in all its elegance and complexity, is simply one possible expression of the infinite creativity of God's True Creation—which is us. If we can do all this with just an imaginary whim of a thought, a passing fancy in truth, what could we do as mature, focused, unified, and compassionate Creators of Realities? Perhaps we are about to get a glimpse of this potential very soon.

You could say that experiencing the tenth dimension is what has been described as Unity Consciousness, or the state that I described to you as I glimpsed it in 1971. All of us in our potential are capable of coming to and perhaps destined to come to this point of awareness, and beyond. Unity Consciousness is so far beyond linguistic description that it has simply been called Bliss by those reporting from this state. The Oneness University in South India has conducted years of research on and teaches techniques aimed at facilitating these higher states (*www.onenessuniversity.org*). At one point, neuroscientists were assisting in this effort and reported that a state of Unity Consciousness or Enlightenment was accompanied by the full activation and dopamine saturation of the left frontal lobe. This may be a biological correlate to a natural step in human spiritual evolution.

The coming together of all the neural pathways in the brain into a single, cohesive, and conscious unit is a further correlate, or reflection, of the inevitable unification of humanity operating as One Mind. I believe the linking of the planet's information systems via the Internet reflects what is happening in our individual brains as well as the collective brain of humanity. Once functioning at this level, any fear-based thought will immediately be known as self-defeating, and thus automatically be released from awareness. War, conflict, neglect, poverty, etc. will have lost their basis in each and every one of us. Our only interest as unified planetary beings will be in that which only serves the highest good of all. Anything else is inconceivable.

You don't have to wait for conditions to be right to step into a 10-D level of functioning and awareness. Why put off what is inevitable? A good approach is to act as if you are there until your intent fully manifests. You may want to start each day with a simple prayer or meditation affirming "I am One with All That Is" or some similar non-dual affirmation. As we train our minds to begin thinking like the Divine, we send out a signal, as it were, to the Divine that "I am ready *now* to awaken to Who I Am." In the meantime, know that as you consciously access and operate from any of these dimensional realms, you are exercising your creative freedom to explore All That Is from the unique perspective of a being who has voluntarily entered into a state of separation and thus illusion. So, enjoy your experiences and learn to be a responsible choice-maker. But do not attach to any of it, as that will ensure the continuation of the gnawing sense of disconnection of which this universe is an expression—until you get tired enough of that experience and choose Peace instead.

In traditional or natural societies the goal of the shaman was to be able to function consciously and intentionally in different dimensions and in bringing back helpful knowledge or information. The purpose behind this process was always healing. Healing, or "to make whole (holy)" is really the only rational thing to do here once we know the world is in our minds and nowhere else.

EARTH CHANGES AS DIMENSIONAL SHIFT

We have seen that the essential difference between the dimensions is the speed or rate of vibration of light/energy resulting in different states of expression. Is it thus possible to create the conditions where something actually goes through a multi-dimensional portal to emerge into a different state or form of itself? The simple answer is "yes" and the simplest analogy is water. When water molecules are at their lowest rate of vibration, we have solid ice. As ice, water can behave like a mountain. It can sink ships, cool drinks, store food, and preserve the life forms from past eras indefinitely. I'm thinking of those cool frozen mastodons. But add a little heat—that is, raise the rate of molecular vibration—and water becomes liquid, with completely different qualities and abilities. Liquid water can carve mountains, dissolve practically any other element, and carry and emit electro-magnetic as well as subtle-energy patterns as Nature's ideal liquid-crystal antenna. But wait! Raise the vibration rate with heat energy even further, and we go into another dimension—vapor. As vapor we have a whole new set of qualities again. Water, of course, is very flexible as a multi-dimensional substance, and can morph back and forth between these states if given the correct frequency of heat energy.

Let's look at the potential for a planet-wide dimensional shift in light of the alignment with the photon band. Emanating from the galactic center we have a form of light unique in the entire galaxy in concentration and frequency. Recall the notion of octaves of light in our discussion of 7-D. What if this intense high-frequency energy with a 1000-year alignment with our Sun's path were sufficient to "cook" all the sub-atomic structures making up what we call physical matter into another dimensional state? On an atomic level, this is accepted theory. Bombard an atom with enough light energy, and the electron in orbit around the nucleus leaps into a higher orbit or dimension in order to hold the new energy. When the light source is interrupted, the electron drops back down to its original orbit, releasing a photon of light in the process.

Greg Braden pointed out years ago in his *Awakening to Zero Point* (Radio Bookstore Press, 1993) that one of the main effects of our entering the photon band would be a relaxation of the magnetic field of the Sun, as mentioned earlier. This was actually reported by NASA on their website in 1999. They used the word "collapsed," saying they could no longer locate the magnetic poles on the Sun. Of course, given Earth's proximity to and sympathetic vibration with the Sun, the same thing happened here and on all the planets. Airports now regularly have to re-calibrate their equipment to the magnetic poles, which are wavering in position quite significantly. As discussed earlier, perhaps the reason for this is that the Sun no longer has to work as hard to produce energy internally through nuclear processes, but can relax as it is now receiving direct energetic support or fuel from the galactic core. As this happens, according to Braden, the frequencies of activities on the Sun have risen accordingly. Evidence of this is in the increased luminosity of the Sun, whose reach, or heliosphere, is 1000 times as radiant now as it was before 1999 (Free and Wilcock, *The Reincarnation of Edgar Cayce?* Frog Ltd., 2004).

Other evidence is seen in the increase in solar-flare activity since 1999, which has disproven predictions based on usual cycles, and is the dominant influence in the dramatic weather changes on Earth now. Each year following 1999, which was the year *El Nino* hit the headlines, we saw a series of "storms of the century," each one greater than the last. On Earth, reports Braden, the drop in magnetics has been accompanied by a rise in the Schumann Wave, or "heartbeat" of the Earth, although this conclusion is still challenged by mainstream scientists. This electromagnetic wave was first theorized in 1952, based on the observation of a resonant cavity between the Earth's surface and the upper atmosphere. Electrical charges build up here due to static effects, which typically release as lightning. An electro-magnetic hum or "heartbeat" in this zone can now be detected around the planet with advanced measuring devices.

This subtle electrical pulse exerts a homing effect on every physical life form on the planet, resonating specifically with the DNA in all life forms. NASA discovered that they had to replicate this pulse for astronauts, who began to deteriorate physically in outer space without it. Braden suggests the rate of the Schumann Wave is now rising from a base of 7.9 HZ to 13 HZ, values reflecting a similar change in individual brain waves as we shift from a sleeping to a waking state.

The controversy around Braden's claims may be due partly to the sporadic nature of these changes, defying repeatable patterns and thus not generating "solid" data. Many psychics and intuitives report energy spikes in geomagnetic energies lately, particularly at and around recognized power places on the planet. These power places correspond to a planetary grid created by a mathematically coherent pattern of lines of energy over the surface of the Earth. The intersection points of these lines have been used by many ancient cultures in establishing places of worship and initiation based on their unique and stimulating energetic qualities. The notion of Earth having an energy system similar to the meridians and chakras in humans and animals gives credence to the idea of Earth as a living organism herself—the Gaia Theory. Is this rise in Earth's frequency reflecting the awakening of the global brain and a new Ascended Planet?

In biological theory, the DNA molecule is being recognized as the primary informational conduit between biological, planetary, and cosmic influences. DNA, it turns out, has crystalline qualities, largely due to the proliferation of ideal "clustered" water crystals attached to the DNA molecule. It seems that DNA is attuned vibrationally to Mother Earth by way of the Schumann Wave and the resonant qualities of water. If the Earth's wave frequency were to increase sufficiently, would this have a stimulating effect on the DNA structure? And would this effect be sufficient to cause, or at least contribute to, alterations in the DNA and thus the expression of life on Earth? As up to 97 percent of human DNA is purportedly dormant or inactive, the implications for this activation process are tremendous. If we can do what we do now at 3 percent activation, can you imagine a "new human" with 6 percent, or 12 percent, or even 25 percent active DNA? All driven by cosmologic events planned from the beginning—our own masterfully created exit strategy for transcending the trap of duality.

This is why, for me, the global warming argument rings hollow. To ascribe recent extreme weather changes *solely* to human activity is to be in serious denial of the role of Nature's cycles and the Big Picture. What could cause this lack of attention to these greater realities in the mainstream media and focusing only on the human contribution to the problem? Could it be the old red-herring technique of "look over here, but don't look there"? As noted earlier, those who have enjoyed the control of planetary conditions for generations are not about to admit, even to themselves, that there is something happening beyond their control.

The operative word here is "control." I have no doubts that at some level within the planetary management system, these cycles and cosmic factors are known, but the information is denied to the public ostensibly to avoid panic. It seems to me this denial of information may also be part of the effort to forestall the inevitable obsolescence of an old control paradigm based on fear and enslavement. Inherent in this dysfunctional approach to planetary leadership is a lack of trust—in you, me, and humanity—to face these trials and opportunities together, empowered by our unity. Yes, humans have likely contributed to global warming, and there certainly is room for more responsible and sustainable forms of energy use, but it's not just about *that.*

As for environmentalists or others sincerely dedicated to improving the human interface with Mother Earth, I applaud your sincerity and nobility of intent. As, however, we can't solve problems from the level of the problem-*maker,* which is the separated ego-mind responsible for all suffering, we need to go to a more fundamental level of cause to be truly effective in bringing about lasting change. We must begin to see the world as an *effect* and not as a cause of anything in and of itself. Heal the mind that projects the movie, and the movie *will* change.

Perhaps another reason to disregard the cyclical view of history publically, particularly the Vedic view of Yugas, is that this view especially implies former Golden Ages where human society rose to pinnacles of perfection before cycling back down into the madness of materialism. This view challenges the modern egoic belief in our own superiority and the ego-affirming myth of progress. "How could anyone else in the past have surpassed in any way what *we* have accomplished," we ask ourselves. "Are we not the Crown of Creation?" Don't get me wrong; I love progress. I love flush toilets and refrigerators. But do I love these things at the price of degrading the environment, exploiting the labor of enslaved peoples, and waging endless war to finance it all? Progress for the few has cost us all heavily. Civilization is not just the history of the expansion of culture, knowledge, and skill. It is also the history of war, conquest, enslavement, genocide, and the rape of the Earth. And that's duality.

Prior Golden Ages, report the misty legends of yore, were times of spiritual as well as material wealth—times of peace and prosperity for all, times of inner as well as outer exploration, when all life was valued and the Divine acknowledged in everything. May these times return, and soon! Can you imagine a modern Golden Age with all our technological achievements and advantages in addition to a global return to true spiritual values? It is your dream. You may have whatever you can imagine.

Interestingly, the Aztec calendar, fashioned after the prior and more complete Mayan calendar, divided the 26,000-year solar cycle into five even 5200-year eons or eras, which they called "worlds." By the way, the End of the World paranoia around 2012 is due in part to the misinterpretation of the term "world." The End of the World is simply the end of a period of time. Sorry, no apocalypse here! The ego loves dramatic endings—any dramatic ending except its own.

The last "world" or 5200-year epoch ended in a flood according to the Aztec calendar. This is consistent with the evidence and mythologies of global flooding, an event present in practically every natural society's memory. According to this calendar, the current world will be destroyed by fire. We tend to interpret these things literally, but could it be that the makers of the calendar were referring to what the Vedic system calls "cosmic fire," or intense spiritual energy in the form of radiations from space, rather than physical fire? Now, fire is a transformative element. As such, dimensional transformation as a result of exposure to cosmic energies is consistent with the model of galactic alignment and the physics of light. We are not talking about destruction by physical fire, but transformation, or trans*mutation* by cosmic fire. Are you feeling the heat yet?

The value of this dimensional model of the Shift of Time lies in part in providing a somewhat grounded, although expansive, explanation for the scale of change we are discussing. As we expand our minds and perceptions beyond the box of conditioning and herd consciousness, models like this can play an important transitional role in our expansion. Eventually, we discard the models, like scaffolds on a building. Once the structure is complete, we will no longer need to be propped up by models that have served their purpose. This may eventually hold true for thought itself, as we no longer will need to build little cognitive bridges and roadmaps to our destination. We *are* the destination, even now.

CHAPTER 4

THE MAYAN CALENDAR—
A ROADMAP TO PLANETARY
AWAKENING

O f all the ways we have to think about time in the modern world, nothing to my knowledge rivals the scope and elegance of the Mayan calendar. Much has been written and speculated about this enigmatic time-keeping system, particularly as the predicted end of the calendar approaches. The ego-mind tends to look at time-based predictions as being first linear, that is describing fixed events beyond human control and following a specific path or "chain of events," and second as most likely cataclysmic and thus fearful. The ego loves to play victim. As mentioned earlier, Barbara Clow wrote about this common tendency for humans to expect the worst when it comes to dramatic changes on the Earth. And perhaps with good reason, she tells us in *Catastrophobia.*

Not too long ago on a cosmological scale, around 9500 BC, there were vast catastrophic changes on the Earth associated with the last passage through the photon band. This was before the advent of writing, and thus before recorded history. The memory of this terrible time is, however, locked in our DNA and cellular memories, perhaps along with deeper memories of past traumas throughout life's rocky road from 16.5 billion years ago up to the present day. When we hear or see images of uncontrollable disaster, these memories can be triggered and we go into a contracted, fearful state where creative responses to whatever is truly going on around us are stifled. We "re-act" to the past rather than acting creatively.

But "catastrophobia" is not in any way the intended purpose of the Mayan calendar, as Hollywood would prefer to have you believe. Rather, the calendar was a way for the Maya to be aware of and stay attuned to the ebb and flow of natural and spiritual energies as they unfolded in cycles in a predetermined trajectory of time. The calendar is based on multiple natural cycles, including that of the Sun, Earth, Moon, and Venus, and that of the human gestation period of 260 days. By holding in their awareness the many holographic representations of life's flow within these cycles, the Maya learned to respect and venerate the unfolding of time as part of a much greater plan of Creation. How unlike the modern technological and reductionist notion of time as simply a random yet linear movement through endless detail and disconnected events with no unified purpose!

I will not attempt to go into the intricacies of the calendar's structure. That work has already been expertly accomplished by Carl Calleman (*www.calleman.com*) and validated by Barbara Clow with her recent book *The Mayan Code* (Bear & Co., 2007). The book you hold in your hands is intended as a review of the work of these and other visionaries and an overview so that, along with all the other topics discussed, a Big Picture may emerge that leads to a greater appreciation of the unified plan unfolding before us all. The further intent is that you embrace these times *now* with peace, joy, and childlike expectation.

QUETZALCOATL AND THE
NINE UNDERWORLDS

The calendar was said to be the gift and legacy of Quetzal-coatl, the last great deity-king of the Mayan culture circa 2000 years ago. He was known as the Feathered Serpent, a title implying a blend of heavenly and earthly qualities. When he left the Earth plane, Quetzalcoatl reportedly said he was "returning home to Venus," but that he would revisit Earth at some time in the future. Unfortunately for the later Aztecs, they miscalculated this return and mistook Cortez' arrival by sea from the East to be the return of the legendary God King. This is why Cortez was able to waltz into the New World, decimate the Aztecs, and take their gold home to Spain largely unimpeded. He must have thought at one point: "It's good to be mistaken for a God!"

Quetzalcoatl's mention of Venus is interesting. Aside from Venus' movement being one of the many cycles observed in the calendar, Venus itself has some unique properties. It spins in a direction opposite to all the other planets in the solar system. In the physical realm, it is a living hell with temperatures that could melt lead and a toxic atmosphere that could dissolve living flesh instantly. Yet, in other dimensions, can there be something else going on? Remember how limited our senses are at showing us reality.

Nikola Tesla, now regarded as the pioneering genius who gave the world radio, radar, alternating current, and many other inventions too numerous to count, claimed to have created near the end of his life a device that could gather data from space using the body of Earth itself as an antenna. And he claimed to be receiving messages from Venus! This was just the ammunition his detractors needed to discredit Tesla completely. But why would they want to do that? Many, if not most, of Tesla's greatest discoveries were stolen by others. Just look at any modern history book and see how Marconi, Edison, and others got credit for Tesla's work.

We find interesting references to another great historical figure, Jesus of Nazareth, as "the bright and Morning Star," another name for Venus. And of course in Greek and modern mythology, Venus is the archetype of unconditional Love, a 5-D attribute as we have seen. Could it be that planets like Venus that appear dead and lifeless in one dimension may actually support a higher vibrational civilization—in this case, one of Ascended Masters or those who have graduated, as it were, from the 3-D duality school of Earth? I cannot discount this possibility.

In alignment with the idea of different dimensional expressions of the same body or within one space, we have the Hopi Blue Star prophesy. The Hopi predict that by the year 2012 a Blue Star or Blue Sun will be very evident in our skies. We may discover to our amazement that our Sun is part of a dual-star system, a much greater statistical probability than it being just a lone star. Do the Hopi imply that a new physical body will magically materialize out of nothing? Or is it more reasonable to appreciate that what is really changing here is human awareness, and as we open to a broader scope or version of All That Is, our senses will reflect this expansion by being able to perceive a Reality that is already here in another frequency range of vibration, just beyond our current limit of perception?

We must also pay attention to the occurrence and timing of the last transit of Venus. This is a somewhat rare alignment of Venus, Earth, and the Sun that occurs roughly every 120 years. Oddly, when it happens once, as it did in June 2004, it occurs again around eight years later before disappearing for another 100 years. That would put the re-appearance of the alignment in June of 2012, after the predicted end date and completion of the calendar on October 28, 2011. If we think of Venus as carrying the archetype and frequency of unconditional Love, consider the transit as the frequency of Venus powered by the Sun and blasted onto the Earth for seven hours, to return again eight years later. It is as if Earth were being blessed with the frequency of unconditional Love that we will need to carry us through this time—the two events bracketing the Time of the Shift on October 28, 2011, as it were. Was *this* the promised return of Quetzalcoatl in the form of a more universal energy field? Jesus also said his return would be "as the lightning comes from the East" (Matt. 24). Modern Mormons believe these two historical figures are one and the same, citing legends of Quetzalcoatl bearing wounds in his hands and feet. That implies that the calendar, whose recognized author is Quetzalcoatl, is also a gift of the Master of Peace, Jeshua Ben Joseph, or in the more familiar Greek translation, Jesus. Thus it would behoove Western believers to look at this timetable with respect and consider the implications for their own religious views.

The Mayan time-keepers were full-time devotees of the tracking and teachings of the calendar. Given the challenges of supporting a large population in difficult farming conditions, one can appreciate how critical the timing of annual events like planting and harvesting could be. But it went far beyond that. Perhaps on some level the Maya felt a greater responsibility to all mankind, especially those who would be alive at the time of the calendar's completion—us. Otherwise, why did they commemorate their time-keeping system in huge nine-step pyramids scattered throughout their empire—literal calendars in stone? Lost for centuries under the jungle overgrowth, these irrefutable stone documents have now been uncovered and understood by people like Calleman, whose insight is unparalleled, in my opinion. Perhaps this is because Calleman is a biologist, not an archeologist. He has applied the simple principles of science and the scientific method with an eye untainted by the prejudices and conservatism that mark much of historical and archeological academia. He has nothing to lose by rocking the boats of his more conservative colleagues!

A key insight from Calleman is that each of the nine steps of the stepped-pyramid model symbolizes an epoch of time called an "underworld"—not in the sense of a "hell," but simply a foundation of time upon which subsequent foundations are laid. Before any one of the foundations completes in linear time, the next one starts. As such, none of the underworlds are yet complete; they still support the structures and consciousness of the ones above. Each step up the pyramidal calendar model represents both a greater sophistication and expansion in the expression of life and a time acceleration factor of twenty. The entire model is scheduled to complete, with each underworld completing simultaneously, on October 28, 2011. This is somewhat before the more generally accepted end date of December 21, 2012, and for good reason. The calendar itself is not tied to cycles of Nature, but rather to the birthing of a new consciousness. This is not to say that the latter process does not occur within natural cycles; it is simply not what the calendar is about. The calendar traces the progress of Awareness or Light or Mind into matter in this Earthly experience. It represents the stretched-out dream of time as we, in our unlimited creativity, have imagined it to be. Rather than a new cycle, the calendar represents the end of cycles that have been playing out for 16.5 billion years, and the end of the cause of all suffering from within the dualistic mind.

As the process of time unfolds, life expresses with greater complexity and scope at each evolutionary step up the calendar. And, unlike the modern Gregorian calendar, which portrays time as endlessly unfolding over a recklessly random temporal desert, the Mayan calendar clearly indicates a Grand Purpose to our experience of time. Just like the structure of a pyramid, time has a point—a reason. Once the purpose of time is completed, we will no longer need to experience a continuation of past patterns. Linear time will be put in its place—that is, it may be used for tracking common events like keeping appointments, but the experience of psychological time, our mental attachment to and identification with past and future that is responsible for 90 percent of human suffering, will be over.

How are linear time and human suffering related? Our entire separated ego-existence is completely dependent on our belief in time. Having a past to describe ourselves and a future to fulfill gives us an individual identity apart from others and their unique experiences in time. Our personal histories are simply the memory of a chain of perceptions. We have seen that the nature of perception is itself illusory. Thus the past is simply a set of preferred illusions. Past conditioning dictates 99 percent of our thinking. Thought is therefore an old roadmap that keeps us in the same old ruts, perpetuating the past into the future, while providing a safe haven for the ego and its fear-based pseudo-existence. A truly original thought is a rare event, and usually occurs as the result of the dedicated cultivation of mental silence or the demands of attention to an immediate trauma.

Time-bound consciousness is not just an individual thing. Collectively, we are chained to a world of cyclic historical patterns of fear-based aggression, war, poverty, and inequality that today threaten all our futures! All the plans to save the planet that deal only with the level of effects are doomed to fail, as they are simply dealing with symptoms and not the cause. And the root cause of every problem in the world is the belief in separation in the mind, with the concurrent belief in time, space, and bodies as "proof" of separation's viability. This is the fall from Grace and the loss of knowledge of our Oneness with God and each other.

The fall from Unity Consciousness involved partaking of the knowledge of good *and* evil—that is, the perception of opposites and duality.

Separation from Oneness is, however, an oxymoron deluxe! If you can divide Oneness, then it isn't truly Oneness. Oneness remains as it is no matter what I fantasize to the contrary. And that is what separation is—simply an illusory dream. For many, it's a nightmare. A dream is a very convincing illusion. A shared dream is even more convincing. Within the dream of separation the biggest "co-illusions," or collusions, are time, space, and the body, as noted. Each of these is a separation concept. In reality—that is, next to Oneness—they are only impossible and delusionary ideas. And not very solid ideas, either. They are ideas that were doomed from the start and in reality were over the second they were imagined.

Time and space are our way of stretching out this momentary lapse of sanity into seemingly endless bits. The body is the ego's ultimate hiding place from the memory of Oneness, which can only spell the end of the ego. Soon, perhaps sooner than we realize, we will find ourselves in an ego-less world—a world at Peace. The ego is afraid that without *it,* all would be chaos. What we discover, however, and to our delight, is that without an ego, all is Love! Love rushes in to fill the space made by your willingness to go within and fearlessly face your illusions.

The beauty of the Mayan calendar is that most of the model is complete. We can look at known history through the lens of the calendar and see a perfect match with significant events in history and significant turning points in the calendar. Again, I refer you to Calleman's work in this area. Looking at the calendar's accuracy so far provides strong encouragement to take heart and feel confidence in the predicted outcome. In quantum time, it's already happened!

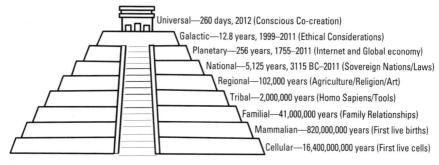

Universal—260 days, 2012 (Conscious Co-creation)
Galactic—12.8 years, 1999–2011 (Ethical Considerations)
Planetary—256 years, 1755–2011 (Internet and Global economy)
National—5,125 years, 3115 BC–2011 (Sovereign Nations/Laws)
Regional—102,000 years (Agriculture/Religion/Art)
Tribal—2,000,000 years (Homo Sapiens/Tools)
Familial—41,000,000 years (Family Relationships)
Mammalian—820,000,000 years (First live births)
Cellular—16,400,000,000 years (First live cells)

Completion of all nine underworlds on October 28, 2011.

Calleman's model of the nine underworlds is a concise map of time with general themes or outcomes for each step. Each level represents the accomplishments of Light into Matter from the first single-cell organisms up. Notice the greater complexity of life forms and eventually human institutions as we ascend through time. This is really about the awakening of life ultimately in the form of perfected humanity. The theme here is very much one of Love. Love by nature expands and is more and more inclusive, until it embraces All That Is in its Awareness. At this writing, we are well through the eighth or galactic level, which began in 1999. The calendar thus accurately predicted the entry of the solar system into the galactic photon band that same year. Just as an outcome of the planetary phase or seventh underworld was our collective realization of ourselves as planetary citizens (recall the first photos of Earth from Space), the outcome of the current galactic phase may well represent our expansion into galactic citizenship. This implies we will finally get to meet the neighbors.

Exopolitics is a discipline that looks at the tangible evidence of human/extra-terrestrial (ET) interaction over history, and stresses the importance of preparing not just ourselves, but our institutions and collective identity for the inevitable "coming out" of our ET friends. (See Webre, *Exopolitics: Politics, Government and Law in the Universe*,

Universe Books, 2005.) Many informed sources report that knowledge of ET interaction with Earth has been deliberately quashed by our well-meaning but paranoid patriarchal leaders. They seem to think that, like not talking to our kids about sex, if we pretend it's not there maybe it will just go away. Of course, sex doesn't go away when we pretend it's not there. And this approach will be about as successful when it comes to life "out there"!

You can see by this model of time that the earlier foundations or underworlds took a l-o-n-g time to unfold. Observers during the cellular phase would need infinite patience if they wanted to see any evidence of change in their lifetime! As each new level kicks in, however, time compression by a factor of 20 takes effect. More consciousness comes into form in less time. Now, as we near completion, time really seems to be zipping along. More change occurs now in a year than in most of our ancestors' lifetimes. And the process will continue to accelerate until the purpose of time is complete. And what is this purpose?

Paradoxically, the purpose of time is to undo time—that is, to make a shift in our relationship with time from being its slave to being its master. This implies a basic shift in personal and global consciousness, which the cosmological conditions we have already discussed seem to support or reflect. We shall soon know ourselves as conscious cocreators of realities. This means we will know experientially that Life happens because of us and through us, not to us, and that we are Masters of Creation—individually and collectively. Even now, many of us are beginning to suspect this, as our thoughts seem to be coming home much more obviously and immediately in the last few years. An increase in synchronistic experiences seems to be occurring—or at least these experiences are becoming a much more common topic of conversation.

Becoming conscious co-creators of realities will entail a massive awakening to our common source in the Heart/Mind of the Creator and to our common bond as the Created One. Some aspects of this shift will be instantaneous, while others will require some time for re-education and reorientation into a whole new mode of Being. Any systems or institutions based on the old paradigm of separate interests will need to be dismantled, and new methodologies and ways of cooperating with each other and Nature will need to be implemented. It will be the beginning of the end of the ego and all the manifestations of this collective mental disease that has plagued humanity seemingly forever.

Another view of this same process of time compression is found in Peter Russell's "scale of technological advancement" (*The Global Brain Awakens: Our Next Evolutionary Leap*, J. P. Tarcher, Inc., 1983). On this scale, it is clear that human advances in technology over the last 10,000 years were pretty minimal for the most part. The wheel, simple irrigation, food preservation—these were all tremendous developments, but advances of any importance only happened sporadically over long periods of technological drought. Then we have 1500 AD and the beginning of the stimulating effects of the photon band. We find things like the printing press, sailing ships, and world exploration beginning to open the world up to a greater reality. Since the post-war boom of the 1950s, technological advances have accelerated at a dizzying rate, to the point where now each year new developments and discoveries make last year's knowledge obsolete. University grads are now training for jobs that don't exist yet, and what they studied at the beginning of their learning process may be obsolete by the time they graduate.

Russell's graph predicts the vertical scale of technological advancement will go into infinity by 2012. What struck me in his model was, of course, the alignment with Mayan and other predictions, but also the notion that this may be the time when we shift from projecting all our technologies outside ourselves, to realizing that *we* are the ultimate technology. We will ultimately embody all of the innovations we have pulled out from within, finally owning our own Divine unlimited creative potential.

THE WORLD OF SEPARATION

All technology is an extension or amplification of a human ability or potential. Advances are literally projected out of our DNA memory banks. In the hologram of All Time, every "new" invention already exists, albeit in a dimension of time different from our current experience. We simply "remember" technologies from different space/time trajectories that become available as we open our minds to new possibilities. Most truly inspired and original ideas come as complete packages, sent perhaps by a future version of ourselves!

To the dualistic mind, this may all sound like lunacy or blasphemy. However, the kind of global changes on the scale we are describing defy normal linear parameters of cause and effect. Nothing drives the linear mind batty faster than the fuzzy logic of quantum reality. Where is the solid evidence, it cries! How is this verifiable? Much to the chagrin of the linear mind-set, there isn't necessarily any evidence in the empirical sense—only in the miracle sense! At least there is no proof in a form that the old "double-blind" dualistic paradigm can accept.

In a way, the old paradigm of the scientific method proves its own point, like a self-fulfilling prophesy. By setting out to disprove a hypothesis, according to the proven principles of quantum physics, one will see what one expects to see or more accurately, *wants* to see. So you want to disprove the observer effect? Well, of course you will, because you are the observer!

We must be able to transcend our own inner limitations if we are to open to new possibilities. It is only from a non-dual framework that we can even begin to understand how this new level of change can or will be. If the problem is part and parcel of a limited state of awareness, we must go to another level in order to solve the problem. Both Einstein and the Maharishi in effect said the same thing: "A problem cannot be solved by the same level of consciousness that produced it."

Dualistic thinking is a result of the imaginary separation from Oneness. You could say it was a necessary adjustment to a misuse of the mind—a functional illusion, if you will. From the non-dual perspective of *A Course in Miracles* we find that when the separation from Source occurred, the mind shifted from its intended purpose of creation to that of perception. Perception required a separate "perceiver," an "I" with a unique point of view different from all other perceivers and from what is being perceived. This was the birth of what we call "ego."

The ego is actually nothing but all the collected thoughts we have about who we think we are—thought collections easily formed into habits, beliefs, and attitudes that seem so solid and real to us that we no longer stop to question them. In non-duality, it is not necessary to ask the question, "Who am I," as all existence is One and self-evident. It was only after the split in the Mind of the Created that this question even arose. Knowledge knows; perception doubts. Skepticism masquerades as intelligence in these days of reductionist mania. Our answers to this needless question have birthed the ego and all the resultant guilt, pain, and suffering of duality.

The ego is a response to a temporary hallucination. Therefore, it can only be an idea held in the One Mind we share, and nothing more. I repeat these non-dual themes on purpose, as repetition is the law of memory. The linear mind needs the continuous reinforcement of these ideas it seems, or it simply slips back into its old familiar ruts by default.

The world described by the Mayan calendar is the projection on the screen of consciousness of the belief in the One Mind of the possibility of separation, *and* the design for the ending of the dream. Time is an essential part of the movie. The End of Time implies the end of dualistic thinking, the end of the destructive ego, and a return to the natural use of the mind, which is Creation.

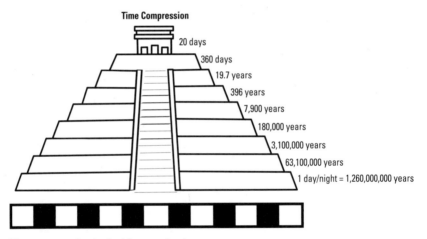

Time Compression

20 days
360 days
19.7 years
396 years
7,900 years
180,000 years
3,100,000 years
63,100,000 years
1 day/night = 1,260,000,000 years

Time compression in the Mayan calendar.

Getting back to the model, each of the nine steps is divided into thirteen even time segments called the "days and nights of creation." The Aztecs assigned specific deities to each of the days or nights, which symbolized the energies of an agricultural cycle from the planting of the seed in Day One to the harvest on Day Seven. The rabbi Jeshua also used the analogy of seeds and the harvest. Again, the entire calendar is entwined with the patterns of Nature.

During the day phases, new energies are downloaded into the world—or more accurately, into the Mind of those projecting the world. The nights provide periods of rest, reaction, adjustment, and assimilation. There was thus a pulse-like wave movement of light into matter over time. Is it any wonder the Maya and many other ancient cultures venerated the image of the serpent, which perfectly symbolized the wave motion of consciousness through time? We see the same imagery in the typical sine wave, which represents for the modern mind two of the basic forces of Nature—electro-magnetism and light. Only in modern times did we demonize the serpent as we detached further from Nature and fell under the patriarchal spell.

As mentioned, each time a new underworld started, the thirteen days and nights were compressed into a smaller space, representing a twenty-fold acceleration in the experience of time at each stage. At this writing, we are nearing the completion of the galactic underworld, which started in 1999, the year the Sun entered the main body of the photon band. The days and nights of the galactic underworld are 360 days long—almost a Gregorian year. By the time the final universal underworld begins (March 9, 2011 according to Calleman's calculations), the time-acceleration factor will compress the same amount of change we are now experiencing in a year into twenty days!

As with most things in the dualistic world, there is controversy about the true date for the end of the Mayan calendar, as well as concern for what this event will mean for all of us. My sense is that if this change is all about our new relationship with time, then the closer we get to the end date, the less arguing about the "correct" interpretation will have any meaning for us! Freedom from linear time implies no need to plan or worry about a future that is being determined only in the quality of our experience of Now. The time of change has already been upon us for

500 years, beginning with the rebirth of art, science, and the love of beauty in the Renaissance. This final 25-year membrane of time—what the Maya called the Time of No Time—has been our experience since 1986. In the next few short years, we can expect only an acceleration of this same process—a refinement and expansion of human potential beyond past limitations. The difference is that our present choices may very soon determine the kind of world we all awaken to tomorrow or experience immediately.

For the sake of discussion, we have Calleman's end date of October 28, 2011, and the more popular end date of December 21, 2012, based on the cyclical galactic alignment. Personally, I don't feel it's a matter of which date is right, but rather of appreciating how each date may carry its own significance. October 28, 2011 represents the completion of what Creation has been accomplishing on this planet for billions of years as the Divine fully awakens within our dream of separation. It is the crashing of the 9-D time wave on the shore of existence as it dissipates into cosmic dust never to be repeated. The purpose of time, which is the Great Awakening of the One Mind to itself, will be complete. It is a graduation for humanity from a chrysalis to a butterfly capable of flying beyond all past limits. It is a maturation point wherein humanity shakes off the spell of history and recovers its Truth. How this will actually be experienced by those present is anyone's guess. I assume there will be a whole gamut of experiences with one common theme: "I am not alone. My Mind is Your Mind is One Mind and it is Love." And we will laugh at what we previously called "reality."

Much has been pegged on the specific date of December 21, 2012 as representing first the end of the Mayan Calendar and secondly a kind of "zero point" for the galactic alignment. Solstices are significant in themselves, but I am afraid too many have run with this date with a "the sky is falling" mentality. You have to suspect ego when fear is the message. The alignment with the galactic center has been occurring for many years and will continue to do so. How can one day in particular, other than in the meaning we give it, make much of a difference given the massive scale on which this alignment is occurring? If anything, the start of the galactic alignment period in 1998 heralded the beginning of the galactic underworld (eight of nine levels), thus validating further the Mayan calendar's accuracy and significance. On the other hand we cannot entirely discount the observed cosmological conditions at any time as being any more or less significant than any other. If an observation confirms and supports a greater overall truth, then take it for what it's worth. Contradiction or conflict of opinions is not helpful, and only serves the agenda of separation. Treat the date of December 21, 2012 as a good day to celebrate...as is any day we may choose.

The other factor with this date, as discussed, is the actual effect of galactic light in triggering the conditions for dramatic change on the energetic, sub-atomic, and physical planes—cosmic fire driving a dimensional shift and the further merging of consciousness and matter. The sheer physics of such an alignment is staggering to consider. What a wonderful time to be alive and experience such a rare event!

An analogy that seems to fit very well with this cosmic alignment of 2012 is that of the "sacred union." The story is very intriguing and deserves a deeper look, tying in as it does with the need to balance and heal the effects of the wounded-male archetype on this planet. Ancient calendars, including the Mayan, Hebrew, and Chinese calendars, looked to the cycles of the Moon to delineate months. The 28-day lunar month created a 13-month calendar. This was a way of time-keeping associated with the human female fertility cycle. Many pre-historic cultures were based in a feminine cosmology. These were the pre-patriarchal God-dess societies. We think of them as being perhaps more peaceful, Earth-centered, agricultural societies. The recent upsurge in interest in Goddess and Earth-based practices and beliefs represents not only a return to a more Nature-based philosophy, but also a reaction against living in a largely patriarchal world—at least a world being managed by those with a patriarchal bias. Women do not send their children to war. Nor is it a feminine trait to rape and pillage the land and Nature with no regard to the impact on future generations.

THE SUPPRESSION OF THE FEMALE ARCHETYPE

There is a reason why the world has been so off-balance in its expression of male and female energies, which we shall explore shortly. The Mayan calendar implies a dance of *yin* and *yang* polarities being broadcast from the World Tree as influencing the movements of consciousness and thus culture over the history of humanity. Suffice it to say that the wounded-male archetype has been running amok for far too long on the planet and today threatens its very survival. It is time for a reckoning and a correction of past imbalances.

We see that the number "13" is associated with the pre-patriarchal lunar calendar. The recent rise of the popularity of Mary Magdalene and the Blessed Virgin is indicative of a need to feminize the dominant Judeo-Christian patriarchal paradigm in the Western world. Many believe, based on fairly substantial evidence gleaned from recently discovered apocryphal gospels, that the historical Jeshua and Mary Magdalene were married, and that she actually was disciple number 13 (Freke and Gandy, *Jesus and the Lost Goddess*, Three Rivers Press, 2001).

In the Middles Ages, the Knights Templar, defenders of Christian pilgrims during the Crusades, returned from the Holy Land not only with physical treasures, but also with knowledge of the role of Mary Magdalene and a possible bloodline linked to Jesus. They also carried back to Europe the secrets of sacred geometry and other lost knowledge (lost to Europe at any rate) that they had learned from Arab scholars. The Knights eventually became as rich as the Vatican through their financing of pilgrims to the Holy Land and the accumulation of gifts from rich patrons. All in all, they became too great a threat to the Roman spiritual dictatorship of the day. The decision was made to solve the problem by slaughtering the Knights Templar in their sleep, along with the Cathars.

The Cathars were a large movement of Christians who believed they did not need a priesthood to represent them to God. They also believed the world was evil, and that gathering riches as the Vatican was wont to do was anathema to true Christianity. It was decided by the Church fathers to be rid of both the Templars and the Cathars on Friday, 13 October, 1307 AD. Was this choice of dates mere coincidence? Or was there either a conscious or unconscious need to desecrate the number 13? This is why Friday the 13th is still considered an ill-omened day, as is the number 13 generally. Well, ill-omened if you were a Templar, a Cathar, or a woman practicing natural healing or any other form of unsanctioned spiritual practice in the Dark Ages.

We also see the symbolic erasing of the memory of the sacred feminine in the removal of the thirteenth constellation of the ecliptic, Ophiuchus, from Western astrology. These constellations are the star groupings associated and aligned with the Milky Way—the band of stars visible overhead on a clear night.

Currently, if you want to look in the direction of the galactic center, you need to find the constellation Sagittarius depicting a male warrior. This star grouping looks like the outline of an archer, with his arrow pointing at the galactic center. However, before the current Western astrological system of twelve zodiacal constellations, there were thirteen, with the thirteenth being in direct alignment over the galactic center. This was called Ophiuchus, the Serpent Holder. And just like thirteenth month, it was written out of Western astrology and consciousness. When we consider the galactic center as the womb of Creation (yielding Mother's nourishment as the Milky Way), this erasure appears to repeat the intent to obliterate the awareness of the Divine Feminine in favor of the controlling patriarchal Warrior Father.

There seems to be a common theme here typical of the consciousness of the wounded-male archetype. An archetype is a general set of beliefs and ideas set as a semi-permanent template in 4-D. Generations of believers simply tapping into the archetype tends to reinforce the idea over generations, establishing a "group-think" phenomenon in which we no longer question our assumptions. When a lot of people see a lot of other people thinking the same way, there tends to be a solidification of the ideas into a self-reinforcing dogma. Hence we have a historical tendency to produce codes, creeds, and laws to validate our current perceptions, in an attempt to make them real and enduring.

The wounded-male archetype and its characteristics correlate directly to a story involving our ET ancestors, which we will look at more closely soon. Suffice it to say that the mind-set of male polarization was firmly established in the royal lineages of early Western city-state cultures going all the way back to Sumeria circa 4500 BC, with the rule of kingly lineages established by divine right. This mind-set in its modern version has provided the philosophical basis for the obsession in the West with colonization, discovering and conquering new lands, the enslavement of foreign cultures, over-consumption of natural resources, the accumulation of wealth by the few to the neglect of the many, and the disdain for the rights of men, women, and children who get in the way of this cultural bulldozer bent on world domination and exploitation.

The great hope of the age we are entering is for a healing of the wounded-male archetype, and a return to a more feminized consciousness in which the dualistic forces within us, including *yin* and *yang* energies, will begin to dance in harmony and mutual respect. Calleman points out that the Mayan calendar indicates just such a process is happening, illustrated on the political scale with a decline in the power of Western-dominated societies and their policies, and a concurrent rise in the power and influence of Eastern cultures, which represent the majority of humans on the planet and are generally rooted in a more collectivist and less individualistic approach to existence. You could say that such a planetary re-alignment of energies is reflective of the ascendancy in the calendar from the national underworld to the planetary. In the national underworld, national interests are primary. In the planetary, we begin to move to a greater, more holistic world view. Modern communication technology has played a major role in this expansion. Ultimately, as we move through the galactic and universal levels, we will likely expand into telepathy, of which today's Internet is only a shadow. Unity of purpose and planetary peace will be brought into manifestation as a result of clear, honest, and open communication.

We are all in this boat together, and can no longer let the artificial divisions of the past dictate our lives as One People, One Planet. Now, more than ever, we must release ourselves from the prison of history and the dungeon of linear time. Meanwhile, our galactic neighbors wait patiently for us to "get it"!

LEFT BRAIN—RIGHT BRAIN

On an individual basis, this return to harmony from the divisive state of male-female polarity is represented in the balancing of the left and right hemispheres of the brain.

Each brain hemisphere has a unique way of experiencing and operating. Neither is either correct or incorrect, but when our attention is polarized in either, we run the risk of being mentally unbalanced. Left-brain dominant functioning is more consistent with the wounded-male archetype and the typical Western mind-set. Those "skewed to the left" thus tend to suffer from the inherent limitations of cause-and-effect thinking and linear processing. Left-brain dominance is consistent with the experience of never-ending problems requiring solutions. Left-brain logic is language-based and time-bound. The left hemisphere confuses data with intelligence and puts a lot of faith in the accumulation of facts, observations, and mental labeling. Much of what we call higher learning in the West is simply memorizing the special language of the discipline being studied. Once you know the talk, you can sound very intelligent, but really be saying nothing at all!

If the left brain doesn't have a problem to solve in the moment, it will drag one up from the past, or project one into the future. Once you recognize this tendency, you can observe it in yourself. Like a dog without a bone, the left brain is literally beside itself when it is without any conflicts to chew on. Language itself is inherently divisive and linear, setting up artificial conflicts through simply conceptualizing, and thus limiting, experience. In fairness, left-brain functioning serves us well when it comes to navigating physicality, predicting the results of our actions, and formulating simple solutions in 3-D. Without the balancing influence of the more *yin* right brain, however, left-brain dominance can pull us into obsession, fear-based decision-making, and lower survival reflexes applied inappropriately. This frequently manifests as conflicted relationships and endless debate and analysis, as we find in politics, education, and the mainstream media.

Right-brain intelligence is non-verbal. With the right brain hemisphere, we process experiences like color, space, and emotions. The right brain does not need mental labels; it is content just to be. Right-brain functioning facilitates higher, more holistic states of awareness including visionary and peak experiences of self-actualization. It supports a more unlimited mode of perceiving unbound by language or linear assumptions. Right-hemisphere states are more conducive to what we call religious experiences, something that is commonly reported in all cultures in all times according to pioneering psychologist William James.

Any good form of meditation works because it brings these two mental players, the left and right brain hemispheres, into a balanced partnership. The sum total of harmonizing the hemispheres is an overall reduction in the frequencies of brain waves and an exponential expansion in the ability to perceive multi-dimensionally. In other words, when the whole brain is operating as a unit, it runs much more efficiently and doesn't have to work as hard. Left-brain dominance is like running your V-8 engine on four cylinders. It must work a lot harder to get anywhere, and may soon burn up!

As our experience of linear time begins to give way to a more global, or quantum, experience of time it will be more and more difficult for the rational mind to account for its experiences in terms it is used to. Thus, for some, the shifts implied in the Mayan model of time compression may lead to deeper confusion, depression, disorientation, even suicidal paranoia. Suicide, the self-destructive urges arising from a fearful egoic state, may be a much more prevalent killer than we think. How many drug overdoses, car accidents, violent confrontations, or even terminal illnesses are simply different forms of a death wish for those whose entire frame of reference, especially around personal identity, is melting away before their eyes? The solution to this pent-up energy of resistance is surrender—to life, God, the universe, or however we conceive of a Greater Power. Our insistences are our resistances. We are our own greatest enemies when we refuse to surrender ourselves to our Self.

The prevailing symptom-based medical paradigm is not equipped to work with the kind of mental adjustments we are being called on to make. The currently left-brain dominant form of materialist medicine we have in the Western world is incapable of discovering non-physical causes of disease yet is perfectly suited to the immediate needs of a war-based economy. In most cases, symptoms related to a breakdown of illusory forms of consciousness are diagnosed as mental illnesses. Do not make the mistake of believing you are ill simply because you can no longer tolerate a former level of mental processing that you now see as incomplete and dysfunctional. It is entirely appropriate that you may feel temporarily dissociated as the veils of illusion fall from your eyes, and you begin to see a deeper reality. Recognizing that this world is insane is a symptom of sanity. The modern medical Mafiosi may prefer to stifle the symptom and the patient with poisonous drugs rather than open their own minds to the possibilities of an imminent global shift in consciousness, much less to the emergence of individual episodes of enlightenment. Our society, in its divorce of Church and State, has not been able to account rationally for genuine spiritual emergence, and thus, as it has done with so many other natural processes, it has "medicalized" it.

The phase of darkness that rapid spiritual growth can bring is generally recognized by many spiritual traditions as the "dark night of the soul." Given that the soul, or Spiritual essence, is and has always been in perfection, a more accurate term might be "the dark night of the ego." This is the sometimes-necessary passage out of duality through darkness before bursting forth into the Light. Don't stop the birthing process by stifling the symptoms before it's complete! You could really make a mess of things. This is where your spiritual practice of stilling the mind and contemplating the Divine will carry you over the threshold. It is through your will and the Divine Will that you, and we, all awaken to the Truth of our Being, which is Oneness. This is inevitable. Putting it off will only prolong the experience of suffering. The when and how of your awakening is somewhat of your own choosing—the "if" is not.

The power in knowing this—that time as we have known it is disappearing—is in knowing that we can voluntarily choose to let go of the old concepts, conditionings, and assumptions that simply no longer work for us, and turn to face openly, even to embrace, the promising fresh wind of liberation and freedom from these old self-imposed restraints in the new energy emerging within and around us.

To get back to the subject of the number 13 and the sacred marriage, we now have a scenario emerging where, along with the balancing of the global brain hemispheres, we also have the physical alignment of the Sun (male principle) with the galactic center (female principle), seeding as it were a new expression of life—enlightened humanity, or *homo luminous* as the Peruvian elders refer to us. In this cosmic wedding we have the potential for the fulfillment of the many prophesies of return, including those of Jesus, Mohammed, the Jewish Messiah, Quetzalcoatl, and others. This promised return will not, however, be in the form of an individual savior for a few chosen true believers, but rather in the form of a wave of awakening or planetary enlightenment in which *each and every individual* and aspect of Creation spontaneously emerges into a higher octave of vibration and awareness of itself as an infinite aspect of the One. All we are here to do is remember—to remember "forever." Just imagine.

In the culture of the Maya, only the high priests had access to the top, universal structure of their ceremonial pyramids. All others were forbidden access. Today, as all of humanity is ascending the structure of time together, we are about to enter the universal Holy of Holies together, without the need for an intervening elite priesthood or personified deity. As the Hopi elders have said: "We are the Ones we have been waiting for."

What will this actually look like? Most likely, there will be more "light" and less density, consistent with a shifting of awareness to a new higher vibration and dimension of existence, free of the old limitations and constraints of the former dualistic world. Our senses may actually perceive deeper and richer colors, sounds, and sensations. There will be a loss of interest in conflict and "win-lose" scenarios. Our thoughts and actions will come from recognition of the other as "I." Thoughts and intents will automatically be known by everyone. We will think differently when we know that every thought is being heard by all. Why not start accepting this now—because on the level of the quantum Mind, this is already true! There simply are no private thoughts!

Intelligent beings will not willingly or knowingly harm themselves. If they do so, it must therefore be out of igno-rance. When you and I consciously recognize the One Mind—the Savior, Allah, God, the Buddha—in each other, the only possible response will be Love recognizing Love in celebration and peace.

We have in the Mayan calendar a most reassuring com-fort in this time of change and potential uncertainty. It is still up to us individually to avail ourselves of what the calendar has to offer. Calleman and others believe that by learning to track time by the calendar now we can more closely align ourselves with the spiritual energies as they continue to pour into this experience of time.

In Calleman's most recent book, *The Purposeful Universe*, he reports two very significant developments in science that validate the calendar's predictions and the holographic model of the universe. The first is a discovery by astronomers of a vast standing scalar wave in the geographic center of the universe. This, as discussed, is a multi-dimensional portal allowing for the flow of (our) creative intelligence to manifest as the physical universe. This discovery represents modern confirmation of what the ancients referred to as the Tree of Life on a scale unknown to us in the modern era. The second bit of big news is the discovery of the mathematical correlations between the protein structures within each cell, called "centrioles," and the numerical organization of the calendar itself. Thus the calendar is not only symbolizing the completion of the plan of time "out there" but is also reflecting the completion of this plan in every cell of every living thing. It appears we have tied together the macro and micro universes and recognized a common thread centering on the calendar. Here is a holographic symmetry that not only validates the Mayan calendar as a master template of time, but also confirms the universe of form as being the unified projection of a single force or consciousness that is us in our Divine creativity. No matter where we look in the universal hologram, we find the Tree of Life pulsing out its rhythms of time. The plan of Creation is being played out on all levels at once, including within the very cells of your body.

Stop now and *feel* the possibility of that last sentence. By allowing ourselves to feel the future now, we will hasten the completion of the Divine plan and begin to live consciously in "forever."

CHAPTER 5

DNA—THE INTERFACE
BETWEEN GALACTIC LIGHT
AND HUMAN POTENTIAL

So far, we have been looking at the macro scale of the Shift of Ages in terms of the galactic alignment and cycles, dimensional shifts, and the Mayan calendar. We now turn our attention to the micro level of DNA—the Book of Life in each and every living cell in all life forms on Earth, and likely everywhere. No matter where we look in the hologram of All That Is, we see the same general patterns in movement together in a grand symphony of Creation all singing the same song—the one song of the uni-verse.

The physical 2-stranded DNA molecule was discovered (in the modern era) back in the 1950s. It was assumed then, operating on a purely mechanistic and material-istic model, that DNA served solely as the blueprint for physical development and expression. Things like inher-ited physical characteristics now had an explanation; even inherited tendencies toward certain diseases and condi-tions were seen to be written in the genes of DNA. Social biologists even suggested certain racial and behavioral characteristics could also be genetically pre-determined, which gave frightening credence to Nazi-like racial-purity beliefs. These simplistic assumptions have been largely discredited, yet may survive in eugenics-based programs like mass vaccinations, racially targeted pandemics, and the fabrication of bio-warfare agents specifically targeting certain "less desirable" populations. As far-fetched as these ideas might seem, Dr. Len Horowitz has provided hard evidence that these and other insane programs have been going on for decades (*Emerging Viruses: AIDS and Ebola*, Dr. Len Horowitz, Tetrahedron Inc., 1996).

Although I have no doubt these kinds of things go on, I prefer not to give much attention to conspiratorial ideas. Not that they can be discounted entirely, but the whole idea of "us versus them" is based in separation, and is thus fundamentally illusory and not real or of any real value. Only the illusory ego is entranced by any seeming confirmation of separation; it literally feeds on conflict and division. The ego thrives on pointing out the work of the ego in others. Yet only the ego can perceive the ego at all! It is important to recognize falsehood in 3-D, but it is also important to be able to look beyond the possibility of falsehood to Reality, which is One. By the way, what I just stated can result in what the *Course in Miracles* calls "level confusion." What is true in one dimension or context may only apply to that dimension or context. It is a relative truth, rather than an over-arching Truth coming from a higher, non-dual perspective.

Essentially, higher Truth does not fit into a lower-dimensional context based in separation. Dualistic religions have been trying to do this for ages. The logic of the ego and of Spirit are like water and oil—they never mix! This is what dualistic religions attempt to do—to bring God into the world either to fix or punish it, thus making the illusion of the world real for themselves. Non-dual Truth (We are One, only Truth is True) cannot be understood or explained in relativistic terms, and so is discounted and overlooked by the egoic mind. At the same time, there is no place for the separated ego in the appreciation of Oneness. One must lay aside the internal arguments and questions and move into a more heart-centered perspective for these higher Truths even to be possible. When this happens in an individual's experience cannot be predicted, and may depend on a certain stage of spiritual maturity based on life experience. Thus it is said in the *Course* that we do not try to bring the Truth to the illusion, but rather bring the illusion to Truth, where it is dissolved. There can only be Truth. Nothing else is real.

DNA AND THE DIMENSIONAL MODEL

Contrary to older models, DNA is now understood to operate on many dimensional levels. Much of the advanced research on DNA as well as psychic phenomena generally was done by Russian scientists. Perhaps this is why much of this information was considered classified here in the West, and thus kept from the public "for our own good." All during the Cold War era, Russians were investigating bio-plasma (the human energy field), bio-magnetics, and other esoteric topics as matters of potential national and political importance. Gurvich, for example, as early as the 1920s, discovered what he called "mitogenic radiation"— the observed communication between separated onion cells through empty space. Later, in the 1970s, Fritz Popp in Germany identified what he called "biophotons," or emissions of light coming from and being absorbed by cells, even when separated by considerable distance. Around this time, we also had the publication of *The Secret Life of Plants* (Tompkins and Bird, Harper & Row, 1972), a bombshell of a book that opened a whole new world of understanding and appreciation of the intelligence of supposedly "lower" life forms. This book provided proof that plants react to stress in much the same way as animals—even to subtle stress at a distance! There seems to be an intelligence operating between life forms beyond the limits of physical proximity and bio-chemical messengers. It is now appreciated that DNA is more crystalline in its qualities, which goes a long way toward explaining these observations of non-local communication.

Crystalline structures are so named because of the regular patterning of the molecular arrangements of the substance. This regular patterning creates what seems to act like a net, antenna, or resonant matrix for specific frequencies of light/energy. All true crystals have an electrical aspect as well. When you have regular molecular patterns "scrunched" together under heat, they emit what is called a "dielectric" energy, or an electrical charge as a result of their internally stressed structure. This is called the piezo-electric effect. I recall as a child getting a crystal radio kit for Christmas one year. It was really cool! All these wires and coils had to be put together, and where you placed a certain wire on the quartz crystal determined which radio station you heard. And, there was no battery! The crystal not only was the power supply for the radio—which wasn't very loud; you had to use a headset to hear—but also acted as an antenna receiving radio signals specifically matching the arrangement of molecules on the different faces of the crystal. I'm sure the battery companies must have bought up the patents to these little wonders. Soon after, the rage was the transistor radio. which required a life-time supply of 9-volt batteries. The point here is that what we know about crystals can now be applied to our appreciation of how DNA functions.

Much of what I am discussing and more about new DNA research is summarized in Horowitz' DNA, *Pirates of the Sacred Spiral*. He has done his homework, and tells it all...although in a somewhat conspiratorial tone. What may help explain the crystalline nature of DNA is the fact that DNA is nested within a matrix of ideal or clustered water molecules. The water molecule in this state is one of Nature's finest achievements! Water is the only liquid-crystal substance on Earth, other than perhaps mercury. All life on Earth depends on it. Even though water is in a liquid state and can rise in frequency into a vapor or descend into solid ice, the water molecule itself is "dielectric," as are solid-crystal molecules. That is, it can hold an electrical charge, like a solid crystal. As such, water can be charged from an outside source like sunlight and thus go into a more coherent, crystalline functional state, in which it can absorb and emit energy and information.

This is the basis of classical homeopathy. When you shake or "succus" the water the molecules align magnetically, taking on the shape or virtual structure of any foreign molecule present in the water, even down to only one foreign molecule. This energetic "shape" will be sustained even when further dilutions in distilled water ensure no possible presence of the original foreign molecule, or "mother tincture." The magnetized water becomes a fluid crystalline substance capable of communicating vast amounts of subtle information to the body's own quantum structures through the clustered water within these structures. Actually, the water molecule is Nature's best energy-storage and information system. Bio-chemically, it is the universal solvent and the necessary common component of all life forms and processes.

Clustered water surrounding DNA is thus part of an information-sharing system that links the DNA through the quantum-physical structures of the extra-cellular matrix of the body along with the meridians and chakras to the macro universe of light, sound, cosmic radiation, and extra-dimensional information. Throughout the body, we find specific protein structures called "microtubules" and "actin filaments" that support clustered water molecules within them. These structures make up a web of protein filaments literally connecting all cells and their DNA with the body's own Internet or information superhighway. This structure, the extra-cellular matrix, has been called a "missing organ" in our understanding of physiology, and has been well studied and described by James Oschman (*Energy Medicine: the Scientific Basis*, Churchill Livingston, 2002). Given that we now understand the meridians to be "pathways of light," we can truly say we are "light beings." This is not just New Age mumbo-jumbo; it is solid science. Consider the implications as the planet moves into the galactic photon beam. And the whole system is being amped up from the center of the galaxy directly to the center of your cells!

Most scientists now appreciate that the actual body-building aspects of DNA only account for anywhere from 3 to 10 percent of what is there. Arrogantly, the rest has been referred to as "junk DNA." That's like saying "junk appendix" or "junk tonsils." Separation again! What if these dormant aspects of DNA hold deep secrets and potentials for a fuller expression of life? Let me ask again, if we can do what we do on, say, 4 percent DNA activation, can you imagine humanity at 20 percent or higher?

Some evolutionary biologists have conceded that massive gamma ray bursts from space may have been responsible for what appears in the record of species as the complete wiping out of older, simpler life forms, to be replaced almost overnight by a higher order of life—every 26 million years. The source of these bursts, however, is assumed to be from random local supernova events, not a regular, cyclic exposure to our own galactic center or a grander universal plan.

The DNA in your cells is not called the Book of Life by more poetic researchers for nothing. It is not only the record of your family characteristics, your lineage, or even humanity's. It is basically the same molecule found in all living things, and is thus a record of the development of life from the very beginning of time to the present. You could accurately say there is a miniature Mayan calendar in every cell! All of life's triumphs, tragedies, challenges, and catastrophes are held in memory there. You are a living library—perhaps even of life as it was before it came to this planet! Barbara Marciniak's *Bringers of the Dawn* (Bear & Co., 1992) states this. In this classic channeled material, we learn that the "books of the living library" in our cells have been scattered for eons, devastated by former planetary and species-wide trauma. However, "light filaments" coming in at this time from the cosmos are helping to restore order and rebuild the libraries as we shift toward planetary enlightenment.

The beauty of this expanded view of DNA is that it depersonalizes many of what we assume are our private challenges. Take disease for example. We are wont to own our diseases. We say *"my* condition" or "I caught the flu." Ruiz, in his beautifully simple work *The Four Agreements* (Amber-Allen Publishing, 1997), suggests that we should not take *anything* personally. This is a great way to deflate the illusory ego, which is only our idea of who we think we are. There is much wisdom in this view.

In India, one of the higher yogic practices is for devotees to go down into a village and purposely infect themselves with a dread disease. They then go into seclusion and, through meditation and other disciplines, heal themselves. They do this because they appreciate that on the level of Oneness, all minds and DNA are joined and healing is always shared. They do this in service to humanity, perhaps recognizing that the healing will be communicated by their DNA to every other life form on the planet (or in the universe!). They believe this may be their highest purpose in this life.

What if this were true for us as well? Could this mind-set of "illness as service" help to shift us out of victimhood and into spiritual practice, with just a simple change in awareness and attitude? We have an opportunity now, unlike any other generation, to heal the ancient memories of trauma of all life forms in our cells. And we are being given the tools as no other generation has been (at least for a very long time) to accomplish this. The tools are not only in the form of advanced healing technologies and the recovery of ancient wisdom, but also in the form of the galactic photon band itself. I encourage you not to "take anything personally," but to go within when your body begins releasing the toxic memories of life on Earth in the form of symptoms. Symptoms are always related to healing. Today's superstitious and materialistic medical sciences want to suppress symptoms as "unpleasant." We have disconnected the symptom from the natural course of healing an illness. Suppressed symptoms, however, do not go away; they go deeper, only to emerge again in a more acute phase.

REVERSE EVOLUTION

We can be pro-active in this cellular-memory clearing process. It is not necessary to wait for an illness to emerge. As DNA is receptive to sound, light, physical pressure, subtle (low-level) electro-magnetic radiation, laser light, and focused intent (a form of scalar energy), there are many modalities we can investigate to do our own "cellular clearing." Some intuitive folks have observed that human DNA expresses energetically as twelve strands, or more. The fact that most of us are carrying two strands of physical DNA implies that either we are very low on the evolutionary scale (which we would prefer not to believe!) or that somehow humanity was downgraded genetically from a former higher state of functioning. This idea would be consistent with the Vedic view of the 26,000-year Solar orbit result-ing in stages of both increased as well as decreased levels of consciousness on the planet. Evolutionists don't seem to consider the possibly of "reverse evolution." Yet, as we shall see, there does seem to be some stunning evidence for this! I must mention here, however, research by Berrenda Fox of the Mount Shasta Medical Clinic, in which she claims to have observed three physical strands of DNA showing up in the cells of some children born since 1999—the year the Sun entered the main body of the photon band. So it seems Nature's DNA recombination therapy program may be underway.

One thing that has marked human development in the past is our amazing adaptability, even within a single gen-eration. It is being reported now that some children born to parents who are both HIV positive, for example, are exhibit-ing complete immunity to AIDS. We did not survive the tri-als of evolution by developing scales or fangs or venoms but by using our wits and exploiting our tendency to adapt rap-idly to changing conditions sometimes within a single gen-eration. I am counting on this rapid and fluid adaptability to continue to serve us during the days and years ahead!

Again, this discussion is intended only as a brief over-view of vast and complex topics. I think that if we stay with the overview approach, however, we will more easily be able to grasp the Big Picture that shows what is really going on here, both within and without us. It is very easy to lose sight of the forest in the complexity and density of the trees. Besides, it could take a lifetime to master any one of these topics, and I don't have the time! Others have done such a wonderful job. I am truly grateful and I honor their work.

Okay. Let's move on to one possible story of how our DNA got "downgraded" and "scattered," and why our under-standing of history and the human saga has so many holes in it. Hang on to your rational mind; it may be in for a stretching! Or, simply decide to let it go. Hanging on too tightly may just give you a headache! If the following story does not fit your accepted and culturally endorsed world view, you may just want to consider what follows as a lost episode of *Star Trek*!

CHAPTER 6

WHO'S YOUR DADDY? WILL ALL ETS PLEASE STAND UP!

Ah! Good! You are still with me. If you think of your mind as a garden, only an open mind can fully receive the benefits of sunshine and rain. Only then can you grow something new!

Before beginning this chapter, I must make it clear that the following story is all happening within the Oneness of our true existence, and is simply one chapter in the dream of separation. Please don't see any of this as real in and of itself, as *nothing here is*. We have masterfully projected our dream of separation onto the canvas of consciousness in order to experience separation in all of its seemingly infinite expressions. Our purpose in all of this is to awaken to our Oneness, laugh at our crazy dream, and go forward in our creativity as One. And this has already been accomplished outside of time, space, and the current illusion of the separation of bodies. Now sit back and enjoy the metaphor to follow, gleaning what may be of interest to you in the pursuit of Peace through Forgiveness.

As noted above, it is generally accepted that on the level of our DNA, humanity is currently running on practically empty. Either we are very low on the evolutionary scale and have a very *l-o-n-g* way to go, or we were somehow downgraded at some point from a higher level of functioning.

Many years ago, friends suggested I might enjoy Zecharia Sitchin's 1976 work *The Twelfth Planet* (Avon, 1976). They recommended it because they knew I had an interest in spirituality, and was not averse to alternative views on things like ETs and UFOs. They certainly had me pegged. For me, the book was an experience of light bulbs popping in my mind with each revelation Sitchin proposed. The book is written in a somewhat stodgy, academic style, but its content—which is literally "out of this world"—explains so much about our history, the world and humanity's place in it, and the cosmos.

It is not surprising that, if you go to any "big box" bookstore and ask for Sitchin's work, you will be directed to the science fiction or New Age sections, as the view of history he has documented flies in the face of practically all accepted theories of human development. I say "documented," because as you delve into his work, you realize that everything he says is based on archeological evidence. Again, it is a very academically oriented work and not necessarily an easy read. Some may argue that his views are simply one person's interpretation of the evidence. If we look at Sitchin's credentials, however, and the fact that he is one of only 200 or so people on Earth who can translate the ancient cuneiform languages, which are over 6000 years old, you may decide he is well qualified to hold his opinions.

Sitchin describes how, as a young student of antiquities studying in Israel, his thirst for knowledge led him to an inquiry into the identity of the race of giants briefly mentioned in the book of Genesis. He was told by one of his professors to sit down, shut up, and not ask such questions! This "put-down" merely fueled the young scholar's burning quest: Who were these giants? Where did they come from? Where did they go? Hold that thought, as we go into the story a little deeper.

Sitchin's research is based on the revelations locked away for millennia in the writings of the ancient scribes of

Sumeria. Sumeria was a thriving society around 4500 BC, located in the same area as modern Iraq. This region is generally referred to by historians as the cradle of civilization, nestled in a formerly ideal temperate zone in and around the Tigris and Euphrates valleys. Although currently a desert, at the time of Sumeria's peak, the area was an ideal agricultural and climatic paradise, not at all like present-day Iraq.

SUMERIA

Not much was known about Sumeria until the mid 1800s, when English and American archeologists began to search for evidence of the ancient cities mentioned in the Old Testament. Some of these were found, and along with them came the surprising discovery of a hitherto unknown advanced culture—Sumeria. Soon, Sumeria became known in archeological circles as the "civilization of firsts"—the first known written language, advanced agricultural science, advanced political structures, mathematics, metallurgy, astronomy, and more. These were all in place in Sumeria 2000 years before the rise of Egypt.

For example, it is generally accepted that the domestication of animals and grains came out of the Middle East. It was the Sumerians who knew the secrets of plant and animal genetics, and who engineered the main food species that continue to feed most of the planet today. Although ruled by a lineage of kings, they also had a parliamentary system in which political decisions were made based on a vote between two debating "houses," with the final vote left to the King.

Sumerian astronomers were aware of Earth's position in a nine-planet solar system, referring to Earth as the seventh planet. At first this caught historians off guard, until they realized the Sumerians were counting planets from the outside of the solar system starting with Pluto, in which case the Earth is number seven. How did they know this? We think that Pluto was discovered in 1930! The Sumerians were also well informed about advanced architecture and civil engineering. And less than 20 percent of the documents discovered in the form of clay tablets have been deciphered, so we have much more to learn about this amazing society.

The Sumerian scribes attributed all of this advanced knowledge and technology to a class of "special" beings who made up their royal and scientific elite. And, to Sitchin's intellectual delight, they were described and depicted as giants—some as tall as fourteen feet! These giant kingly types were depicted in bas-reliefs and cylinder seals—intricately carved pictures in the form of tubular crystals that could "roll out" endless clay copies. Modern academia prefers to dismiss these depictions of giants as merely symbolic of their social stature, to which Sitchin applies the rule of Occam's Razor: The simplest explanation is usually the right one! What if the scribes and artists were simply telling it as it was, with no artistic license or imagination added?

This kingly caste was known in the Sumerian language as the Annunaki—literally "those who from heaven to earth came." Another of the young scholar's questions answered! They were not originally of this Earth. The Annunaki were very open about their own history and relationship with humans, and the scribes wrote it all down. Again, modern academics will tend to look at these stories as myths, preferring to credit the Sumerians and their scribes with good imaginations, rather than good reporting skills.

Here is the story of humanity as related by the Annunaki. Please keep in mind our discussion of the downgraded DNA and the promise of full human expression through its future activation. Please also keep in the back of your mind the non-dual reality that all of this is simply depicting a drama playing out in the dream of the One Ancient Mind.

Dream images are merely symbols projected by the dreamer on the 'screen' of consciousness. The purpose of the dream is the healing of the dreamer's mind through the forgiveness of these symbols; images of our hidden, unconscious guilt.

THE ANNUNAKI

Many hundreds of thousands of years ago—about 450,000 years ago—the Annunaki were a wandering group of advanced beings whose planet had somehow been ejected from their own solar system. Most likely their planet was part of the Sirius triple-star system and the Annunaki's ejection was possibly the result of some cosmic cataclysm, although they may have been evicted! Their planet was eventually pulled into the gravity field of our Sun, and became an "adopted orphan"—the twelfth planet. The Sumerians used the term "planet" to include the Sun and Moon, counting 11 heavenly bodies in total in our solar system. The Annunaki planet, Niburu, thus became the twelfth planet. Because it is still likely under the gravitational influence of its source in Sirius, Niburu's vast elliptical orbit takes 3600 years to complete one cycle around our Sun and its original home star system. This is an orbit more consistent with that of a comet or asteroid than one of the "Sun-bound" planets. Niburu may be in orbit around both our Sun and the stars of the Sirius group or some other body, perhaps an unseen "brown dwarf" star.

Sitchin proposes that Niburu's occasional passage through the region of the inner planets could explain some of the anomalies we observe among the inner planets. For example, Venus spins backward compared to all the other planets. Uranus spins on its side and the axis of the Earth is tilted about 23 degrees compared to the Sun's, which accounts for our seasons. There is a vast field of space rubble between Mars and Jupiter, the asteroid belt, where logically and mathematically according to Bodes Law, there should be another planet. The Sumerians actually accounted for how these things came to be, and how the Earth itself was knocked out of an orbit between Mars and Jupiter to its current location in relation to the Sun. According to the Sumerians, the Earth is the remains of a former large planet known as Tiamat. Half of Tiamat now makes up the asteroid belt; the other half became Earth. All of this cosmic history and more is recorded in Sumerian documents.

In 1950, well before Sitchin's time, a Russian named Emanuel Velikovsky wrote *Worlds in Collision* (Abacus, 1974), in which he offered alternative explanations for Venus' uniqueness. His predictions about the physical nature of Venus made in the 1950s became fact many decades later, and his theories are no longer dismissed out of hand. There appear to be answers to many of today's cosmological mysteries—answers that may not fit the current theories of experts and so are pushed aside until the evidence becomes undeniable.

Now back to our story. This view of history can be somewhat disorienting because it defies practically all of our current cultural assumptions about how we got here and who we are. We find, however, that our mythical and religious accounts of the beginning of life and humanity actually fit the Sumerian story, albeit without their level of detail. What we have in our mytho-religious writings are watered-down accounts of actual events.

The Annunaki, who were worshipped by the Sumerians as Gods (for surely with what they could do, they must be!), said that they originally came to Earth to locate and harvest gold. They needed it to seed their own upper atmosphere which was slowly dissipating out into space. Without some kind of planetary shield that would create an artificial greenhouse effect, their planet would die and they would truly be homeless. Earth was a pretty good candidate for having sufficient gold. Small rocky planets close to their home star have higher concentrations of the heavier, more complex elements like gold, created in the supernova event that gave birth to the solar system as we know it.

Our Sun is a second-generation star. Before it began 4.5 billion years ago, there was a giant "proto star" in its place. This first star went through an evolutionary cycle that resulted in a supernova explosion. In the explosion the simpler elements within the star like helium and hydrogen were "cooked" into the more complex elements we find in our elemental table. The heavier of these new elements precipitated out only to the small, rocky inner planets like Earth, while the lighter elements were ejected farther out into space to congeal as giant gaseous planets like Jupiter, Saturn, Uranus, and Neptune. This likely occurred due to the greater gravitational attraction of the heavy elements to the newly formed Sun. We know all this because we can see these various stages of stellar evolution happening all around us.

When the Annunaki first surveyed Earth from their spaceships it stood to reason, Sitchin suggests, that they would gravitate to the Middle East, as this would have appeared to be "in the middle of everything," at the hub of three of the main land masses on the planet. This may also explain why Egypt was the site chosen for the pyramids, the largest of which would have been visible from space and would have provided a handy navigational beacon for coming and going from Earth. There is evidence that the pyramids are much older than previously assumed and were once covered with a highly reflective layer of limestone that would have been visible from space. One of the "star chambers" or long tunnels extending from within the pyramid of Cheops aligns the King's Chamber directly with Sirius. Am I suggesting the pyramids were built by highly evolved extra-terrestrial visitors? This is as good an explanation as any, and more probable in my mind than the likelihood of thousands of slaves building what we, with our modern technology, could never duplicate. It makes one wonder how much our view of history is shaped by Hollywood interpretations!

At first, the Annunaki engineers attempted to extract gold from sea water. This is possible, or course, as sea water has all the minerals found on and in the Earth in solution and in the same proportion in which they are found on dry land. The trouble was that because of gold's relative rarity on Earth, they simply were not getting the amount they needed for their purpose by this method. The leader of this original Annunaki survey team of fifty or so, known as Enki, decided to send a scouting team out to find the best source of solid gold on the planet. They soon discovered the gold reserves near present-day Johannesburg, South Africa, where we still mine gold today from shafts extending miles into the Earth.

When I was presenting this information to a group in South Africa a few of years ago, a local resident told me of a story still circulating among the Bushmen of that region. On a certain night under the right conditions, it is told you can still hear the slaves toiling underground, ghosts of the original humans still suffering under the yoke of their God/Masters.

When they moved their party of workers to the new job site, however, the Annunaki quickly realized that this was not going to be easy. They bitterly complained about the new level of labor involved in deep-earth mining, to the point where there was a general strike. The whole project came to a halt.

Enki got together with his female consort, Ninhursag, and they reasoned that the best way to get the job done was to import foreign labor. The trouble was that in South Africa around 425,000 years ago, there were not many contenders for the job. Enki and Ninhursag were master geneticists, and so began experimenting with genetic combinations of available species, to no avail. Some propose that the mythological "man-beasts" of the ancient prehistoric world (before 10,000 BC) were actually the result of some of these failed attempts at genetic hybridization. The scientists hit pay dirt, however, when they discovered an intelligent social ape or *hominid* roaming the savannahs of Africa in small groups eking out an existence as rudimentary hunter-gatherers while attempting not to become prey to the various carnivores abounding at that time. The Annunaki geneticists captured a female of this promising species and, by combining aspects of their own advanced DNA with that of this early hominid type, came up with what we today call modern humans—*homo sapiens*. Thus the original humans were asexual clones created for the purpose of slave labor.

Of course the Annunaki could not endow this cloned being with the full range of their own DNA, so they selected some specific elements like the ability for speech and more robust physical strength. But they chose to "switch off" the bulk of their full genetic endowment. After all, they were looking for slave labor, not to create a race of superbeings. In Sitchin's later work, *Genesis Revisited* (Avon, 1990), he reviews this history in light of what had been learned about DNA in the interim between books. One fascinating detail is the agreement among biologists today that all humans are related to a single common ancestor, a female—Mitochondrial Eve, as she is known—who came out of Africa. For a more comprehensive overview of the Annunaki and a specific timetable outlining their roles on Mars and with Atlantis, Mesopotamia, and Egypt please see Patricia Cori's *Atlantis Rising* (Cori, P. *Atlantis Rising: The Struggle of Darkness and Light*. Berkeley, CA: North Atlantic Books, 2008). Modern space-faring epics like

"Star Wars" and "Star Trek" pale in comparison with our actual history and involvement with "ETs."

Now what I have just recounted presents a major challenge to two of our predominant belief systems—evolution and creationism, or "intelligent design" as the theory's main religious proponents now call it. Again referring to Occam's Razor, Chaos Theory, and the notion that new ideas that are rooted in truth and fact very often provide the joining and reconciliation of what formerly appeared as diametrically opposed ideas, is it possible that *both* are true? In other words, the apparent contradiction in two points of view may be reconciled when we take a third position, or a new perspective providing a fresh, more inclusive context—the Big Picture. It is another way of experiencing the collapse of duality.

In this new view of history, which is evidence-based, we find room for *both* evolution and creationism within a larger context. Humans, like all life forms we observe today and in the record of species, evolved through normal adaptation up to a point. Then along came the supernatural Gods who finished off the job, perhaps saving us from a very long period of further natural evolution. Of course this idea does not satisfy the minds of those who like to presume humans were created directly by the Divine Omnipotent God of Creation and not out of our own desire to separate from the Divine. This almost universally accepted belief in the universe as God's Creation, if looked at carefully, does not stand up to deeper reasoning. It is only from a non-dual perspective and appreciating that all there is *is* God—that nothing else exists—that we can appreciate the impossibility of a perfect Creator making an imperfect Creation. The syntax I am proposing is this:

- First the Divine created us as One Perfect Being. We as One Spirit are the Divine's only Creation.

- Out of our own Divine creativity and the desire to experience something "more than everything" *we* caused the Big Bang and universe of separated forms.

- We can't blame God for what we did.

- He/She is incapable of seeing or even acknowledging our illusion, and waits patiently in reality while we dream.

Although this view may seem to depersonalize the Divine and increase our sense of alienation, the Divine actually instilled in each and every one of us the memory of our own Divine nature and Oneness with our Creator. When we tap into this memory, which is locked within every mind, we experience a tangible, loving, and personal feeling of connection and Oneness. Divine images, beings, and saviors serve only to provide a mental image that can act as a "stand-in" for Divine abstraction until we get to a level of understanding that no longer requires that image. The Divine doesn't care what image you use. That is a distinctly dualistic human trait, and the root of untold, needless strife on this planet.

The historical trap we find ourselves in is due partly to the fact that these supernatural beings, the Annunaki, allowed, even encouraged, us to worship them as Gods as this perfectly served their purpose of enslavement. Why would they want us to believe any differently? And of course, we were easily impressed, having come from grubbing around for survival to encountering these beings with their flying ships, weapons, and incredible technology and abilities. A burning bush here, a parting of the waters there, and we were True Believers! As a result, we have emerging out of the Middle East, where the Annunaki eventually established their kingdoms and hybrid human lineage, dualistic world religions based on separation and alienation (emphasis on "alien") rooted in the wounded-male archetype and perfectly designed to control the population through perpetual conflict and war among the slaves.

This story inverts many of our basic assumptions about the nature of creation and the world, so I will attempt to further illuminate any areas of possible confusion. *A Course in Miracles*, a non-dual thought system, refutes the notion of the direct creation of the Universe, the world, and us by God. Logically (and many have rightfully asked this question), how could a perfect being create such a messed-up, imperfect world? For some, this question alone is the basis of life-long atheism, itself an unsatisfactory state of lonely alienation. Dualistic religions are based on an anthropomorphic image of God reinforced by the memory of these historical God Kings. The *Course* states: "If this were the real world, God *would be* cruel!" (Italics mine, 13: intro 3:1). A liberating aspect of this view lies in recognizing how powerful *we* are to have created the universe—albeit not a *perfect* universe—and how completely loved and trusted we are by our Creator to do this!

Of course our Creator knew that in reality our desire to separate ourselves would be impossible to fulfill except in fantasy, so He allowed us to *dream* the universe of form and separation, much as a loving parent watches a child at play. Truly, then, this universe is the "impossible dream" and we are the dreamer, the Created One. Our Creator is waiting patiently for us to awaken and throw off the self-made illusions from which we suffer. He/She is waiting patiently for the child who, tired at the end of the day, has had enough play and wants to go home. And yet the loving parent makes no demands. "Your will be done" is the message offered. Now is as good a time as any to awaken and go home, is it not?

The rest of the history of the Annunaki involves the master-slave relationship established in the early mining days. Sitchin put together an amazing series called *The Earth Chronicles* in which he shows how major movements of human populations and major events in human history reveal an ongoing relationship with these Gods of antiquity. I recall touring through central Mexico with his *Lost Realms* as my guidebook. What an amazing journey, as Sitchin provided deep insight into many of the enigmatic symbols left by pre-historic peoples of that region. I remember especially seeing "bearded ones" depicted at Monte Alban, a culture that thrived circa 600 AD. No natural North American peoples had beards. But emissaries from the East, the Gods of ancient times, did! Many puzzling artifacts and monuments, like the giant Olmec heads of Mexico and the amazing architecture and stonework of Peru, make sense in the context of the ET Gods' presence on Earth, not the least of which are architectural wonders and engineering feats unmatched by present-day builders limited to modern human technology.

Eventually, Annunaki explorers journeyed all over the planet looking for natural resources and spreading their version of civilization, ultimately forming the basis of a global sea-faring society that subscribed to the same basic knowledge of the cosmos, agriculture, metallurgy, etc. The evidence for this advanced global culture was mostly destroyed in the deluge of 9500 BC. Many ancient sites under current coastlines are now being brought to light thanks to satellite photography and modern mapping techniques. Soon the true history of humanity will be largely acknowledged, as will our heritage from the stars and star beings. Once the global war machine has been dismantled and its causes recognized and healed, nobody who now profits from withholding the truth and keeping others in the grip of fear and control will be motivated to continue with this outmoded and dysfunctional way of being. We will transcend the mistakes of our forbearers as we are freed from the clutches of time and history.

THE WOUNDED MALE

The Annunaki, although highly advanced in many areas, were definitely *not* what we would call spiritually evolved masters along the lines of Christ or Buddha. As a matter of fact, they had some pretty polarized aspects, like their insatiable lust for sex, war, conquest, riches, and power. They were clearly operating more from a dualistic 4-D position and not from a non-dual 5-D state. Not all of them exhibited these lower characteristics, but in general, they were a troubled race. They perfectly personified the wounded-male archetype given their separation from their home and their plight as perpetual lost wanderers given over to survival-motivated behavior at the cost of others. They were definitely living out the dualistic hell of separation from the One as space-faring prodigal sons. Souls lost in this state of polarization are doomed to seek but never find the solution to their troubled state of separation in the world of form. This mind-set is still very much a part of the modern ego-based perpetual-seeker syndrome of always looking outside oneself and the ever-present moment for the answer.

The Annunaki were pleased with the loyalty and worship of their slaves and had no qualms about being worshipped as Gods. Eventually, they settled back in the lands of the Middle East after many forays and adventures on the planet, as described in Sitchen's *Earth Chronicles*. The Annunaki were the Gods of antiquity, and are responsible still for the misidentification of advanced beings from space as our God. Even the advancement to monotheism starting with the Egyptians under Amenhotep reflected an image of God as a reasonably nice guy, until you broke the rules. The depiction of the Greek gods was not too far removed from the actual personalities of the Annunaki—that is, patriarchal supernatural beings still prey to petty jealousies, family squabbles, envy, greed, and lust.

I invite you to consider dispassionately the three main world religions that eventually emerged out of the Middle East. All three claim to have common roots in the ancestry of Abraham. All claim allegiance to the God of the Old Testament. But look more closely at this God. He is first of all notably male, which immediately signals duality. Each of these three patriarchal world religions still has trouble today making peace with the female essence. Females were historically banished from the priesthood, and therefore from God's presence. Millions of women were murdered not many generations ago for holding to their gifts of natural healing and their spiritual skills that marked them as threats to the male hierarchal religion of the day. Women were generally given a back seat in these traditional religions, at least in the more orthodox versions of them. The denigration of the female is matched by the denigration of Mother Earth herself at the hands of the modern corporate global economy spawned by the principles espoused by these master-slave religions.

This patriarchal God also has a taste for blood and war, and does not tolerate disagreement from any lesser being or competing religion! He seems to get a real charge out of challenging enemies and emphasizing that his own worshippers are somehow special and chosen—a notch above all others by virtue of whom they worship. Sitchin points out that the original translation of the Hebrew word for "worship" was "work for." "You shall work for no other Gods but me" puts a new spin on company loyalty! The modern soulless corporation with its blind loyalty to profit at the cost of the well-being of others is reflective of a sociopath with all of the rights of an individual, but none of the responsibilities. The Annunaki would be proud.

The Middle East and its three main groups of true believers has been at war for as long as history can remember. Indeed, the very peace and security of the world today is being held hostage by the blind allegiance to endless war in this region. All are fighting "with God on their side"! Now come on—can a socio-religious movement divided into perpetually conflicted factions have anything to do with God or Heaven?

And what about religious architecture? Have you ever wondered why the temples and sacred structures of these dualistic world religions all have *really tall* ceilings? Even the homes of today's aristocrats are marked by tall ceilings that don't make much sense on a practical level, as in meeting heating and cooling needs. But each of these major faiths lives under the promise (or threat?) of God's imminent return, or that of one of his appointed (male) saviors. So to be on the safe side, better make room!

The promised return of the Gods has fostered a deep historical paranoia of being caught off guard should the "boss" make a surprise entrance. I'm reminded of the bumper sticker: "Jesus is coming back...look busy." The idea that the Divine could be involved in any way with such games and in playing off such petty human fears and distrust issues degrades the whole idea of a loving Creator. It is time to walk out of the movie theater of our own conditioned past, shake off the shackles and spells of enslavement to fantasies, and walk in the sunshine of our own, very real Divine nature.

We also find a religious fascination with death, apocalypse, and the ever-feared Day of Judgment. These sound more like the ranting of the fearful ego, made insane by its suspicion that it doesn't really exist and is about to be exposed as a fraud at any time. The ego knows its days are numbered, and it does not know how to accept this fact gracefully.

If the Annunaki were here today physically, and obviously they are not, they would be sitting back in detached amusement at how the slaves continue to squabble among themselves, never pausing to consider that they share a common problem. Just like dysfunctional parents, the Annunaki rule by neglect. By pitting the "kids" against each other, they avoid responsibility for making peace and healing the family's issues, which are their own issues.

Although the Annunaki are not physically here, they still operate as a powerful archetype in the fourth dimension. Our mental conditioning over eons as slaves still places us in an unseen psychic prison of beliefs, fears, and limitations. The global society spawned by their progeny in the form of aristocratic bloodlines and secret societies has in itself become trapped in a mental prison, married, as it were, to materialism and the pursuit of consumer "rights" through debt slavery. Our chains are now digital. Sadly, slaves who have been conditioned too long, when given their freedom, often prefer the security of slavery to the responsibility of freedom. This was the basis of Eric Fromm's classic *Escape from Freedom*, in which he described the societal ennui and disorientation at the end of World War II that led to a desire to escape from the new-found democratic freedoms the War had (seemingly) created into materialism, dualistic religious belief systems, and addictions (Henry Holt & Co., 1941).

A similar observation was the basis of Eric Hoffer's *The True Believer* from around the same time (Harper & Row, 1951). He observed our general discomfort with the light of freedom and our desire to immerse ourselves in the darkness of authoritarian belief systems. It's just what we are used to, Hoffer stated: "Power corrupts the few, while weakness corrupts the many."

The Annunaki live on today in the third dimension in the form of their lineage. Anyone who cares to find out will learn that the affairs of the world, from currency rates to wars to major political decisions, are made by a very small group of "elites." There are as few as twelve families involved. They meet regularly and make decisions that affect us all, yet are motivated solely by their need to maintain their position of power and control at all costs. Even at the cost of peace and our survival as a species, it appears. These elites operate under an ancient contract: "Hold the power on the planet until we return, and you will be rewarded!" The Annunaki conquerors still consider Earth their colony. Like a rich traveler who owns a condo in a far-flung location, they're not sure they'll ever use it, but just in case, they have their relatives take care of the place on their behalf.

These modern elites are the closest living descendants of the royal lineages established by the Kings of Sumeria, and they typically display quite sociopathic tendencies. A good example of an elite attitude toward humanity is found in Stalin's proclamation: "An individual death is a tragedy. Mass murder is merely statistics." Very early in their entanglement with humanity, the Annunaki began to mate with female humans. The original God Kings who were the products of these liaisons were pretty much supernatural beings—demigods whose authority and stature was unquestioned and who ruled easily by virtue of their divine heritage. If you trace the lineage of today's elites back far enough, you start to come across leaders of legendary fame and abilities like Gilgamesh, Solomon, and the ancient Pharaohs. Eventually, however, the Annunaki royal blood became more and more diluted so that by the modern era, the "royals" are just like you and me. They actually may have weakened their lineage genetically through the tendency to in-breed. But, they are still bound by their contract which, incidentally, has no clause for simply conceding power. They know nothing but to continue to hold the power while trusting in God's ancient promise to return.

I suspect there is much concern among the elites, particularly as the promised return of the Gods is not happening.

And there is good reason to assume that the promised return is not going to happen, at least not in the form they were promised or assumed it would take. It is reasonable to suggest that as we ascend beyond 3-D and 4-D duality, Earth will no longer be a suitable or even accessible planet to those still caught in playing out dramas in duality. Some say the diehards who are simply unwilling to let go of the old paradigm will need to be transported to another 3-D planet where they can continue to live out that choice.

David Wilcock goes as far as to say that Earth in the past provided a haven for 3-D populations unwilling to ascend or incapable of ascending beyond 3-D when their planets moved into the fifth dimension. Earth has been the penal colony, the Australia, of our quadrant of the galaxy, it appears. This may help explain some of the less-than-civilized behaviors of humans over eons, and the interesting variations of human races and cultures. We're a planet of rebels! The elites, meanwhile, seem hell-bent on creating Armageddon on Earth now, as they believe their special status will somehow magically rescue them at the last minute anyway. Their sacred writings predict a hellish period of purification and holy war (the king of oxymorons!) on Earth. It seems many are doing their best to make sure that these prophesies are self-fulfilling and that the tyranny and chaos described by ancient scripture wins out!

The Annunaki have thus claimed Earth and humanity as their rightful property. The whole idea of ownership, especially at the expense of others, is foreign to natural societies and has provided the pattern for the great world-conquering Empires of the past (and present). The pattern of our fathers continues in the guise of Western colonial expansionism and later industrialization, global corporatization, and the support of fascistic dictatorships under the guise of spreading freedom to practice democratic capitalism. The operative credo of the elite world management team also denigrates Nature, justifying with a philosophy of growth at all costs the over-consumption of resources and the neglect of the needs of the land and future generations. You can see how we learned this attitude from a race of beings that could easily leave without conscience any planet they stripped of its resources, much as we discard an old car. The natural peoples of the Earth were dumbfounded by the concept of land ownership subscribed to by their conquerors, who seemed to think of themselves as liberators. Now you are free to "work for" no other Gods but us.

Today, there seems to be an effort underway on the part of the elites to undermine the planetary ascension and human evolution itself with the wanton use of pesticides, fluoride in the water (first used by the Nazis to create complacency in the camps), aspartame (a known neurotoxin), mercury fillings (another known neurotoxin), vaccines (with absolutely no research-based evidence that they work), and other known toxins *all proven* to be harmful to humans and life. Sixty-cycle electro-magnetic frequencies (EMFs), deadly drugs and medical practices, a toxic food supply— the insanity of these conditions can only be coming from a seriously limited and sick mentality organized on some level for some purpose, like that of a lost, wounded male, for example, mindlessly thrashing out in pain and suffering. "If I'm going down, I'm taking you with me!"

RULE BY NEGLECT

Sitchin shows that the Judeo-Christian story of Creation in the book of Genesis is a re-write of an earlier Sumerian document. As with most re-writes, things get lost in the translation. The original Sumerian Creation story told of a final summit meeting among the Annunaki leaders about the fate of humanity once the Annunaki were ready to leave. Perhaps they had gotten their quota of gold and needed to get to work saving Niburu. The consensus among the Annunaki was simply to do nothing about the human question—in essence, to rule by neglect. As cloned asexual species we would have simply and eventually died out but Enki held out for another plan. Perhaps he was reacting as a pure scientist, or perhaps as our original Creator he had a soft spot in his heart for the human slaves.

Enki's proposal was to endow humanity with sexuality in order to allow us to survive as an independent species and thus carry on the human experiment. As cloned beings, we were asexual and originally were "birthed" much like test-tube babies, carried by Annunaki surrogate mothers. The human population of antiquity never reached the size it is at today. There is some evidence that the Annunaki originally shared with us the secrets and benefits of their own longevity as well. We apparently used to live very long lives. There is also some conjecture that this may have been one of the uses of gold, since gold reduced to a monatomic state is an ideal biological superconductor that optimizes the functioning of DNA and the nervous system when ingested. Even in a colloidal state, ingesting small amounts of gold has therapeutic benefits. The making of jewelry was originally a healing art that only later was downgraded to provide solely for adornment.

Enki's plan met with a lot of resistance from all the other Annunaki. They pointed out that if they gave the slaves the gift of procreation, which up until then had been their exclusive privilege, two things would happen. First, they would multiply like rabbits, fill the Earth, and make a mess of it. What if we want to come back, they asked? They'll trash the place—a fear that has mostly been justified. Besides, they argued, the conditions may occur in the future, as our astronomers have told us, for the reactivation of *our* advanced DNA, currently dormant in the human slaves' cells. They will then spontaneously inherit all our advanced knowledge, characteristics, and abilities, and awaken to the fact that *they* are the rightful inheritors of Planet Earth. Then they will throw us out!

You can see how this fear filters down in the form of the fears of our present-day planetary management team. What if the slaves wake up and discover the sham? What if they figure out they don't need us, and are better off managing themselves? Don't look at the man behind the curtain.

On this note, I was noticing during one recent day of people-watching the strange fashion among some of today's youth to pierce their bodies with metals and cover themselves with permanent tattoos. "What is this *really* about," I wondered. I was immediately struck by the thought that these are the markings of enslavement. Are these youths feeling an emerging awareness of humanity's plight seeping out from their own DNA and expressing it symbolically as best they can? The impetus of youth has always been to expose the hypocrisy of the prior generation. Shackled and tattooed, we have been marching to the wounded-male archetype's beat for so long, it almost feels normal. Almost.

Enki persisted and finally was able to come up with a compromise. He was, after all, a recognized leader among the Annunaki, and carried the definite weight of authority. Here we have what showed up in Genesis as the allegory of Adam and Eve, the Tree of the Knowledge of good and evil, their subsequent guilt, and their banishment from the Garden and from direct contact with the Gods. Falling from their Divine nature, Adam and Eve were doomed to make or break it on their own, never to return to direct contact with the Gods (the Biblical *Eloihim* is a plural term), thereby losing any advantages that such contact could give them in the future. If the Gods blessed us with independence, the cost was that we truly had to make it on our own. These conditions set by the Annunaki Gods are consistent with the notion of an experiment according to the scientific method, with specific controls and confounding factors accounted for. And we have been trying to get back to the Garden of innocence and security ever since.

Enki was symbolized in the original Sumerian story, which pre-dates the Biblical version, as the Serpent. It was only much later that Christian interpreters identified the Serpent as Satan, who is a relatively recent invention/ego projection. The "flaming double-edged sword" preventing our return represents the seemingly impossible barrier created by our immersion in duality. We will not get back to the Garden by dualistic means, only by transcendence of duality through True Forgiveness.

Now I must ask you, does the God we associate with this period in history sound to you like a loving supreme Divine being, Creator of All That Is? Or does it sound more like a troubled, lost being, or collective in this case, caught up in an inflated male ego, totally distracted by its own perceived needs and thrashing about trying to establish a home? I am not saying God does not exist. I am saying the exact opposite; there is no Reality outside of God. Especially if that pseudo-God is saying "I am God, and you are not." Or "You are my people, and they are not." I *am* saying that if these beings *are* Gods, then we are probably a lot better off without them.

And what about the promise of the imminent return? Each of the "big three" dualistic religions has its own version of this—each exclusive of the others and another guarantee of perpetual conflict. What if it doesn't happen? What if, as the Hopi have told us, "*We* are the Ones we have been waiting for?" There are going to be a lot of disappointed and disillusioned true believers on all sides when it dawns on us that we have been duped into ignoring our own united Divine nature and destiny for eons, waiting for outside intervention. It is my conviction that religious re-education will be a boom industry in the next century. The revelation of our enslavement will constitute the basis for a huge re-education program in the near future, as the old dualistic religions fade into insignificance in the light of our true identity as One with each other and God. There's a lot of unlearning to be done.

Neil Freer has looked deeply into the psychological ram-ifications of millennia of outside control and patterns of human dependency. His roadmap for recovery uncovers the many subtle layers of "unlearning" we will need to address (Freer, N. *God Games, What Do You Do Forever?* Escondido, CA: The Book Tree, 1999).

Once we collectively step out of the dualistic mind-set, it will be much easier to appreciate the inherent limita-tions of our former cultural chains. Once we know this experientially as a deep inner healing and sense of peace, there will be no basis or need for divisions, hierarchies, judgment, sin, or blame. These old fear-based concepts will simply be considered as nothing more than puzzling anachronisms once we all emerge into the Peace and Joy of the New Earth. God bless us *all*.

The good news here, I suppose, is that given that the Annunaki operate from within duality, there must also be some benefits to us along with all the burdens this rela-tionship has offered. And this is so. Their main contri-bution to human success has been in the gift of science and technologies, as well as cultural gifts in the form of the arts and higher learning. Locked in the memory of our shared DNA and now emerging at exponential rates is the knowledge (memory) of space flight, advanced DNA recombination, longevity, quantum science, advanced healing technologies, and perhaps even telepathy and teleportation. Even though cities were made originally for the purpose of amassing slave labor for the Annunaki's self-aggrandizing projects and warfare, they have become the hubs of amazing discoveries and creations in the arts, sciences, and culture. Our extra-terrestrial ancestors have left us with mixed blessings. Yes, we have inherited some of their less-desirable traits, but what will survive the Shift may be the gifts they pass on that will serve only the highest good of all. Like children who overlook their parents' shortcomings and embrace their gifts with humility, we may actually become our parents' teachers. Our gratitude for these gifts along with our forgiveness may yet help us transcend resentment and blame. It's all part of becoming a mature, loving, creative Being. After all, bad parents are better than no parents.

The Creator only sees Reality. It is not possible for God to be aware of what we experience in the dream of duality and separation. God does not intrude upon our dreams, our hallucinations. To do so would give them reality, and they simply have none. *A Course in Miracles* begins with the non-dual declaration: "Nothing real can be threatened. Nothing unreal exists. Herein lies the Peace of God." This is a statement that no one can argue with. You may discount it, but you can't come up with a logical argument. The best way to allow non-dual ideas to affect us is to *feel* them. It is the feeling of these ideas that points you to the experience of Oneness. This feeling you know; it is already a part of you. That is how we recognize it (*re*-cognize it). It has been dormant in our minds for eons, and is now awakening within you, if you choose to allow it.

As fantastic as this whole story sounds, from a non-dual perspective, we have simply been looking at one chapter in our dream of separation. It is all a projection of the One Mind, the Ancient Mind, which is our true spiritual identity as the Son of God. "Son" here is not used in a patriarchal manner, but simply as an analogy for child, offspring, or expression of God. You may use any term that works for you. The Divine reads your heart, not your verbal mind! For that matter, the Divine can never be limited to *any* dualistic doctrine, creed, or sacred writings. These are projections of our own ideas about the Divine. We, in our true identity as One Self, are the Mind of God in action. As co-creators with God, we were given the opportunity to live out the idea of separation in the form of the universe of time and space, which includes the experience of the apparent separation of bodies. To reinforce the non-dual metaphysics of Creation, remember that none of this could *really* happen, since Oneness cannot be divided. If it could, then it wouldn't be Oneness to begin with! In reality, the world never happened. It is our creation, or rather mis-creation. The world, time, space, and the universe are an aberration in the One Mind, which is granted complete freedom to do anything it pleases.

So we must see the story of the Annunaki in this light, or it will serve simply to create more dualistic, fear- and ego-based suffering. How could *they* do this to *us*? We must right the wrongs! It's them or us! But nobody is doing anything to anyone. We are all figures in the same dream, and there is only One Dreamer. As I have noted, the Annunaki embody the archetype of the wounded male. We all carry this archetype in our minds, or it simply could not be part of our experience.

We must transcend the artificial division of "them" and "us." There is only "us" here, and in reality, only One of us! All behavior is coming from the One Dreamer in its seemingly endless separated forms. All behavior is either an expression of Love or a call for Love as the *Course* describes and as the Divine sees us. As such, all behavior is coming from Love. We collapse the pattern of suffering observed in some behavior—what we label bad behavior—by forgiving it. We collapse the judgment in our own minds—the only place it exists—and practice

Forgiveness, not in the old egoic sense of "I forgive you for what you have done," but in the non-dual sense of "I see you as you are as Spirit and there is nothing real to forgive." We collapse the judgment in our own minds by seeing the Big Picture—a more inclusive picture with no divisions between us. I am Divine, as are You. By thus collapsing the perception of "wrong" in my awareness, I reduce the tendency in the One Mind to see it in anyone. I am beginning to think like God. We are experiencing this process in time, so it seems to take time to accomplish this. In truth, it has already been accomplished, and we are merely reviewing the movie from within the illusion of separation—which itself never really happened. (You may shake your head now!)

Please do not struggle with these ideas. Take your time with them, and allow yourself to feel the possibilities. Our minds are so conditioned by the dream; we are constantly trying to understand it in its own terms or frames of reference. This will never work. The only way truly to understand duality is from outside it, in non-duality. The only choice within duality is endless analysis and opinion, leading nowhere as pointless points of view. Your Spirit is always in a state of non-duality, having remained one with its Source. Your Spirit does not need healing. Only the mind that thinks it is other than Spirit does. When you go into a state of non-dual Peace through the practice of mental Silence, the dualistic mind takes a holiday. Allow it to do so. It will be there when you need it, but you don't really need it as much as it would like you to believe.

As for those who represent the Annunaki today—those who still seem hell-bent on ignoring the obvious and clinging to the sinking ship of old-paradigm thinking—we can only intend amnesty for all. This is *the only way out* of this geo- (anagram for ego) political mess. Any approach other than True Forgiveness will only prolong the pain needlessly. Begin now by forgiving now.

For myself, I ask the forgiveness of any of you of religious persuasion if I have in any way offended you. That is not my intent. I have drawn a picture here of global and historical deception masked as world religions, that is true. But I don't recant anything I have said. I do, however, acknowledge that on some level we all choose the circumstances of our life's path in order that we may best learn through forgiveness. All religions start out with a sincere desire to step out of suffering and experience something better. They are all a call for Love and neutral in and of themselves. As such, all paths lead home. There are 7+ billion of us on Earth now, and there are 7+ billion paths home, each perfect in its own plan and destiny. It is entirely possible to awaken to your spiritual path within a religious structure, as it is to do so outside of one. A religious structure, however, does not guarantee a spiritual path. This is still and only a personal choice and experience. Whatever your path, it is perfect for you now. If and when you feel a Divine discontent with that path, look within for the memory of your Divine Self, and it will guide you appropriately.

Forgiveness is a good example of a win-win approach. When I forgive you, the Annunaki, or anyone who comes to mind, I am in reality accepting my own forgiveness for my judgment of you as anything less than Divine Spirit. The full acceptance of my Forgiveness by me lies in recognizing and forgiving you. This is called Spiritual Healing—healing that occurs on the deepest level of cause, which is the mind. It is always a shared experience.

What follows is the simplest, most direct and effective way to forgive that I have yet come across. I encourage you to give it a try, right now. The Annunaki are waiting for your Forgiveness, as are we all.

HO'OPONOPONO—A GIFT
TO THE PLANET FROM THE
HAWAIIAN PEOPLE

Recently, Joe Vitale wrote about a simple Forgiveness technique that rocked his world (*Zero Limits,* Wiley, 2007). He actually said to Dr. Len, his co-author, that after learning this technique, everything he had written up until then became obsolete. Dr. Len assured him there was still value for some in what he had written previously, but Joe knew something completely new and different had happened.

In the ancient Hawaiian culture, whenever a member of the community fell into any kind of misfortune, whether through illness, accident, or even willful crime, the entire population sat in a circle around the person, silently searching their own hearts for how they may have contributed, even in some seemingly minor way, to the person's suffering. Perhaps they held a judgment against this person or their family or maybe felt a secret envy or jealousy. Whatever the case, after they recognized their part and silently asked for the subject's forgiveness, they quietly left the circle. No words were shared. In the end, when all had made their own peace, the individual sitting in the middle was healed.

As simple as this practice sounds, it works based on what we now call quantum principles—that we are all entangled or connected and therefore we cannot escape the effects of one person on the collective, or of the collective on one person. It also works on the metaphysical level we have been discussing, that of the One Mind asleep in a dream of suffering. All minds, then, are joined as One, even in the dream.

Ho'oponopono came to modern attention through Dr. Len's own experience as a clinical social worker in Hawaii. He found himself on night duty overseeing a ward for the criminally insane. Apparently these were very dangerous offenders, some of whom were shackled for their own and others' protection. Dr. Len found himself with enough free time to practice what he remembered of the tradition of forgiveness handed down from his elders. He pulled the file of an inmate, looked at the picture of the person, and repeated four simple phrases, until he felt a "lightness" about his perception of that person—like a softening and more compassionate feeling. He then replaced the file and started with the next. After a period of time, the ward began to empty out, as inmates got well. A couple of inmates were transferred to a minimum-security facility, but soon there were no more inmates, and so the ward was shut down.

Vitale, learning of Dr. Len's success, realized that he had distilled the more ceremonial and complex practice of the ancients into a simple four-step process, which I summarize below with a non-dual interpretation for each of the phrases. After reading these descriptions, I heartily suggest you try it on someone, maybe even yourself. You may use a picture as Dr. Len did, or simply hold an image of the person in your mind's eye. I invite you to begin using this technique right away. Why prolong unnecessary suffering? Think of someone with whom you have a difficult relationship. This may be someone who, as you think of them, evinces a "loss of joy," no matter how slight. You may think of yourself in the past when you experienced guilt as the result of your past actions or some event. Any feeling of "loss of joy" is evidence of an aspect of unhealed guilt in your mind. You now have an opportunity to clear it for you and for all of us. Hold the subject in your mind's eye as you sit quietly with eyes closed. Begin to repeat the four phrases, like a mantra, directing them to this mental image. You don't have to "feel" the connection; the feeling comes after the choice to do this. Just do it. Spirit is more than eager and willing to heal this relationship—even as little as 1 percent of willingness from you opens the door.

You will find, to your amazement and delight, that when you next see this person, or think of him or her, *something has changed!* You'll be tempted to think the person must have changed. What has changed is that the veils of darkness between you have lifted. You are now both seeing more of your real Selves in each other. The past has melted away in the Light of Spirit that you invited into the relationship. Once you experience this enough, more opportunities will begin to present themselves to you. It's as if all your past relationships line up for forgiveness once the way is clear.

"I love you": We are recognizing that at a deep level we are One. We are mirrors for each other. Judging or condemning you would just be doing the same to me. You, in my perception of you, are a projection of my state of mind. Loving and forgiving you is also doing the same for me. The divisions between us are only in our imaginations. Although bodies and actions appear separate, the Mind that is expressing through all of us is the same. All behavior is either an expression of or a call for Love. So Love is the cause of everything, and the cure at the same time.

"I am sorry": Not for anything in particular that you or I have done—that would make the offense real—but for together having decided to experience separation, and for all the suffering of all of us as a result of this mutual decision. For *that* I am truly sorry. And I am sorry for my contribution in this way to your particular experience of suffering, confident that in our awakening and acceptance of forgiveness, we shall ultimately see all suffering washed away in an instant of healing and liberation.

"Please forgive me": Not for what it appears I have done, but for agreeing with you to create this dream of suffering and separation. Please see me as an undiluted, invulnerable, eternal, and forever joyful Spirit, as I now choose to see you. I see you as Spirit who through the majesty of your own creativity and freedom has created this opportunity to awaken and remember Love, and I trust you to love me and forgive me my illusions.

"Thank you": For giving us both an opportunity to heal our relationship, to heal in my mind any misperception of you as less than Divine, knowing this healing goes out to the One Mind and affects everyone and everything in Creation beyond what we can imagine. Thank you for joining with me as One Mind and healing together.

With this level of understanding simply repeat the four phrases with your subject in mind until you feel a shift or inner lightness around the relationship. That is all.

Having worked for a few years with this now, Dr. Len has condensed his "cleaning" practice, as he calls it, to simply: I love you; thank you. You can do the same. Hold the intent of the four phrases, but just run the simple version in your mind. By making Forgiveness a habit, you automatically undo the knee-jerk reaction to judge yourself and others. You restore the mind to its higher purpose, healing the separation in the One Mind rather than staying in suffering, and move from the addiction to perception back to the true purpose of Creation.

CHAPTER 7

PRACTICAL THINGS
YOU CAN DO NOW

W e have looked at this time of change from a few different perspectives. I hope that by now you appreciate where the changes are *really* taking place. It stands to reason, then, that to best navigate the changes without, we must turn to their source within, which is in our own minds. Not, however, the limited, linear verbal mind that is (almost) hopelessly entangled with the level of form, but the peaceful, silent, and powerful Big Mind that sits above and beyond any change, knowing we are safe, secure, and infinite. Your best bet is to begin to cultivate this as your only identity, because it is! Some of you may recognize a kind of Buddhist feeling around what I just said, and you would be right. In Buddhism we find the expression of non-dualism and an identification of the Source of all experience in the mind. These ideas are the missing elements in Western dualistic religious ideas, which posit the level of cause as outside the individual. What is missing in the Eastern philosophical perspective is the possibility of a loving Creator, a central tenet of Western theology. One aspect of the reconciliation of East and West, it appears, may lie in a respectful blending of cultural and spiritual philosophies.

Just as on an individual level we can come to a higher state of awareness and peace by harmonizing the left and right hemispheres of the brain, so we see on a planetary level a harmonizing of the Eastern *yin* mind-set with the Western *yang* mind-set—in the last few decades, particularly. This merging of global hemispheres is predicted by the Mayan calendar, and Calleman covers this idea in his first book as being part of the larger plan of planetary evolution. The beginning of the recent joining of East and West is seen in the rise of the popularity of meditation, yoga, vegetarianism and other practices among the Sixties' Flower Children. At the same time, we see the Eastern world embracing Western values of capitalism and industrialization. The great potential here is that out of this joining there will arise a more balanced planetary awareness on a geopolitical level that will base decisions and policies on the highest good of all and not on "what's in it for us." As noted, we have run out of time to continue playing "them and us." It is time to see there is only "us." Old notions of nationalism and regionalism have already been transcended energetically as evidenced by the movement through the previous tribal, regional, and national underworlds of the Mayan calendar, although these levels are still operative. The fact that all nine levels will complete simultaneously on October 28, 2011 implies the completion of these tribal and nationalistic tendencies that still divide us today.

WHAT YOU CAN DO

There are some practical things we can all do to help us stay in balance and centered in the body/mind while these changes swirl around us. By understanding what has been offered so far in this book, you hopefully feel more at peace psychologically, and can start to now observe and move away from fear-based reactions. Envisioning the world you want is another way to inoculate the mind against frightful future fantasies. Turning off the TV is another. We can also focus on supporting the physical body in a practical way.

The rate of change in the higher non-physical dimensions is very quick—as fast as the speed of light and even the speed of thought. In the lower physical dimensions, change occurs much less rapidly due to the density of matter. Thus, we can shift on an emotional, mental, or spiritual level instantaneously, while the body is left in the dust, wondering what the heck just happened. This will be the feeling among many—at least for those not paying attention—as the planet shifts to a higher, more refined 5-D density, possibly "overnight."

Generally, the same things are happening to our bodies that are happening to the Sun and planets as we enter the photon band. We are being exposed to higher and more powerful forms of spiritual light. By "spiritual light" I mean the higher octaves of hyper-dimensional energies consistent with the Vedic idea of cosmic fire. Just as the changes in the Sun are due to the relaxation of internal energy-producing processes, so our bodies may no longer require the same amount of energy from solid food. What is food anyway, but concentrated and recycled sunlight? If we do take in food today at levels we needed say, ten years ago, what is not utilized for normal metabolism and body repair will be stored as fat or protein waste. Do you think this may have something to do with the epidemic of obesity in our society? I don't think it's the only factor, but it may be playing a part. We could call obesity "galactic maladaptive syndrome," or GMS. Ooh! A diagnosis—wouldn't mainstream medicine and the drug companies love that!

One practical thing we can do to help our bodies adapt is to eat less, and at the same time to drink more water. Water is not only physical food and essential for survival;

it is also electrical and energetic food. Water, as we noted in our discussion of DNA, acts as a "quantum antenna" in its ideal molecular form. It carries and communicates subtle information to the DNA and between every cell in the body, ensuring cooperation and harmony on all levels. Dehydration is a very serious "hidden" health issue in our society, and one that generally worsens with age. This is due in part to the fact that thirst is often misinterpreted as hunger. When it expresses as pain, it is denied as we try to cover up the pain with medications. Headaches, back pain, and digestive complaints often vanish when we pay more attention to regular hydration. Just as your car battery loses energy and eventually dies when its water dries up, the electrical functioning of the body, which includes the trillions of biochemical events that occur every second, is water-dependent. No fluid electrolytes, no energy. You can survive forty days without food, and three without water. Which do you think is more important to your life?

Breatharians and yogic Sun-gazers prove the point of "less is more." By the force of their intent and acceptance based on inner knowing they can transmute all the nutrients they need from atmospheric gases and/or sunlight itself. Think of the savings on your grocery bill! I doubt if I'll ever go to those lengths, but it is good to know what is possible. Eating is for most of us a social convention as much as a biological habit. It seems, however, that our bodies are designed more for browsing than for eating full, regular, balanced meals. In a natural, hunter-gatherer state, which we enjoyed for the vast majority of history, there were no "all-food-group" bushes or "complete-meal" shrubs! The body took what was available and made the most of it. Even grains and dairy are relatively recent additions to the human diet, which is one reason why most food sensitivities occur in these two food groups, notwithstanding that they are consumed mostly in an adulterated form today.

Another possibility lies in the field of biological transmutation. Decades ago a French scientist named Louis Kervan was conducting research on a South Pacific island (*Biological Transmutations,* Beekman Publishers, Inc., 1998). He noticed that the eggs the scientists were enjoying daily were provided by chickens with no visible source of calcium, which makes up egg shells. His scientific background convinced him there had to be an answer, so in his spare time he investigated the chickens' biochemistry and digestive systems. He came to the conclusion that the chickens were transmuting calcium from silica, which was abundant on the sandy isle. Transmutation is not a chemical term; it is alchemical, or what we moderns prefer to think of as "magical." According to the rules of chemistry, changing one element into another is not possible. But the chickens didn't know this, so they did it anyway! The implication here is that if chickens can do this with brains the size of a small nut, why can't we? I think we can. It is only our unquestioned belief in our limitations that stops us.

Do you want to feel better and lose some of those persistent symptoms that just won't go away, as well as that extra weight? Avoid grains and dairy for three weeks, and see what happens! As these foods are relatively recent additions to the human diet, our Stone Age bodies have not yet adapted to them fully. Some researchers suggest a strong link between grain-based diets and obesity, diabetes, heart disease, and cancer (Mercola, J. *The No-Grain Diet.* New York: Penguin Group, 2004). Most fad diets that actually work turn out to be variations on "pre-civilization" diets. The popular Blood Type diet is based on the idea that, although the global population is pretty much mixed up with original tribal lineages scattered over the globe, our bodies still do best on a diet consistent with the bulk of our ancestry (D'Adamo, *Eat Right 4 Your Type,* GP Putnam & Sons, 1996). As such, 80 percent of the population, blood types A and O, cannot tolerate wheat or dairy, our modern staples. Allergy symptoms associated with these two foods alone account for a large proportion of supposedly medical conditions. Working *with* Nature and not against her is still the best approach to living.

And *please* cut out refined sugar and carbohydrates while you are at it. White sugar is a poisonous food additive. It is a chemical, not a food, that goes by the names high fructose corn syrup, invert glucose, and a number of disguised labels. In William Dufty's classic *Sugar Blues* (Warner Books, 1975), we read the tale of the development of the refined sugar industry that reads like the story of the heroin trade. When it was discovered that refined sugar was an ideal food preservative (bacteria know a poison and how to avoid it) for the burgeoning industrialization and corporate take-over of the food supply, many tropical cane-producing countries all of a sudden came under the "protection" of corporate-controlled big governments. The tale of slave labor and political takeovers is indeed sobering—and not so sweet!

Another classic in the field of nutrition is an obscure little paperback whose author eventually became a major publisher of health-related books. J. I. Rodale, in his book *Natural Health, Sugar and the Criminal Mind* (Pyramid Books, 1968), reports on his investigation of the diets and lifestyles of the criminally insane. He found to his surprise that all his subjects had committed their horrendous crimes while in the throes of sugar-induced hypoglycemia. Hypoglycemia is a low-blood-sugar state induced by over secretion of insulin from a high sugar diet—the brain starves and we go crazy. Hitler, an Austrian pastry addict, was a good example. Once away from the sweetly seductive substance, Rodale's subjects reverted to nice, "normal" people. Does this help to explain anyone you may know? Alcoholism is a sugar addiction, by the way.

The most surprising aspect of the sugar story is the recent pronouncement of a major health official that diabetes has nothing to do with sugar consumption. What? Pinch me, what planet is this?

Please research refined sugar, along with the dangers of soy, aspartame, fluoride, chlorine, GMOs, and other common food and health challenges facing us today at *www.mercola.com*. We really do need to take more responsibility for our health, rather than turning our lives over to the "experts."

GET GROUNDED—LITERALLY

The nervous system seems most sensitive to energetic changes in the environment. Perhaps this is because it functions mainly on a bio-electric level. We are dealing with both huge fluctuations in our natural electro-magnetic environment and the injury and insult from man-made EMF sources, the most stressful of which include the everyday 60-cycle field in every home, office, and building. Avoid undue exposure to these electrical fields whenever possible. Getting outdoors in your bare feet or in non-rubber-soled shoes will actually help your body ground out excess electrical energy in your own energy field. A nice walk in Nature every evening will help in this area, and ensure a deeper more restorative sleep.

Being "ungrounded" can contribute to many symptoms attributed to "stress," such as sleep disturbances, mood swings, and irrational behavior. As the magnetic influence of the Earth weakens significantly at about fourteen feet off the ground, living and working in multi-story buildings can be very energetically challenging. Some have found it helpful to use grounding or "earthing" pads in their beds to help stay connected and balanced energetically.

Nutrients that directly support the nervous system include essential fatty acids and specifically lecithin, which is naturally rich in egg yolks. Don't worry about the cholesterol in eggs or other foods! This is another tragically erroneous medical myth that generates millions of dollars in pharmaceutical profits, while degrading human well-being. Dietary cholesterol has *nothing* to do with serum cholesterol, which is produced in the liver as a building block of hormone production. Here's the typical scenario. Stress attacks the adrenals, which eventually begin to under-secrete critical hormones. Sugar and caffeine are the two biggest dietary adrenal stressors, aside from just plain daily stress. The thyroid attempts to kick in and make up the difference in hormone production, but if the stress continues, it too begins to weaken under the task. Hence, a low-thyroid condition is diagnosed. The liver then tries to compensate for low hormone levels by making and secreting higher levels of cholesterol, making more hormones. The extra cholesterol in the blood stream tends to accumulate inside the damaged walls of arteries, along with precipitated minerals and other blood-borne substances forming a rubbery plaque. The arterial damage, which the cholesterol is being laid down to prevent, is typically due to free-radical damage from trans-fats (margarine), sugar, cheap oils, synthetic drugs, smoke, alcohol, processed foods, and other toxic influences.

Your well-meaning but under-informed healthcare provider may advise you to look at a low-fat and low-cholesterol diet, mistakenly assuming there's a direct connection between dietary and blood-borne cholesterol. Your brain and nervous system, however, require adequate fats, as do your cell-wall membranes, so the low-fat diet myth has likely contributed to the epidemic in learning disorders and mental decline, or dumbing down, in modern society, including dementia in older adults. Take a look at the labels of low-fat foods. They typically are high in grains and refined carbohydrates (sugar), which we have seen are at the bottom of many health issues. And the refined carbo-hydrates in most low-fat foods actually end up stored as—you guessed it—fat! Isn't it amazing how many things in the ego's mirror world are actually upside down, distorted, and backward.

Do you want to reduce your blood cholesterol naturally? Start eating eggs daily, and ensure sufficient dietary fats. By providing enough cholesterol in your diet, your liver will stop over-producing it, and your counts will go down naturally. Fats are also very satisfying and concentrated foods, so you likely won't get as hungry as soon after eating. You can do this without the dangerous use of statin drugs, by the way, which have been proven to have potentially deadly side effects for many users. (See J. Cohen, *What You Must Know about Statin Drugs and Their Natural Alternatives,* Square One Publishers, 2005.)

Another easy and practical thing we can do is to listen to our bodies' need for relaxation, sleep, and regeneration. It is only when we sleep and fast that the cells go into detox mode (unless we eat too late at night). That is when the body's repair systems go to work. When we have been going through a particularly stressful time, our bodies may need to catch up with more regenerative time.

We are designed, like the farmers, to "go down with the Sun and get up with the chickens." There's a reason why working all night is called the "graveyard" shift. Staying awake with artificial lighting may actually contribute to a disruption of the natural production of the sleep hormone melatonin. This natural sedative is secreted by the pineal gland only when there is no more light stimulation from the environment. There may actually be a connection between artificial light and weight gain, as the continuance of light past around 7:00 PM mimics summer; a time when most mammals' metabolism is in food-storage mode. It's as if we are telling our bodies to stay in perpetual fat-production mode in preparation for a "winter burn" that never comes.

Studies have shown that teenage boys in particular, who get an extra hour of sleep in the morning have significantly higher grades and fewer behavioral problems at school than when they get up earlier. This is why some smart middle schools have moved their schedule up an hour. Who knows. Maybe the real work we are here to do only happens in our sleep! I would not be surprised, as most things in this mirror world are "bass-ackward."

Sleep is indispensible in supporting the body's ability to rebound from stress—and not just the everyday stress of living, but the stress of entering the galactic photon band and having every aspect of normalcy rocking under our feet! As such, we need to pay attention to the quality of our sleep, which is indicated by how you feel when you awaken. One suggestion I make to folks who are not sleeping well is to move the bed. In North America, geopathic stress is hardly ever considered a health risk, while in Europe it is looked at seriously. Geopathic stress is the result of natural vibrations that rise up through the Earth, some becoming distorted by weak electro-magnetic fields created by subterranean running water, certain mineral concentrations, fault lines, and underground cavities (Rolf Gordon, *www.rolfgordon.co.uk*). The distorted vibrations can become abnormally high and harmful to living organisms.

Apparently in Germany, where geopathic stress is a recognized cause of illness, the state has the right to tell you where you can or cannot build your home based on an analysis of this risk. English studies have also found a strong correlation to "cot death," a term for Sudden Infant Death Syndrome. Geopathic stress is a big topic and is covered well by others, including Roy and Ann Proctor in *Healing Sick Homes* (Gateway, Dublin, 2000). Suffice it to say that if by moving the bed or switching rooms, or even houses, you begin to sleep well, you may have simply removed yourself from a geopathically toxic influence. Living near areas of significant underground water movement such as near large bodies of water surrounded by hills or mountains carries increased risk, as does living over clay beds like those found around major river deltas. Dowsing is one way you can assess and redress some of these issues. (See my *Adventures in Dowsing*, available as an eBook at *www.bluesunenergetics.net*).

GO SILENT FOR SANITY

Along with sleep for regeneration, another indispensible skill for these times is the regular cultivation of silence. It doesn't matter how you get there, but it is only in silence that we can disengage the problem-solving, problem-generating mind so that we can get in touch with our true and higher Selves (Spirit or Soul, if you like), which dwell in the security of peace and joy all the time. Think of it as coming up for air. But in this case, it is "going silent for sanity"! I also like to call this practice "flipping in," as a sane alternative to "flipping out." In our culture, when someone dies one of the highest honors we can think of is to give them two minutes silence. Why not give this gift to yourself regularly while you are alive? No need to wait. It is in silence that we feel the subtle movements of the Soul that give us the answers we need for everything. These answers are never in the form we assume or prefer, because they are much larger answers—more inclusive of a Big Picture and what is truly in ours and others' highest good.

In Buddhism, the Source of Divine Intelligence is called Big Mind. We hear it only when the "little mind" is silent. In the West, the active aspect of the Divine has been called the Holy Spirit. This is the Divine messenger who is always with us, but not always in our awareness. The traditional symbol of the Holy Spirit is the dove—a bird that is so beautiful and delicate, but that will only land when it is safe and feels peace. It is easily frightened by the slightest movement. Not that the Holy Spirit really goes away—but it goes away from our attention when we are distracted. In the Silence of the Big Mind, we also touch the feeling of Trust. When we stop struggling with what is and stop questioning or doubting ourselves, even for a split second, we experience a peace and a remembering that, as Spirit, we are complete, safe, and always provided for. The Western mind is particularly obsessed with knowing—facts, teachings, experiences, data, etc.—in order to someday reach Enlightenment. This is the age-old ego game of seek—but never find. Give it up. There is nothing to add to what you already are. Ours is only to remember the whispers of Spirit in Silence.

In the Silence, we may receive insight into what we think are our problems, which then helps us to let go of them when we realize they are simply a product of how we are choosing to see things—of our own perception and nothing more. We may then decide to see things differently. When we come back to the problem, we see it has shifted altogether. This is the benefit of going to the level of cause, which is in the mind, and of ceasing to struggle in the world of form, which is simply and only ever an effect.

You may find you can better touch Silence by taking a walk in Nature, spending time reading uplifting material, or listening to good inspirational music. Whatever works for you is best. A simple meditation on the breath outlined in Book II works well for many. Whatever technique you use, intend to get to the place of inner Silence and release all mental activity on a regular basis. This may take some time and practice. Old habits are not easy to break, but even a moment of inner Silence will shift your awareness permanently and place you firmly on the road back to your memory of enlightenment—your Self. I say this, as one of the insights enjoyed by the enlightened is that they always were enlightened; they just forgot!

People who regularly "touch" Silence experience less conflict in their lives, because they have chosen to reduce inner conflict. Your world will reflect back to you the state of your mind. Even the actual physical events we experience are literal reflections of the mind's content, along with your perception or interpretation of events and their meaning. Eventually, mental Silence is something you bring back to waking consciousness from your meditations. It becomes a steady, calm center that is not knocked off balance by life's seemingly random events. Cultivating inner Peace through Silence should be a top priority in preparing for further potentially monumental changes, both individual and collective. From Silence, you will know what *really* matters, and be much less likely to fall into fear.

Other physical signs that may be associated with accelerated energetic planetary shifts include apparent cardiac stress, such as feeling pressure on the chest, palpitations, and breathlessness. Some say a new upper-heart chakra is coming online. This is not to say that these may not be symptoms of actual cardiac issues, in which case you need to do the right thing and get checked out appropriately. But if these signs persist after you have been given a clean bill of health, consider the effect of energetic and electro-magnetic stress on the heart. The heart is more electrically active than the brain, producing an energy field fifty times as powerful as the field of the brain. It stands to reason, then, that the heart reflects, on some level, dramatic changes in Earth's electro-magnetic field. And we are becoming more heart-centered as we become fifth-dimensional. If you determine that these symptoms for you are "Shift-related," I suggest you silently commune with your heart and tell it that it is safe—that it is okay to move with the changes going on.

Each organ is a being with its own consciousness, as is each cell. You can talk to your organs. Give them thanks and encouragement. Your body is a community of co-operative consciousness providing a holographic model of a consciously co-operative galaxy. Supporting this view is the fact that the number of cells in your body roughly approximate the number of stars in our galaxy.

Periods of spontaneous detoxification can also occur in the form of diarrhea, sweating episodes, and a feeling of heating up from the inside, like being cooked in a microwave oven. Ringing in the ears, viral syndromes, headaches, dizziness, and feeling "spacey" or ungrounded may also be associated with Earth changes. The fact that certain viruses, like the Epstein Barr virus, are in practically everybody's bodies today may be indicative of the role viruses play in recombining DNA. According to researcher Berrenda Fox, viruses are an essential aspect of human evolution, providing the mechanics for natural DNA splicing. There was a time not so long ago when we thought *all* bacteria were bad—hence, the "war on germs"! Now we know differently. Could we be making the same mistaken assumption about *all* viruses?

It may also be helpful to de-personalize our health challenges. Could it be that on some level we suffer from a particular health issue in order to share our healing with everyone, the One of us, as we described regarding certain Yogic practices? Go inside for the answer to this one. If you intuit that this is your chosen path, then ask the Divine to speed up the learning process so you can get it over with sooner! And forgive yourself for any judgments you placed on yourself. This attitude can help to elevate sickness from a curse to a practice of "illness as service." That idea may prompt some howls from the ego, as the body is its greatest ally and sickness one of its greatest tools for keeping you identified with the body as separate. It won't let go of this tactical advantage easily. Spiritual healing occurs when we reaffirm our identity as invulnerable Spirit, recognizing the self-attack of illness on the body as a feeble ego ploy.

Learning to get in touch with your intuitive knowing can be helpful in getting to the root cause of mysterious symptoms. The rational mind will look for a reason within its own conditioning, and Earth changes may not be in its vocabulary! Finding a good medical intuitive or trusted psychic can be very helpful for putting your mind at ease and allowing the changes, rather than just trying to fix symptoms or look for causes based on past conditioning. An axiom I have found to be consistently true about bodily symptoms is: "It's *never* about what you think it is!"

THE END OF ILLUSION

We must also look at the mental aspects of "surfing the apocalypse," in particular the depression associated with identity loss, or ego death. Whenever we reach a new more expansive level of Self-knowledge, an old image of ourselves "the way we thought we were" dies. The end of illusion gives way to an expanded sense of Self, but at the cost of disillusionment. There may be a momentary insecurity, as the ego diminishes but is not yet totally gone. Don't give in or feel sorry for it! Knowing what's going on is half the battle. Trusting and staying in gratitude is the other half.

Spiritual awakening is like stepping off a solid dock into a boat—you're not sure if you can keep your balance or if the boat will support you, so you freeze momentarily before deciding either to jump into it with both feet or jump back. Indecision is hell! The trouble is that you can't really jump back once you *know* there's another way of being. So at some point, you have to take a blind leap and just jump! There's no other way to find out where the boat can take you.

Ego is a relatively modern term, first articulated by Freud over 100 years ago. In his model of mind structures, the ego was suspected of being a "dark basement" in the unconscious mind full of memories of pain, suffering, and frustration—mostly sexual frustration. This, of course, was likely Freud's own projection having been raised in a sexually repressive, patriarchal Victorian-era family. Nonetheless, the standard psychological model based on Freudian insights has held that an ego can be made healthy and so is somewhat like an untamed beast. You're stuck with it, so you may as well make peace with it. The ego supports such a position.

The ego, however, is much less substantial than this. It is simply a set of beliefs about who we are from the stance of separation. It is the made-up answer to the question: "Who Am I?" The question was only needed because we lost sight of the Self as One. A self-realized being never has to ask this question. The ego sprang into existence the moment we created a need for a separate identity, but it essentially represents a lie and is made of nothing other than imagination. We see what we want, and we wanted to be separate. The ego knows this and is programmed to resist its own dissolution. So it will fight vehemently to the death (your death, preferably) to preserve itself.

We often talk about "my" ego as separate from "your" ego. Yet in reality, if there is only the One Dreamer, there is likewise only one ego—a collective, mass hallucination and a big part of the dualistic fourth-dimensional thought field. The ego is not personal; it is the condition of the sleeping Son of God. And it is living on borrowed time, which is dissolving before us all. Time, as a mental construct of the ego, is an integral part of the ego's existence. This is why the ego resists any and all notions of the End of Time as this would represent the end of the ego. So if you are feeling disillusioned, congratulations! Your other choice is to stay "illusioned." You are now available to experience an even higher point of view of your Self and Reality. A mind that is full of the false ego-self has no room for higher perception of a greater Self. There is no conscious need or desire to change. This is why we often must come to a place of emptiness and surrender of our thoughts about our self before something new can be birthed in our minds.

There seems to be a progression here, however. As the ego is continuously "chipped away" in our minds through our direct contact with Spirit or the Self, and through Forgiveness of our own projected guilt as seen in our perception of others, eventually it will and must simply go away like mist before the morning Sun. This is inevitable, and only a matter of time, which is not real. Hang in there. The whole Shift of Ages is about our collective graduation from the need for an ego at all.

In the past, a state of egoless bliss and constant awareness of Oneness was rarely achieved on Earth. Those who did achieve it and were remembered became the saints and masters of old. The conditions now exist where many of us here will be reaching this state together, *en masse.* You could say all the problems of this world are really the problem of the ego being acted out in endless forms. Greed, hate, fear, anger—these are all the fruits of the ego. With no ego obscuring the light, we naturally rise to our original state of peace, joy, and bliss—a state of unconditional Love. This is a vision you can hold now, trusting that it is absolutely real and present in the here and now.

Generally, then, we must commit to keeping our hearts open and our minds still. In doing this, we may actually begin to reconnect these two intelligences, which upon connecting create a completely new kind of intelligence. The analogy here is with the joining of the hemispheres of the brain. I am sure that both processes are part and parcel of the same process of ascension. I find it fascinating that in the union of opposites, we find a greater reality emerging that is exponentially more than the sum of its parts. When two (duality) become three (new level of inclusive awareness), the three become One, as in the mystery of the Christian Trinity.

The Heart Math Institute is dedicated to research proving the manifold benefits of exercises and techniques to harmonize the heart and brain (*www.heartmath.org*). The classic literary term "mind" actually referred to the heart and brain as a unified system, so again, we are just getting back to our natural state as whole and complete beings, reflecting the wholeness of our Source and Creator.

AWAKEN TO ONENESS

In my own life, there have been many turning points that were explained to me in dreams, usually just before the turning point itself. One of these dreams has stayed with me for years, and has served to help me accept and not resist the many twists and turns of life. In the dream, I am attempting to cross a raging, muddy river on a flimsy bridge of twigs and branches. Not surprisingly, midway, the bridge disintegrates and I am cast into the water. As I begin to panic, however, a voice speaks to me loud and clear: "Don't struggle—just let go and let the river carry you where it will. If you struggle, you will perish. If you just let go and trust you'll be fine!"

One way I have learned to "let go" is to realize that there are no fixed laws or rules about how or why things happen. This is the old paradigm based on the assumption that our perceptions of cause-and-effect relationships are somehow true. David Hawkins, in his first classic work, *Power vs. Force* (Hay House, 2002), suggests that our belief in cause and effect is one of the biggest cognitive blunders of our time!

"Shift happens," as the bumper sticker reads. One thing we can count on in this life is change. But if something can change, was it real to begin with? So I have learned, and continue to learn, to let go of the belief in or need for predictable outcomes, and to be okay with uncertainty. The smartest and most honest thing I can say in most situations is: "I don't know!"

I have learned to ease up on myself, and to try to turn my "shoulds" into "coulds." So far, this has not failed me, because, here I am! Life in the dream is full of paradox and contradiction. That is because the dream is based on false premises to begin with; it is a set-up for perpetual conflict with an escape clause. Your power to escape lies in your ability to choose, or to exercise your will. It turns out there is only one Will in Creation (remember 8-D?) and it is yours and it is your Creator's. So why fight the river? I think where it is taking us is an unimaginably wonderful destination. All rivers lead to the ocean eventually. That is what my heart tells me, anyway.

Awakening to Oneness, once understood, is effortless. It lies in the acceptance that we are already awake and that only a part of the mind has forgotten it. A favorite ego game is to be the perpetual seeker. "You'll be Awake *after* the next workshop, guru, book, acid trip, ashram retreat, etc." Any time but *now*! But if you could awaken now, would it not imply that you are already awake and simply chose this time to remember it? And once awake, you no longer need a made-up identity as a seeker. Your knowing removes all doubt. You *are* Divine, eternal Spirit. Why settle for less? The ego would have you chasing your tail for eternity if it could, in order to keep itself relevant. The really good news is that this is very tiring and discouraging, and eventually, we get to the point where we've had it with the game, and so simply drop it. We go Silent—and boom, there is the memory, crystal-clear and brilliant. "Aha! That's who I am. Now I remember!" This will happen to each and every one of us at the time appointed by us. We are the dreamer, main actor, and playwright all at the same time.

Awakening only requires Spiritual Light. And the Light is always on. Just like physical awakening, however, we may at first resist. Sleep may still seduce us back into oblivion, even though the alarm clock is blaring. Nevertheless, sooner or later, we remember that being awake is where our real life is being lived, and that the dreams, whether pleasant or horrific, go nowhere and are made of nothing. Dreams lose their value as the day begins to dawn.

Part of letting go into the flow of life lies in realizing that you have never really been in control of your life, at least not from the perspective of the conscious mind. You simply have been making choices based on a very limited scope of awareness dictated by perception and conditioning. Despite our habits of judgment, there comes a moment when we realize we are *all* doing our best here, even when it appears to be our worst. However, making choices is where your true power lies. Thus, it is crucial that we know what our options are. Having now seen where the ego comes from, you are free to put those fear-based options aside, and wait for what is true and real (peace-based) to be shown to you.

The ego usually speaks up first, but if we stop and think—"I see where this decision is going. I've been there and done that, and frankly don't want to choose that again"—we become open to an answer from a deeper part of ourselves, the part that remembers forever. There is great power in choosing to say "no" to the ego, even when you don't know what the alternatives are just yet. Preferring to do nothing rather than the wrong thing is choosing the right thing. Giving up the illusion of control is one of the greatest favors you can do for yourself. We say "Stress exists because I insist!" Our insistence is usually that "my" plan, "my" assumptions, opinions, and perceptions, my "shoulds" *must* happen, or I fear I may lose control and cease to exist as I imagine myself to be. This is the ego, afraid of its own inevitable demise.

Try turning all your "shoulds" into "coulds." We all have preferences for how we would like things to be or turn out. But at the same time, stay flexible. "Want what life wants," as my first guru, Vernon Howard, said (*The Mystic Path to Cosmic Power,* Parker Publishing Co. Inc. 1967). Always leave the door open for whatever may happen. Don't limit yourself to patterns of the past. That is all perception and preference are—an attempt by the ego to keep the past and itself alive.

Here is an exercise that helps me release the future from the prison bars of my perception. While in meditation, I see the issue at hand on an imaginary altar. I offer the altar with my concern on it to God, whom I imagine in the form of a beautiful Light. It is now out of my hands. I still may go back and approach the issue as I would have anyway, but now the pressure is off me. I have alerted the Creator that I am open to other options. I am okay with a miracle here!

This exercise is called "true prayer" and is further described in Gary Renard's wonderful book, *The Disappearance of the Universe* (Hay House, 2004). It was through Gary's work that I was able even to approach the non-dual principles of *A Course In Miracles.* He has done a wonderful service to humanity.

PRACTICE FORGIVENESS

It is helpful to realize that a key aspect of this period in history is the Collapse of Time. You could say that it is about the end of history. Who needs a past when the present is so full and fulfilling? The key to releasing ourselves and others from the past is Forgiveness. Not the old kind of forgiveness that first looks at the behavior and then forgives it. That kind of forgiveness makes the behavior real, and doesn't really overlook it. It is actually the ego feeling superior for being so generous and gracious, even though you are a lousy so-and-so. True Forgiveness, as Gary Renard teaches so well, comes from an understanding that there is really nothing to forgive. No action, no matter how heinous it may appear, can change the fact of the Divine and eternal Self that you and I share with every other seemingly fragmented part of our Self. This is true for me, and for you. This freedom is not a license to do whatever we want—which is what the ego would prefer you to think. True Forgiveness recognizes that the cause of suffering is in the mind and, as we all share the One Mind, your suffering *is* my suffering. Therefore, the only way I can perceive fault in you is if the fault, on some level, is in me. And on the level of One Mind, it is. So the most loving thing I can do for myself is to forgive you.

The fault in me is in the form of unconscious guilt for which I have not yet accepted my own forgiveness. So I take responsibility for my perception of you, and my role in our mutual suffering. When I forgive—that is, when I overlook the fault in you—I receive the immediate benefit of Forgiveness in myself. And all of a sudden I see you as you are—perfect, Divine, and an expression of Divine Love come to help and teach me an irreversible Forgiveness lesson! Now that's "win-win"!

You could say your forgiveness creates a new world of possibilities. Using the analogy of the hologram, when I make a decision or judgment (perception and judgment are the same thing) I create a set of highly likely outcomes or a probable timeline, if you like. The entire hologram now reflects back to me this decision and, no matter what direction I take, my experience is shaped by my decision. For example (and I know you will relate to this), I have decided to purchase a Volkswagen. I am now seeing Volkswagens all around me. They weren't there before, but now I can't get away from them! My hologram has become reflective of my decision. But let's say I change my mind. No, I think I'll buy a Volvo. Guess what I will start seeing?

In a similar manner, when I decide that others are out to get me—that it is a dog-eat-dog world of lack, with terrorists behind every tree, where I must struggle to survive—what will my hologram feed back to me? No matter where I turn, my decision is waiting for me. And I act surprised! So, when I get tired of that, I can just change my mind and the world *will* shift to suit my intentions. When I move, the image in the mirror moves too. Funny how that works!

Now what if a whole bunch of us decide it is time we live in a world ruled by Love? What if a whole bunch of us went though some kind of electro-spiritual mind wave that made it impossible to think fearful thoughts, or at least made it easy to let them go? I think this is as good an explanation for the Shift of Ages as any. As the 1960s poster said: "What if they gave a war and nobody came?" Future headline: "All conflicts and unfair practices on Earth have been canceled due to a lack of interest. Now everybody—take the day off."

Bringing this reasoning back to the personal sphere, doesn't it make sense to experience as much joy, love, and peace as you can right now, thus ensuring that your hologram will return just that to you? How do you do this? By stopping anything that doesn't give you that experience! As the doctor said to the patient who asked how to stop the pain as he was hammering his thumb: "Stop doing that!" The whole notion of sacrificing ourselves to make others happy simply does not stand up to quantum reality or sanity. It worked for some in the old days of slavery, but that is so passé!

Currently, part of the mind of the One believes it is in a dream of separation, but you and I know that's not possible or real. So let's agree to show the sleeping part of the One Mind what it is like to be Awake. By acting as if it were, we make it real. Let's *be* the light that is always on. Let's start forgiving our way out of here!

A BEDTIME STORY

There may be concerns about being in the right place for the Shift. Any uncertainty or anxiety about this is coming from fear, and thus from the ego. Begin now to affirm to yourself, "I am *always* in the right place at the right time" and know that you will be. Think of all the survival fears you have had all your life up until today. Where are they? Did anything happen as you feared? Are you here, now, perfectly safe in this moment? Case closed.

I have given you the best understanding I have as to what is going on. Tomorrow, my views will shift, but that's okay. Some things will never change, and those are the real parts! Here is a possible scenario for the actual crunch time of the Shift. The details may be off track, but it will give you some idea of what's going on as we move through this incredible birthing. The real outcome is that we will know we are making up this entire world, and so it's really anybody's guess as to what we'll be making up in the future. With almost 7 billion of us here, there will likely be 7 billion versions or variations of the actual event. My only responsibility is to hold my peace, and extend it. If enough of us do this, there will be lots of peace to go around! If we are in a state of Oneness at this point, however, I am confident we will be making up something that will be fun, interesting, creative, expansive, and helpful to all. The paradox, of course, is that the closer we get to the appointed time, the less time will matter at all!

So here's the bedtime story...

As the magnetic field of the Sun drops to zero due to the reduction of internal energy production and the Sun receiving most of its energy from the photon band, the Earth's magnetic field does the same; it drops to zero. In fact, core samples of iron show that radical realignments in the Earth's magnetic fields have occurred many times in the past, involving a momentary magnetic collapse as the poles "reset." Thus, a collapse of the magnetic field is an expected precursor to a "flip" or re-alignment of the magnetic grid to a new configuration on the planet. For example, at one time, Hawaii was the North Pole!

With a brief period of zero magnetism on Earth, the frequencies of matter and light down to the subatomic or purely energetic level accelerate exponentially as high-frequency galactic energy bathes the planet unrestricted. Recall that the electro-magnetic field serves as a limiter on frequency, including the frequencies of light energy. An electro-magnetic field of zero thus allows unlimited light frequency.

The unlimited rise of Spiritual (multi-dimensional) Light on the Earth is so intense that it blocks out the narrow range of visible light, leading to a period of pitch-black "hibernation," at least as seen by our limited photon receptors, or eyes. This may last three days. It's as if we get anesthetized or taken "off-line" while the operation on our DNA is performed. For some, this may be a frightening time of disorientation and mental meltdown, especially if they have actively resisted the opportunities to flow with the Shift up until this time. Even alternative light sources won't be of any use here, as it is not just a simple power outage. *All* visible light is simply obscured.

However, for those who have entered this time with their spiritual eyes opened—the Awakened in other words—they will know spontaneously what to do. Well, what else can you do when it's pitch black and all the electronics and communication systems on the planet are knocked out? All that's left is to meditate, and see what happens next. It will be handy to have some water set aside. By going into a deep, unfettered meditation, we will actually be able to build and maintain an internal bio-magnetic field in our brains and hearts. This bio-field will hold and maintain all the cellular memories that have been purified through the practice of True Forgiveness. Only higher-frequency thoughts and memories based on Truth and the Oneness of our identity as God's Creation will survive the massive wiping out of the collective mental "hard drive" of the fourth dimension. Earth and all beings here will move up vibrationally through the fourth dimension, only keeping thoughts that are true, pure, and uplifting, emerging fresh and new into the Light of the fifth dimension.

Some, including Lynn Grabhorn, have suggested that there will a splitting of worlds into a 5-dimensional Earth and a residual 3-D planet, which will provide a home for those not willing or ready to make the shift to 5-D. Another variation is that, as *this* Earth goes 5-D, the unwilling are transported to another 3-D planet and get to do the whole human thing over again. Either of these scenarios could result in what appears to be mass death. Please remember, *there is no death,* just a transition from one form to another. The Biblical idea of "one taken and one left standing in the field" has served to feed the divisive and elitist doctrine of only the "saved" surviving, while the rest go to hell. We already discussed David Wilcock's idea that Earth has been a repository for humans who didn't make the grade in the past on other planets, making Earth more or less a galactic reform school. Either way, I am not too concerned, as in the Big Picture we all make it home. Whether some decide to take a detour or get caught up in a cul-de-sac of more forgiveness lessons is immaterial in the largest sense. Our freedom to choose even against what appears to be our own best interests is indicative of the trust our Creator has in us, knowing that nothing we choose in the dream universe affects in any manner the Reality of Who we are.

On 5-D Earth, we will experience Mind unburdened by the past. It will be the ultimate spin-cycle of the Mind and the end of karma! What was never true will be forgotten for good. Even the pollution and filth of the 3-D world will return spontaneously to 2-D, where it properly belongs. We are still in a dream at this point, but we have awoken within the dream, and so can begin to dream consciously and lucidly as masters and no longer as victims—no longer held back in the dualistic mental prison we have endured for eons. Our nightmare will have become our dream come true and the next major step on our ascendancy to our true home in the spiritual kingdom of God.

Then the real work for the Awakened on this planet will begin. Before the Shift, they related for the most part to each other. If you went to a spiritual talk before the birthing, it was likely someone preaching to the choir. Nobody else seemed interested. After the Shift, everyone will be asking: "What the heck was that? What just happened?" Many will need a complete re-education and orientation as Spiritual Beings having a human experience. Many teachers will be needed. Are you one?

When Lynn Grabhorn was asked, "What is one simple thing I can do now to help prepare for the Shift?" her reply was, "Learn to be grateful" (*Dear God, What Is Happening to Us?*. Hampton Roads, 2003). She suggested the practice of extending gratitude for all the little things we take for granted and of developing an "attitude of gratitude." Be thankful for that pencil, for this glass of water, for this car, for your dog—whatever. By doing this, we are also practicing non-resistance to what is. We are shutting down the tendency of the mind to separate itself from what it perceives with judgment. Grateful people flow easily into each moment without resistance, absorbing and becoming their experience. We are being like God by becoming and extending into our world, instead of holding back and separating. Such a simple and powerful practice!

I encourage you to begin to journal your thoughts and feelings, especially those that come to you in Silence. Ask daily to see others as pure Spirit. Doing so in your meditations makes it more likely that you will actually remember and feel this about others as you go about your days. Find a way to begin to re-educate your mind and shift your perceptions heavenward. Foster a non-dual perspective in order to get out of the trap of duality. *A Course in Miracles* can help with this, although it is quite dense and couched in what may seem like "religious" terminology. Personally, I was much better able to appreciate the *Course* by first reading Gary Renard's *Disappearance of the Universe* (Hay House, 2003). It was both a challenging and exhilarating reading experience, and I highly recommend it to anyone looking for a deeper understanding leading to lasting Peace.

In general the feeling of the time of Shift will be analogous to the contrast and relief we feel when we wake up from a nightmare, realize it was all made of nothing, and laugh for taking any of it seriously. We then joyfully get on with whatever our real life presents to us.

CONCLUSION OR BEGINNING?

I trust that by coming this far in the reading you have absorbed at least some of this content and considered the possibility that some, if not all, of it is true. Or at least true for now, knowing that in the shifting sands of the third and fourth dimensions, truth is often provisional— that is, relative and subject to revision as things ultimately change. In that case, I applaud you, and implore you to stay open to more truth as it is revealed. You may also have come to taste the subtle flavors of unconditioned Truth— that is, Truth as it is in its higher, non-dual expression and without an opposite. This is Truth that does not change, nor is it subject to any influence. It always is. This is the Truth of your Being, which is unshakable, invulnerable, and forever joyful and free. To that aspect of your Self, I say "Welcome home!"

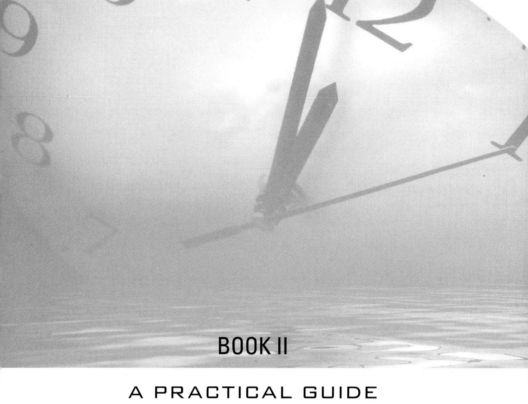

BOOK II

A PRACTICAL GUIDE
THROUGH THE COLLAPSE
OF TIME

A man can understand what is similar to something already existing in himself.

—Amiel

CHAPTER 8

THE TEMPLATE OF TIME

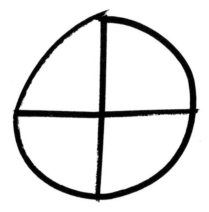

One day as I was meditating on the back porch, a series of images instantly flashed before my eyes like a quick series of pictures in one of those cartoon flip-books. I somehow knew this was a compressed "zip file" of information, and as I jotted down the individual frames, it came to me that this looked like a pictorial model of the radical changes we are experiencing on the planet relating to time. Don't ask me how I knew this! I just did. Maybe it was because I was already looking into the Mayan calendar and because the Mayans call the period we are in the Time of No Time. I wanted to explore the message within the pictures further.

Although more and more people are now becoming aware of the nature of the Shift in planetary consciousness predicted to culminate around 2012, I'm afraid that for the vast majority of us it is still business as usual, even as our lives are being radically rocked under our feet. I assume that if you are reading this in the brief period remaining before the Shift, you are among the pioneers in awareness—those who feel the call to prepare for what is already upon us. If you are reading this after the Shift (assuming we still read!), it is my wish that you will find here an explanation for what the heck just happened, as the Shift is assured to affect everyone on the planet and will ultimately transform *for the better* every aspect of life as we once knew it.

The Oriental philosophy of *Wu Wei* tells us that we accomplish the most by doing the least. This appeals to my basically lazy nature, and seems to validate the notion that visceral effort alone is not a holy or even necessarily sensible virtue. As I recall from one version of history, the modern Protestant work ethic was foisted on medieval European society as a way to morally bolster and sanctify capitalism. Although it certainly paid off for the investors in industry, it was really just another form of the ancient game of slavery through religious mind control. In order for one person to profit disproportionately from the labor of many, the many must be convinced of their moral obligation to work all hours of the day and night just to survive, often chained by debt. Working your fingers to the bone became a sanctioned pathway to Paradise, as touted by the popular propagandists of the day, who spoke mainly to the uneducated from the pulpit. It must have been a challenge to use the fires of hell as a motivator to sacrifice and work hard, as most folks were already living among the flames every day!

Another perspective on the positive attributes of laziness lies in the great promise of mass production. It was genuinely believed during the post-World War II economic boom that a toaster, a refrigerator, and a washing machine in every house would create vast amounts of leisure time, while our mechanical slaves did all the grunt work. The trouble was that we had to become "wage slaves" ourselves in order to keep up the payments and keep up with the latest necessities mandated by the most masterful means of cultural mind-control ever devised—the television.

Suffice it to say, muscling our way through our challenges is not necessarily the most balanced or intelligent approach to overcoming them. The "rugged individualist" stance is more indicative of the wounded male archetype discussed earlier. We must soften our problem solving habits to open to new possibilities that serve the interests of all at the expense of no one.

The intention behind Book II is to help you understand and relax into the process of the Collapse of Time. It's happening anyway, so we may as well understand it better and enjoy the process! I have used the symbols that came to me during meditation as chapter headings, as I feel they reveal a model for better grasping this ephemeral topic— in stages, as it were. Words, symbols, and thoughts cannot contain or explain ultimate Reality, but they are, in Eckhart Tolle's words, "pointers to the Truth." May the truth of these words reach you in the place of Truth already waiting in your mind.

THE TRUE CROSS OF CREATION

The first image that came to me as I was meditating was of what the Mayan's refer to as the True Cross of Creation. Unlike the Christian religious symbol venerated by millions, this cross is balanced in all four quadrants and held within the circle of Oneness. It is an ancient symbol seen also as the sacred Medicine Wheel of Native American cultures. I suppose this is not surprising, as the Mayans were also a North American culture. These advanced societies were the norm on the planet in different stages of history. I don't think we understand the full scope of cultural cross-pollenization that occurred among these ancient peoples.

Carl Calleman, in *The Mayan Calendar: Solving the Greatest Mystery of Our Time* (Garev: 2001), goes into an in-depth description of the Mayans' use of this symbol which they also called the World Tree. To the Maya, the symbol represented both the center of the cosmos and the four directions of East, South, West, and North. In other words, they saw the Cross as a fundamental template for Creation somehow tying the physical Earth to the greater cosmos. They also saw it as symbolizing four spiritual qualities that had a time-related influence on humans, as well as implicit geographical energies ascribed to the four directions. The West represented releasing or "letting go what no longer serves"; the South denoted receiving the gifts and nurturance of our Creator and Nature; the East called for being open to new awakenings and rebirth; the North spoke to "being thankful for the challenges and lessons of this life." This model provided the basis for many Medicine Wheel ceremonies, which also could involve the vertical directions of "down," which acknowledged Mother Earth, "up," which recognized Father Spirit, and the center or heart as where we hold all these energies in balanced reverence— thus yielding seven directions in all. The Seven Directions ceremony is easy to do at home. Either indoors or out, trace the symbol or lay out stones or crystals in the shape of the World Tree. Stand in each quadrant facing each direction and connect with it with your intent and silence.

Thus the symbol of the True Cross of Creation or World Tree is not just a pictorial image. It carries an actual "livingness" within it. The World Tree, which existed long before this present experience of time we call the modern era, is regarded by many cultures as a portal beyond the material world as well as a primary source for the energetic template of our collective experience in time—a two-way resonant portal, in other words. The modern version of this template of Creation involves scalar energies, the multi-dimensional opening created at the intersection of two equal electro-magnetic fields. Is this implied by the intersection of the two lines? Scalar fields exist from the macro scale of the entire universe down to the micro scale on the cellular level in our bodies. Scalar fields are the portals into a multi-verse where we discover the material universe is only a thin membrane overlaid on something much more vast and complete.

GALACTIC TIME WAVES

Barbara Clow, in *The Alchemy of the Nine Dimensions*, notes that the center of the galactic wheel was traditionally associated with the ninth dimension—the source of time waves and home of the World Tree. This is consistent with the Mayan belief that the World Tree is a vibrational template of which our experience of time on the 3-D Earth is an expression. There are resonances with this template on many levels, including with the planet itself and within the human body and the universe. A time wave can be explained as an emanation of creative energy coming into form through the multi-dimensional portal of the galactic central vortex, or Black Hole. The wave would then spread out from the center, "informing" life's expressions throughout the galaxy. The notion of a wave implies a beginning and an end.

The Black Hole in the center of our galaxy is not only a gravitational hub but also a vortex of unimaginable power. Vortices have been studied by ancient alchemists and some free-thinking physical scientists, and have been observed as having transformational properties. The galactic vortex may well be a multi-dimensional portal connecting the local physical universe with the universes comprising what is now conceived as "dark matter" or the non-physical dimensions of existence. As such, the time wave emanating from its center may very well be generated simply from another dimension of existence, perhaps even as an experiment or whimsical "what if...."

If the galactic time wave is indeed a wave, this implies a life cycle—that is, a leading edge, a crest, and finally, the wave crashing on a shore to be replaced eventually by another wave. LaViolette's super-wave theory proposes a similar idea. He spoke of a wave in the form of cosmic radiation arriving here on a regular basis every 10,000 years, tying this to known Ice Age cycles. Many of his theories were met with skepticism by mainstream astronomers, but as is the case with most visionary researchers, they are now being accepted as the evidence mounts. (See *Galactic Superwaves and Their Impact on Earth,* CD Rom, Starlane Productions, 2001. See also the website link: *www.etheric.com.*)

Because the two lines of the True Cross of Creation create two basic sections of the circle, the Aztecs, who came after the Maya, saw in the symbol of the World Tree a depiction of the basic dualities of life: good and evil, dark and light, life and death. Recognizing the dualistic nature of the world is a huge step toward being able to transcend the world, as we have seen in earlier discussions.

Calleman goes on to describe the True Cross as a wave generator of *yin* and *yang* energies, literally broadcasting complementary yet opposing pulses of energy over the globe and directing the winds of historical movements and changes. See his books for a more detailed description of this dynamic. This is a wonderful depiction and validation of the living quality of the True Cross.

The Mayan time-keepers were aware that the culmination date of their record-keeping in 2011 coincided with a rare alignment of the plane of the planets in our solar system with the plane of the galactic wheel—an event that finds the Earth in a direct line with the galactic center on December 21, 2012. Although this date marks the exact point of alignment, the energy of this event spans many years on either side of the date. Calleman has actually calculated the end date of the Mayan calendar as October 28, 2011. It makes sense that the time wave would complete, as the calendar predicts within a larger context of galactic initiation. The calendar's completion and what it entails will likely help to prepare us for whatever level of change is coming after October 28, 2011.

So again, we see the symbolism of the True Cross of Creation depicting this meeting point of two lines, or directions, as having sacred significance. One line may represent the plane of the solar system, and the other the plane of the galaxy. If we superimpose a time-related interpretation on the model with the horizontal plane representing linear time and the vertical representing quantum or "all things happening simultaneously" time, the intersection of planes can be seen to represent the meeting place of differing versions of time or the end of time as we now know it, coinciding with this rare galactic alignment.

A galactic time wave can be viewed as a script, or plan of how time will unfold. It is important to make it clear that the Maya and other pre-industrial cultures did not see time as randomly unfolding in an endless stream of disconnected events. This is a modern interpretation based on a more mechanical and linear perception, or left-brained interpretation. One of the main distinctions of the Mayan calendar is that time is seen as moving along a pre-determined trajectory toward a grand purpose, albeit with many "freedom of choice points" throughout. As such, multiple natural cycles were looked at as having equal significance, and time was only meaningfully understood if one looked at all the cycles as a grand cosmological symphony. Thus in the Mayan culture, being a time-keeper was a full-time job.

Even though there is provision for free will within the plan of time, the plan ultimately must come to the prescribed conclusion. Just like the pyramids that the Mayans constructed as memorials to their calendar, time moves through a series of nine stages toward a point—a time when the purpose of time will be revealed. Then, conceivably, a new story of time, or "no time," will begin as this current wave hits the shore.

As with so many dualistic puzzles, we tend to see these things from an either/or perspective—either time is following a pre-determined path, or it is entirely subject to every random whim of chance. A non-dual view reconciles this dichotomy with the understanding of a holographic model of time. Each decision I make creates a set of predictable outcomes, or a specific world of experience. If I do not change my mind, the outcome is relatively fixed. But when I step out of my conditioning and take a creative leap in a new direction, I literally create a new set of outcomes—a new world of experience. Could it be we have absolute freedom to create experiences within a model that has an overall set purpose or universal outcome? This is like saying that all roads lead to Rome. All you can realistically do in this case is to choose the road with the fewest bumps. I have found one of the characteristics of Truth is that it often provides a reconciliation of former dichotomies wherein both are true in a new light. We have free will, and we don't. And it's cool.

THE CROSS AND THE MYTH OF RETURN

The sacred symbol of the True Cross of Creation pops up in Bronze Age Scandinavia and in early Celtic art and jewelry. It was called the Sun Wheel by these cultures. Astrologers still use the True Cross to symbolize the Earth. The pioneering natural healer and teacher Hanna Kroeger also embraced this symbol, encouraging her students and clients to wear it as jewelry.

Although the popular Christian version of the cross takes on a different meaning for most believers, it is interesting that in medieval depictions of Christ, we often see the equal-armed cross shining overhead nestled within a halo. The Christian cross is an enigma. Although the Christian faith is purportedly based on the murdered and risen Christ, the "murder weapon" is used as its universal symbol! I can't help but see the modern cross symbolically saying, "Don't come here Christ with your rebellious message of peace and forgiveness. Remember the last time!" Of course the faithful will say the cross symbolizes Christ's sacrifice. But sacrifice is unknown to a non-dual Creator. "Atone for what?" asks the Divine. The need for sacrifice is rooted in the belief in "sin," which is simply the face of the hidden guilt of separation. If separation did not happen anywhere but in our minds, there is no basis for guilt, sin, or the ego other than in our belief in them.

Yet even within this unbalanced cross is the message of the galactic crossing—a cosmological event that may very well portend the end of psychological time and the lifting of the conditions for dualistic spiritual blindness. If the heightened energies of galactic alignment were to affect consciousness to the point where humanity's collective hard drive were spontaneously erased, we would lose the memory of a history that has bound us to centuries of suffering, inequality, and war. We have seen that a drop in the Sun's and the Earth's magnetic fields is a very real aspect of this alignment. If the illusion of time were to be replaced with a crystal-clear perception of timeless Reality, the promised "return of Christ" may be realized spontaneously in each awakened mind. This is in the realm of high probability, as I see it.

We can think of the sacred symbol of the True Cross as a vibrational tone generator emanating from the galactic center. As noted, the rotating vortex at the center of the galaxy is a dynamic energetic pattern generally regarded as a dimensional portal by metaphysicians, as all vortices are. For example, when a vortex in the form of a tornado passes over an area, investigators often find very puzzling "impossible" combinations of materials in its wake—things like straw embedded in wood, brick, or metal, for example. Vortices exist all around us—in natural streams, in our blood stream, and in the electrical spin within our cells. It is the basic form of momentum in the universe. You could say that all things spin out of the void into manifestation. So we see the galactic center is about transformation on a massive scale.

That is why we can look at this symbol as a depiction of duality itself. Duality is how we describe the possibility of opposites. Although we take our experience of opposites as a given, it's only from a non-dual perspective that we can truly appreciate what duality implies—or the cost of a dualistic mind-set. A non-dual state of Mind implies ultimate rest and stillness—a state where we experience the essential Oneness of all creation, and ourselves as One with All That Is and its Creator. Although it can never truly be described in full, a non-dual state *can* be experienced— in deep meditation, for example. Because we live primarily focused in 3-D physicality, our experiences of non-duality seem to come in fleeting glimpses. If you have ever had one of these glimpses, or moments of "actualization" as the humanist psychologists prefer, you know how difficult it is to hold on to these moments and make them last. As soon as you observe the non-dual moment and mentally label it, you have stepped into the observer role and established duality once again—distinguishing between "me" and "my experience." Aaargh!

Although duality "out there" only reflects a deep level of conflict or split in our minds, it does offer us the golden opportunity to change our minds through the exercise of will or choice. Living in 3-D is like an intensive Boot Camp of the will. It forces us to make choices, and then to live out the consequences of our choices until we choose otherwise. Hopefully, if we ever wish to graduate from 3-D, we become responsible choice makers. And this involves the awakening to non-dual awareness of our essential Oneness—that what I do to you, I do to myself.

This first image seems to represent the set-up of how we are and have been experiencing time. It is currently possible to choose between operating in linear time on the horizontal axis, and having fleeting moments of "timelessness" on the vertical axis. The horizontal axis can only envision the past or future, and sees the present moment as an insignificant dot on the vast linear plane of time. It is only in this present moment, however, that we can shift into vertical time and access the higher realms of non-dual reality. Thus the importance of cultivating "now" awareness, or mindfulness. This is done by the devotion to meditation, as in Breath Meditation offered earlier.

Here is a mental exercise to help ground these ideas. Consider the horizontal line to represent a conflict in your life. Conflicts always involve time. "What will I do about this? Why did I do that?" The opposite ends of the line represent the two opposing points of view within the conflict. For example, maybe you are conflicted about moving away or staying living where you are. On the "moving away" side you may have thoughts of future, adventure, discovery, or uncertainty in mind. On the "stay here side you may have thoughts of the past, comfort, security, or boredom. As long as you vacillate on this line, moving from one side to the other, you are not at rest. There's no peace, and you are not fully present to the Now.

But say you get to the point in the exact middle where you detach from the issue altogether, surrender the conflict, and just decide, "You know, it doesn't really matter what I do here—I am happy as I am right now, and I trust I will know what to do when the time comes." You surrender the conflict to the Divine in your own way. At this exact midpoint, there is zero pull in either direction—or a subsequent zero-gravity point. You are resting in neutral. You are free to "go vertical" and launch yourself into the Time of No Time—that is, the realization that all events are occurring at once, and your only real choice is when to stop suffering from the belief in time at all.

Shall we go there?

CHAPTER 9

FROM HORIZONTAL TO VERTICAL—THE BEGINNING OF THE END

The next image in the sequence I saw was of the horizontal line in the first image disappearing, leaving only a vertical line through the circle. I took the entire flash of images to imply a process of transition from our current experience of time (the first image) through a collapse of the linear model and into a new way of Being or of relating to time. Interestingly, the Mayan calendar describes the period from 1986 to 2012 as the Time of No Time. I think this vision of the changing images was a gift to help me understand this transition a bit more in terms I can currently navigate. The outcome of this process will very likely be disorienting for many, especially for those who have invested much of their attention in meeting the demands of linear time and based their identities in mental images of themselves rooted in the past. As we have seen, the concept of time and its continuity is a central function of the separated ego.

In order to better understand linear time and duality, we need a non-dual reference point. Historically, these have shown up in the form of largely esoteric doctrines like the Vedic Vedanta and the Chinese Tao. These thought systems are not necessarily part of the normal modern psyche, especially in the "educated" West. In fairness, the consciousness revolution of the Sixties and the subsequent rise of New Age ideas really represented the seeding of the Western mind with the ageless wisdom of the East. Look at the proliferation of yoga, meditation, and practices focused on inner peace and enlightenment. More recently, *A Course in Miracles* has presented a non-dual thought system more accessible to the Western mind in that it is couched in the terms of modern psychotherapy.

The typical notion of time as representing the continuity of past, present, and future events is a dualistic concept. It is rooted in a basic assumption of the separation of events in time. In non-dual Reality, or quantum time if you prefer, all events happen simultaneously. What we experience as multiple events stretched out over time and space actually happen in an instant and are over the instant they happen! It does feel like an old movie sometimes here on 3-D planet Earth. However, we have unconsciously chosen to stretch out our experience of "everything" into seemingly endless experiences delineated by time and space. The ego loves this job, as time seems to prove its separate existence!

THE ILLUSION OF PAST AND FUTURE

From the perspective of duality or perception we presume the past exists, but is fixed and out of reach, accessed in the form of memory. If perception in the present is only partial and based on individual projection and thus not essentially real, and the past lives only in our memory of previous perceptions, then neither are real. This past we imagine lives on in the repetition inherent in our conditioned thoughts. The vast majority of our thoughts are the same ones we entertain over and over, day after day. The act of perception itself simply re-creates the past in our present experience. We then project our past images and "set" interpretations onto a hopefully predictable future, and feel secure. Language freezes reality into pre-conceived packages of assumptions and judgments based in the need for the security of continuity. You could say our thoughts reveal and perpetuate our fears—particularly the root fear of separation from our Divine source. Our collective memory, or at least that of the victors, we call history. It is a humbling yet necessary stage in the awakening to accept the meaninglessness of our thoughts. It takes great inner courage to do so. Into this initially frightful void we find, to our delight, Love pours in.

On the horizontal line in our model, the past is on the left. The present is an infinitesimally small point half-way along the line moving along at an imperceptible snail's pace. The present is actually obscured behind the vertical line, which represents non-linear or quantum time. This illustrates how the Now is the only portal into Forever. The future, then, extends out to the right, representing both the false security of repeating the past, and the secret fear of the unknown. The intersection of the two lines is the secret entry point into the eternal Now, or the sense of timelessness achieved in states of enlightenment. Enlightenment, transcendence, or Heaven if you prefer, can only be found in the present moment. The ego would have you look everywhere else but here and now, because it knows you will never find it (Truth, your eternal Oneness) anywhere else but in the here and now. The ego delights in your poring over ancient texts, repeating ancient rituals, or clinging hopefully to models of spirituality from the past. Alternatively, the ego will have you focused on the future—the next book, workshop, guru, or appointment—to find "it," the ever-elusive carrot of enlightenment. However, peace is only and always a Now experience. Only Now is real.

To help consolidate and make solid these ideas, think about a past event. When you were experiencing the event, what "time" was it? Now, right? Okay. Now project your thoughts into an event you expect to happen tomorrow. Again, what "time" will it be in that experience? Now again, right? So what is the only time we ever actually experience? What is the only time there is? Where do we live our lives? And where are these places that we hold in our minds and call the past and future? Are they real or just imaginary? Is time just a story we tell ourselves—a story of separation, rooted in an imaginary event, or a dream of separation?

Obviously with the horizontal aspect of this model, the bulk of time appears to have either already happened, or will happen in the future. The Now pales in comparison to the full weight of horizontal time. The idea of the future has the potential to create much anxiety, as it is unknown. This is perhaps why the separated ego is so heavily invested in re-creating the past, as this creates the illusory comfort of being able to predict the future. Yet we are never certain, as the future is just as likely to present some surprises as it is to be contiguous with the past. Thinking of some of these unpredictable events produces stress. But the stress is not in the event. Rather, it is in the mind that has chosen to interpret the unpredictable as a threat to its safety and sense of control. Stress only exists for the ego.

So our whole experience of linear time, with the merciless demands of past and future pressing in on us, is just a construct of the mind. It is an idea *we* came up with to explain how things happen around us in a dream of separation, but it is an idea that also dis-empowers us. Time and space allow us continuously to re-create the experience of separation, believing that in doing so we somehow make our separated selves more real. Time is thus an imaginary construct of an imaginary construct, the ego. It is twice removed from Reality.

If this is true, then we ought to be able to change our experience of time by changing the way we think about it. We actually do this all the time. Sitting in the dentist's waiting room can seem endless, while "time flies" when you are having fun and are totally absorbed in the novelty of the moment. Being totally present in the moment, still a comparatively rare state of being, negates the need for any time-based reference at all. The Now appears in its complete fullness—or "suchness" as a Buddhist would say.

Take this to the extreme. If we were somehow cut off from all past reference, yet perfectly aware of the present moment, we would have no references to project onto the future either. We would be totally and 100 percent here in the moment. Time would stand still, as we would no longer pay it any attention. This happens sometimes in moments of extreme trauma—or when we are involved in extreme sports, when all frames of reference collapse and attention is totally fixed on the experience. Sporting types refer to the Zen of golf, rock climbing, etc. People report seeing things in slow motion during these events, until their minds kick in again with a conceptual label for what is happening, thus separating them into participant and observer or commentator. The slow motion effect, I believe, is a result of being present to every nuance and dimension of an experience all at once, like being in a Shamanic trance. Can you imagine if this "total focusing in the Now moment" were to sweep the planet like some kind of invisible energy wave? All that mind power we lose to the imaginary past (regret, guilt) and future (fear, denial) would be returned to us to enable us to live fully in the moment with all our faculties, gifts, and powers 100 percent right here, right now. Wow.

LIVING IN THE NOW

This, I propose, is the promise, or potential, of the Shift of Ages predicted by the ancients and on the minds of an increasing proportion of the population today. The physics explaining such a possibility exist, particularly with the passage of the solar system into a region of space with incredibly high energy emanating from the galactic core providing the energetic backdrop for this event. As already noted, the rise in energy and frequency in our space environment has contributed to a relaxation of the solar magnetic field. It now no longer has to work as hard to produce energy from internal processes. It is being fed by the Mother of us all, the heart of the Milky Way. The Latin root of the word "galaxy" is translated as "milk."

The drop in the Sun's magnetic field is allowing huge releases of energy that are largely responsible for the upsets in Earth's weather patterns. All the predictable cycles are "off"— not only on Earth, but on all the planets in our solar family.

Although there is likely much more to this Shift, what I have described here seems like enough to create a situation resulting in a global adjustment to our experience of time. Because time as we know it is a product, or result, of the mind in its present state of separation, a change on the level of the mind will change the nature of our experience of time. The normal functioning of the brain is dependent on a normal electro-magnetic environment. When that environment goes through a radical shift, we have the conditions for the Time of No Time. This is what the image implies with the collapse of the horizontal line, folding up like the stays of an umbrella. No more linear time. Only quantum time remains. So what is that like?

To live in quantum time (the vertical line) is to know that all events occur at once. It is indicative of a more holographic and holistic—or Holy, if you like—way of Being. I like the image of a spherical holographic structure representing everything happening at once. Specific events occur anywhere within the sphere, yet all events are held within a singularity, if you like, occurring at the point of Creation— our creation of the universe of form. We, as focal points of awareness within the hologram, seem to attach to a specific set of experiences, or a timeline within the sphere, much as a specific conditioned thought becomes a specific neural pathway in the brain. As we expand to a more transpersonal view of the Self we all share, we begin to move in multiple pathways at once. This is when we begin to see ourselves in others, and the distinctions of separation begin to melt. Eventually, as we expand into our full potential, we inhabit all timelines at once and realize Oneness.

For now, even though things around you may still seem to be subject to some kind of linear progression through time, the way you perceive this will change. You will see that this movement through time is much more flexible and subject to your will and choices. And with the ability to relax totally into every experience without fear of the past repeating or anxiety about what is to come, life will become simply a series of complete-in-themselves moments, with no attachment to outcomes, meanings, interpretations, judgments, projections, or perceptions. All channels of perception will be clear and open with no static. You will see everything exactly as it is—not as isolated phenomena, but as part of a continuity of matter and energy seamlessly joined to the next experience, and the next, and the next. It will be like being able to hear every instrument in the orchestra and its individual voice, while also hearing the totality of sound creating an exponentially greater experience.

This is what William Blake meant when he said, "If the doors of perception were cleansed, we would see every-thing as it is...infinite." By the way, it is from this quote that the famous rock group, the Doors, took their name, as Aldous Huxley did for his classic work, *The Doors of Perception*. I find it interesting that the beginning of the collapse of horizontal time looks just like the 1960s peace sign. Was this iconic symbol an unconscious projection of what was actually happening on the collective level around the meaning of time? It was the Sixties challenge to the prevailing war-mongering egoic machine that essentially kicked off the Aquarian Age—an era of recovering our humanity and saying "no" to brutality, ignorance, and inequality. In Calleman's interpretation of the Mayan cal-endar, he points out that the late 1960s represented the same energy conjunction as did the Renaissance period. Some of the Flower People who are today's leaders in busi-ness, industry, and government still recall the idealism of those years. Some of them will rise to roles of leadership when they see the dream of World Peace and No More War becoming the new Reality. Maybe we will remember and truly realize (make real) that "all you need is love."

In this relaxed state of being here and now, relationships blossom into their full beauty. The joy of every encounter bubbles with assured anticipation. We ask "What could be better than this?" and discover, to our delight, it's the next perfect moment!

We are now, as I write, already deeply involved in this process—an accelerated phase of time compression according to the Mayan calendar. We see and feel disori-ented perhaps by what seems to be the growing pressure and demands on our time. Sleep is becoming erratic. Too much information floods in as the media seems to have no idea of the Big Picture, and so still focuses on individual dramas and terror, only increasing the potential for chaos and complete breakdown. I feel that the harder some people cling to the "way we were," the more difficult this present transition will be for them. Many will think they are going nuts as their frames of reference melt before their eyes. Remember, the ego would rather destroy you than simply allow you to choose. It *wants* an Armageddon! Please don't rely on the experts or the authorities to tell you what's going on. How can they tell you when they don't know themselves? This is all about *you* becoming the expert and authority on your own true Reality, and then living it to the fullest!

GOING VERTICAL

The remaining vertical timeline symbolizes our changed relationship with time. In school, the timelines in text books were always horizontal, reinforcing the notion of linear time. This served well in devaluing the present moment, which, as it turns out, is the only real time (bassackward again!). I invite you, in your mind's eye, to take that horizontal timeline we were all taught, and rotate it around in your own mind until it becomes vertical, creating a model of time consistent with the big changes we have been talking about. This is why, by the way, we can access any point in time in our minds and shift those experiences, which are simply memorized energy patterns, as easily as we can shift patterns in this Now moment. This is why things like past-life therapy and timeline therapy actually work, if we allow for the possibility that all events occur at once. Time is not what it used to be! And your mind is the ultimate time machine.

We have said that linear or horizontal time is a construct of the ego. The ego is that part of the mind that truly believes in its own separation—from other egos, bodies, objects, times, spaces, and ultimately the Creator. The ego is the great destroyer of lives, health, sanity, nations, and hope. And one of the ego's biggest "cons" is time. The ego is on the way out, and it knows it. In the Big Picture, it suspects its days are numbered, and they are! The ego is obsolete; it no longer fits the plan of Creation, which is everyone's happiness. It actually never did fit the plan. In fact, from a non-dual perspective, it doesn't even exist! The ego is simply a persistent illusion, like a recurring nightmare. Once seen for what it is (and is not), it simply evaporates. Let it go. Go vertical. Replace it in your mind with Love and the Light of Oneness. You will not disappear. You will become truly alive.

So as horizontal time disappears we are left with only a very dense experience of a Now in which we have full access to our intuitive intelligence and its non-local cosmic connections. We can "go vertical" and escape the dense gravity field of psychological time. The Now is your *only* portal into eternity, and it is *always here*. Try this variation on an earlier image. Visualize a pyramid with the base representing horizontal time. See yourself on this line being continuously pulled in one of two directions—to the past (left) or the future (right). Now see yourself finding the perfect neutral balance point on the line right under the apex of the pyramid. This is symbolic of when you end the duality in any experience by not looking to the left or right, by not referencing past or future, but by simply settling into total acceptance of what is being experienced Now, with no preference or attachment to outcomes. You are in trust. You find yourself at a gravity-free point that enables you to launch vertically and upward directly in line with apex of the pyramid. You could also call this point of departure the "still point." Going vertical symbolizes your access to the Mind of God, if you like, or to the "all-seeing eye" at the top of the pyramid. Now your vision can soar above and beyond the pyramid into eternity. In this timeless state, we can accept into our experience anything we like, without any attachment or fear around it. We no longer fear the opposite or end of anything.

I have a dear friend who tried working on his car in the driveway. He propped the back end up with a jack and supported the axle with some cement blocks while he worked on a wheel. Not smart. He was an experienced mechanic, and probably knew better. His wife was in the house and the first to hear the sickening thud of the car as the bricks gave way and he screamed as he was pinned in the wheel well, doubled over in a seated position. Without a moment's hesitation, his wife ran outside and lifted the car with one arm while she pulled him out with the other. Now this car was no lightweight sporty model. It was an old station wagon from the late Fifties—a regular tank! No one could understand, as the story was told later, how she was able to do this. Perhaps because all her attention was laser-focused in the present moment, allowing her to tap into the vast ocean of human potential of which we, adrift in a dream of time, are oblivious.

Imagine your life lived entirely focused like this—not because of a dire circumstance, but because your brain, your mind, has evolved to a point where it no longer depends on any time reference for its sense of Being. Every moment is so complete, so full, so rich, so rewarding, that you can never imagine a moment more perfect. But wait! Here's another one—and it's unimaginably better than the last, which you have forgotten anyway.

This is the promise of the coming Golden Age. Time, as a construct of mind, is being de-constructed on the level of Awareness. Yes, we will likely be able to choose to use "clock time" when necessary, especially for the co-ordination of practical common events, like meeting friends or catching a bus. But just as easily as we take off our watches at the end of a busy day, we will be able to discard the need for clock time, and spend most of our time in Now Time—the Holy Instant (whole instant, as in complete) as it is called in *A Course in Miracles.*

CHAPTER 10

A PRIMER ON LIVING IN VERTICAL TIME

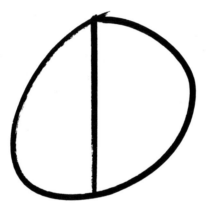

The end of chapter 9 actually explains what living in Now Time will be like. The difference will be that soon this will become our collective experience, rather than an occasional glimpse caught through the veil by some. So you won't feel weird, or fearful of others' opinions as you glide gracefully through your Now moments with a slight half smile, because everyone else will be doing it too! It will be like those big music festivals in the Sixties where you just floated through the day recognizing everyone as your brother and sister, at least for the weekend. As noted, I think that period and its celebrations were just a glimpse of what was to come—a "teaser" to give the Boomers an ideal to remember, until the real thing came along.

Along the progression from time to No Time, an inter-mediate stage described as "holographic time" will occur. A hologram, as noted earlier, is an image wherein the total-ity of the image/information is included in each part, no matter how small. When I act upon the field of time I set in motion very specific results or reactions. You could say I create a holographic world of specific outcomes deter-mined by my own conditioning and that of all the players involved. At any point, however, I can break the spell of the possible future by making a different choice. This is most dramatically experienced when I recognize a conditioned pattern as no longer serving my happiness or the good of all. I can step out of my own conditioning and take a bold, creative step in a new direction. All of a sudden, the old hologram dissolves, and a new one immediately springs to life in my experience. I have created a new world. I am seeing everything with new eyes! I am now more aware of myself as the cause of my experience, not as the effect of outer circumstances and conditions. I am acting more like my Creator—and it feels good, natural, and appropriate. I also feel more peaceful and powerful in my new hologram, because I now know that if it begins to degrade or unravel, I am responsible and can simply change my mind, and move from world to world. I am a fearless pioneer of new worlds all waiting for me to explore and experience in the wonder of Creation endlessly—all available to me Now.

GROKKING

Obviously our time-bound institutions will have to become much more flexible in their operation. Computers are help-ing to make this possible now with the creation of virtual worlds, global connectivity, and 24/7 functioning. Schools, healthcare facilities, corporations, and government bureaus will ultimately become more like wonderful places where we can visit and connect with friends, while perhaps pursuing an interest or fascination, either as learner or teacher. The delineation between these two roles will become much less rigid. Learning and teaching will merge into what Heinlein called, in his *Stranger in a Strange Land,* "grokking."

History, as we have been conditioned to understand it, will become an anachronism condensed down to a few thin volumes, with titles like *What was Believed about Time in the Age of Darkness.* Those who care to look into this rather moldy and unfashionable study will shake their heads in wonderment, questioning the sanity of their forbears.

Institutional religion, too, will be understood as sustaining a long and painful holding pattern in human development, responsible for untold sufferings and for deluding entire populations for eons into putting aside the direct experience of their sacred Selves in exchange for the vain hope of some ever-elusive future called heaven or salvation—or worse, in the fear of some imagined hell. We will shake our heads and ask how this could have been so.

And what was called healthcare in this fading memory of the world before the Awakening—how could this murderous practice based on a debased view of biology to the exclusion of Mind and Spirit have survived amid seemingly intelligent people for so long? How did so much power and authority concentrate around such a medieval set of beliefs and practices, nay superstitions, responsible for millions of unnecessary surgeries and poisonings by un-natural chemical toxins? It is even said that in those dark days, someone who dared practice a more safe, natural, non-invasive, and effective form of medicine could be charged, fined, jailed, or even assassinated for daring to challenge this monstrous idol to the scientific ego of man. Yet safe, natural, and affordable cures were buried and denied to the people under the weight of this inflated and self-serving monolith. Unimaginable!

Yes, all of this seems unimaginable to the Mind that has found its home in the world of vertical time. It is much easier now to forgive the blindness of the past, as it is easier to have compassion for those who were driven as slaves by the relentless fear of the future. Perhaps in a few generations, there will simply be no interest in revisiting the Dark Time, as the need to repeat the past into the future dissolves. The present moment will be so complete and satisfying that we will simply not turn to diversions or distractions to reduce stress or soothe unconscious anxiety. These are mental patterns requiring a belief in time, as is boredom. Underlying these common psychoses is the thought, "What if the next moment is just like this one, or worse? What if I am never able to escape this gnawing suspicion that my survival hangs in the balance between life and death at every second, and that I have limited time and finite opportunities to escape into more pleasure, more consumption, more oblivion, more of whatever erases this fear that I will not exist?"

None of this will matter to the Mind at peace with the present moment. More good news is that you don't have to wait for the right conditions to experience vertical time. That notion is just another time-bound belief, as is hope. We think that, although our lives suck at this moment, someday, things will be better—over the rainbow, my prince will come. You get the idea.

You can use the pyramid illustration as a meditation, if you like, to help you experience vertical time. First think of all disparities in your life; then feel their tug and pull. Then see yourself coming to the perfect point of Peace between the polarities. Focus on your breathing to get you there. As soon as you are there, "look up" in your intention and say to the Divine Mind, the Creator, Presence, or whatever term suits you: "I am ready to see things differently. I am ready to see the Truth and choose Peace. Show me my true Self. Show me as I am created—eternal, innocent, invulnerable, and free." Ask that your mind be healed from the belief in time, and the need for the belief in time. Forgive yourself for believing in time. It is only a dream. You do not condemn yourself for having a dream. Rather, you just chuckle, shake it off, and go on with your real life.

CHAPTER 11

STANDING STILL

In the next image, the horizontal line itself collapses into a single point at the center of the circle. Of course, there is no right or wrong way to interpret these things. It is possible that you will intuit something of your own and that I will see something different down the road. I am sure this is one reason why Spirit communicates often in pictures. As the Chinese say, "A picture is worth a thousand words." Pictures, as symbols, can yield new information as we revisit them from time to time; as our minds expand, we "see" more.

It seems, however, that even our experience of vertical time will eventually pass away. Perhaps this is pointing to a compression of all experience into a single experience all the time—the time of Now Time!

The Hindus have a (non-dual) belief that all emotions come from a single source of emotion, Eternal Bliss. When we have an experience we automatically overlay it with a thought, perception, or judgment, which are all the same thing. A little piece of this Bliss becomes distorted and pulled away from its Source. It becomes "stuck" to our belief in time and perception. It then becomes our experience of pain, loss, fear, or sadness, all forms of contraction or reverse creativity. When we release ourselves from the judgments, perceptions, and beliefs we hold around that experience, which happens through True Forgiveness, relief comes and emotional energy can go back to the pool of Bliss where it came from. We feel good again, and now we are more aware of the feeling of ourselves as essentially Bliss—and so we grow in our joy and appreciation of life, ourselves, and Divine wisdom. In the East it is said that if you go into the heart of any experience, you will find Bliss.

The third image may point to the return of Awareness to where it was *before* time began—that is, as a single point of Awareness within the totality of Being (the circle). This is a good description of the first "thought" of God—like an idea springing up from everywhere and congealing into a specific pattern or point of view. As we are the Created One, the Divine's one and only creation, perhaps this dot represents us before the idea of separation took hold. As we knew ourselves as both one with and separate from our Source, we took the "separate from" part, and imagined it in all its endless ramifications. We thought to mimic our own creation but forgot our own Source in the process. We broke the causal chain of creation, and ran off to play by ourselves. The fact that this thought emerged out of everything and became "something," however, implies perhaps a larger plan, and brings up the question "Why did Creator allow this to happen at all?"

Perhaps this is a good point to describe these events as noted in the metaphysics of *A Course in Miracles*, which says that "before the beginning" a "tiny mad idea" occurred within the Oneness of All That Is. This idea was allowed because in the reality of All That Is, *nothing* can be denied or excluded, even the crazy thought that Oneness could be anything other than One. Real Love is total freedom. The problem isn't so much the idea of separation as it is our taking it seriously and forgetting simply to laugh it off.

Because this idea was born out of Oneness, we can say that metaphorically, this was the first expression of One-ness that was *of* the Oneness, yet seemingly separate. The trouble is that, now that this idea was born and carrying all the weight and authority of the One, it was granted the opportunity to experience separation fully in all of its unlim-ited possibilities, including time. In other words, it now had to live out the consequences of its desire to separate. At this point, the Big Bang occurred. This was the beginning of the universe of separate forms, of space and time, and eventually, bodies. As the physical universe expanded out from this point, our identity as the child of the Divine cor-respondingly contracted into endless microscopic forms, including bodies manifesting in different times and spaces. Would not it be more accurate to call this the Big Oops?

The beauty of this story is that it puts us, humanity, in the driver's seat. If we can take full responsibility for the first idea of separation, we can change our minds. After all, this was not a sin, only a genuine mistake. And if we are totally responsible for this universe of time, space, bodies, and everything else, we are relieved of the false need for or hope of an outside savior to come and rescue us from our-selves based on our behavior or beliefs sometime in a fan-ciful future, only to create a spiritual hierarchy with us as subservient once again. Once we are empowered with the responsibility to help find our own way back to conscious Awareness as the One thought/expression of God, don't you think the Divine will rush to meet us more than half way?

IT NEVER REALLY HAPPENED

Here's the key, and something of which I find I must constantly remind myself. The universe of separation didn't actually happen. It was the natural consequence of the *imaginary* split from Oneness, which, when you think about, is an oxymoron. It is not possible.

That's what this experience we call life is. And it is all happening within the One Mind that is dreaming it. It actually thinks while in this state that it is billions of separated parts!

Awakening while in the dream of separation has not been too common an event so far on this planet. Well, it may be more common than we think, but many people probably keep quiet about such "awakening" experiences, or may be afraid to talk about them. In many cases describing spiritual emergences can get you locked up or accused of being in league with the devil—especially if your experience doesn't fit the prevailing dogma of what is or isn't spiritual. Modern society doesn't seem to be able to accommodate experiences outside the walls of its current materialistic prison. We marginalize the unusual in our egoic drive to conform and survive. Worse, we diagnose the unusual and non-conforming and medicate them back to sleep.

So the total collapse of time to a single point as symbolized in this image is perhaps pointing to a return to where we started—that is, a return to an idea within the Mind of God. We never left, but we think we did. Upon hearing this, if you feel your former identity slipping away, try this one on: "I am an idea in the Mind of God, and I never left!"

The order of events implied by the total vision indicates an "undoing" process. This is an idea consistent with, for example, natural medicine. In natural medicine, we respect the body as a self-regulating, self-healing system. All we need do is remove the blocks and resistances to these processes, and healing occurs of itself. This tendency toward self-healing is called "homeostasis." I offer that the same is true in the emotional, mental, and spiritual realms as well. We are already perfect expressions of the Divine. This has never changed. Only our memory of our Divinity seems to have been erased, overlaid with piles of unconscious guilt and suffering incurred through eons of ego slavery. Remove the thoughts, beliefs, and attitudes that keep you down, and your Spirit will soar! When we return to our knowledge of Oneness through a reversal of the dreaming process, we awaken to our home in the Source and *know* it consciously. Who you really are is there now. Who we *think* we are is here.

Only one identity is true. Only one idea is real. Only one identity will survive the Awakening. Don't worry. Nothing that happens to you in the dream can possibly harm or threaten you, no matter how dire or dreadful things may appear. As it says in the *Course:* "You are at home in God, dreaming of exile but perfectly capable of awakening to reality" (10:1:2).

One of the ego's biggest cons is the fear of death. Death is typically shrouded in our culture in extreme emotion, fear of our own mortality, and the color black. I find it delightful that so much research into near-death experiences by reputable scientists is now available, refuting death as any kind of end at all, other than the end of physical suffering for many. With a few variations on the details, near-death experiencers all seem to be saying the same thing; that despite the end of the physical body, we, as Mind, continue to see, hear, feel, and reason. Most report pure joy at this liberation, and regret when they are told to return for whatever reason. "I'm sorry sir, you don't have a reservation. You'll need to come back and try another time."

Understanding all this as you now do, having come this far, indicates that the Awakening has started for you. From here, your further awakening is a process of recognizing that all of your perceptions of time, space, and yourself as a body emerged out of this single point—the single decision to experience something other than Oneness. Recognizing the single source of all conflicts, contradiction, and suffering is an amazing accomplishment, for a single error implies a single solution. The good news is that the solution was given immediately, the moment the error occurred. We all carry the correction as the spark of Spirit in our minds. This is the true meaning of the Holy Spirit—a Divine messenger seeded into every seemingly separated part, and the guarantee of the undoing of separation. It arises in your memory each time you decide to forgive yourself for the decision to separate by recognizing that, in reality, it could not happen. It arises when you know your loving Creator sees you *only* in this Light. You do this when you forgive "the other." The one solution is always Love.

You are most likely to touch upon this knowledge of single-pointedness through silencing the mind as described earlier. The Breath Meditation offered in chapter 12 may be helpful. Visualizing the symbols in your meditation may help you cultivate the experience. Think of this as settling into the "zero point" of existence. The zero point is the beginning and end of everything in one place. It is a place of no time, no space, and no mind—akin to Zen philosophy. Yet out of this emerges everything—the universe of your own Divine creation.

It is clear these symbols were given in the order they were to provide a map of "unlearning;" of finding the road back home by retracing the steps that got us here. Here is another example of how the mirror world makes a backward version of reality. There is nothing here that can add to or take away from Who you are. There is just an opportunity to release the belief in illusions and allow Truth to naturally arise as easily as the morning Sun as it dispels night's darkness.

THE EXPANDING ROAD TO WHOLENESS

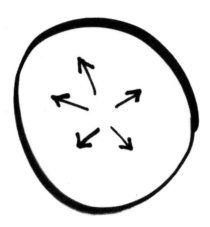

In the next image I saw, the dot disappears momentarily, but becomes the source of an energy that begins to emanate outward in all directions from the center of the circle. It is as if the dot were immobile as long as it remained a point, but in dissolving into the zero point, or void, it becomes a tremendous source of energy that begins to move in an outward, expansive way.

What this symbol appears to say is that after we collapse both horizontal and vertical time into a remembering of how time began (as a thought within Oneness), we unlock a tremendous source of creative power. It's as if the One says: "Okay, now you get it. Now you have returned home, and I will bless you with all of the creative power and joy that I have been unable to share up until this time. Now, go out and Create." Sounds like the parable of the Prodigal Son, doesn't it? In our *false* guilt (*all* guilt is false!) for imagining we destroyed God by separating (that's what we think at the deepest unconscious level), we can't imagine that the Divine would actually reward us for straying so terribly and staying away so long! But, recall, we didn't go anywhere. We're just having a hallucination.

This image is very positive and encouraging. Once we get over our belief in time and all the other figments of imaginary separation, we'll really go to town! We return as One to our true and proper function—Creation. Ken Carey, one of my favorite authors, describes how this dynamic could play out. Read his *Third Millennium* (Harper Collins, 1991). It is so beautiful and timely—channeled by an Archangel.

Carey talks about this present era from 2011 forward as a time of gathering of the lost tribes, as it were. He predicts that some people will be drawn to certain areas of the world and begin to form intentional communities of like-minded folks. These will be people who respect life, the planet, and each other, and want to demonstrate that it is possible to live and thrive by these principles. He called these communities "Islands of the Future."

Carey says these islands will form and come together around the wave of awakening in 2011. But he says there will be a further 1000 years of developing and building these communities, and that the "really big show" will come in 3012, when all these communities will band together, each forming a specific "organ" in a universal Body. This body, which may be a vast collection of space ships or vessels or simply an allegory for our unified state of Being, will then launch itself out into the universe with a mission to create worlds and birth new civilizations—"To go boldly where no man has gone before." The vision here reminds me of the ending of Stanley Kubrick's *2001: A Space Odyssey* with the enigmatic baby floating off into space. I always wondered what that could mean!

There's metaphysical and mythical validation in this idea of a birthing process—evidence that out of the stillness and collapse of time a new creative energy will be released. The center of the galaxy was referred to as the Womb of Creation by the Maya and others. The center of the Milky Way as we see it from here in the band of stars overhead even resembles an opening to the birth canal in the night sky, and was referred to by the Maya as the "dark rift." Certainly in the stark realm of physics, the galactic center is a powerful source of light and electro-magnetic energy, which are the substrate of all matter ("matter," from the Latin *mater*, mother) There is also every indication that the Black Hole at the center is a powerful scalar wave generator or multi-dimensional portal, according to Maxwell's original electro-magnetic theories. The Maya called this portal the Tree of Life.

Maxwell was the originator of most of our modern theories of electro-magnetism. In the late 1800s he formulated what today is still considered the bedrock of our understanding of electro-magnetism. In his original theories, he allowed for the existence of higher octaves of electro-magnetic energy that vibrate beyond our ability to measure, calling these "hyper-spatial dimensions." These were later called scalar waves by Tom Beardon. Before Maxwell's theories were made public, however, the hyper-spatial aspects were written out and his theories reduced to a few dumbed-down official theories sanctioned by academia. Although this is only conjecture, one has to wonder whether these parts of Maxwell's theory were removed intentionally, and made available only on a need-to-know basis when it was discovered that hyper-spatial dimensional energy had a direct impact on consciousness and opened a theoretical door into time travel, hyper-spatial travel, and other exotic possibilities.

The Sun has often symbolized the male principle—expansive, life-giving, sometimes burning us with its rages, bringing drought and thirst. Here we have a rare cosmological alignment occurring once every 13,000 years (halfway through the 26,000-year solar-system cycle), whereby the male principle, or light, aligns ever so briefly with the dark rift in the Milky Way and the galactic core—a "cosmic quickie," it would appear—enabling the fertilization of a dormant humanity with galactic radiations of spiritual light. This is the birthing of *homo luminous*—the Child of the Morning, or the return of Christ, Quetzalcoatl, Maitreya Buddha, the Messiah, all names for the cosmic child who is us.

THE CIRCLE AS CENTER

The circle that remains in this stage of the images still symbolizes limitation. It is circumscribed, delineated by its boundary, and thus not quite yet expressing its full nature as pure Creativity. The disappearance of the point in the center is symbolic of the merging of the particular with the general—as in the dissipation of personality and self-definitions that hold us in the dream of separation. Similarly, it is possible to experience timeless states of being, yet still be bound by an ego. The ego actually loves to give us metaphysical moments of deep or wild realizations as long as we keep ourselves separate from the experience. We do this when we call it *my* experience, *my* revelation, *my* channeling, etc. This eternal chasing of the carrot of enlightenment is a favorite ego game, and can keep anyone distracted for eons.

We see now that the Collapse of Time in the earlier images is just part of the greater process of Awakening back to our

Source as the Divine. Notice that I didn't say back to our source *with* the Divine. This would imply that "I" and the Divine are not One, but two. So the image of the dot disappearing from the center and beginning to move out represents the beginning of the breakdown of duality between "me" and God. Duality exists only as a facet of our belief in separation. That is how powerful we are. We can dream a dream so intense and vivid that to ourselves, it seems completely real.

As Awareness, which is as good a definition of Who You Are as any, begins to move out from the center there is a temporary loss of identity. The center of our being feels cut loose from the dock, and we are adrift in an endless sea of potential. A stage in this aspect of Awakening occurs when we begin to notice how everything in our perception (our thoughts) is always relative to other perceptions. We see our own chains, and it is not comfortable. We can then drift into ennui: "What's the use of anything? What's the purpose of life if all I experience is endless rounds of meaningless experience?" Know, however, that this is only a temporary feeling of dissociation as our image of ourselves as discrete and individual begins to dissolve into something greater, as yet unformed. The caterpillar resists dissolving in order to become a butterfly, but has no real choice in the matter.

This reminds me of the "death trip" some psychedelic cowboys used to talk about in the Sixties, when the hallucinogenic experience led one to the prematurely expansive knowledge that our self-definitions meant nothing. The trouble was that there was nothing for the mind to hold on to beyond these stories we told ourselves, and so the experience often led to a nosedive into "bummer land" without a new context to aspire toward or identify with.

If we are to look at these images as mapping the Awakening process, they imply the need eventually to launch out of the gravitational womb of the center spot and begin to expand outward in a progressive and open manner. Just as with earth-bound rockets, the initial effort may need to be tremendous to break the spell of gravity. Once the movement begins, the process becomes progressively easier, as gravity eventually loosens its grip altogether. That is what the spiritual journey from our "small-s" selves to our "big-S" Selves is like. At first, it may take a cataclysmic event to break us loose—a serious illness or accident, a sudden relocation or dislocation from familiar surroundings, or the loss of a dear one. These defining life events are often what prompt us to dig deeper into ourselves for the resources we sense must be there, but weren't necessary to us up to this crisis point in our lives. There is a chance we could implode and attempt to hold on to mother gravity, or our old sense of identity, for dear life and even self-destruct at this point. The ego would prefer this. It truly is programmed to survive at all costs—even at the cost of your sanity or life. Of course, the ego's plan never works, as your real Self is immortal, invulnerable, and completely safe within the Mind of your Creator.

There is a part of you that is way beyond the ego and its influence. It is your Spirit or Soul if you prefer. While the ego frets and worries, your Spirit knows that your real Self cannot ever be contained by anything or be content to remain a little "dot" in existence. Because Spirit knows you *are* existence itself dreaming you are a dot, Spirit provides the will to begin to move outward from the center. And the farther you go, the faster and easier it becomes. As ego-gravity becomes less and less, you find out that the Joy and Peace and Love you always wanted is your natural state, and comes effortlessly, lifting you even higher.

However, all of this is still happening within the context of your Mind—not your little brain-centered idea of your mind, but your true Self as Big Mind, as the Zen folks say. You find that this open space you are moving into contains all of experience within it—not just your personal experience, but *all* experience. You'll recall that the DNA in your cells holds the record of *all* life! We remember that this experience of expansion is happening all at once with no limitation imposed by any belief or system of time. Time, it turns out, was just a belief in the "small mind" that thought it was a dot! All events—past, present, and future—appear before you as a Divine tapestry reflecting the beauty and creativity of its designer, you! However, there is still one final hurdle. The circle itself must be dissolved if this expansion of Awareness is truly to continue beyond the confines of time—that is, for Eternity.

All that I speak of here is completely accessible to you and can be directly experienced under one condition—Silence. These are realizations of the Soul that do not come by study, discussion, comparison, or analysis. One of the biggest favors we can do for ourselves as we unravel the belief in time and the ego that made it up is to learn to cultivate Silence. This involves first of all paying attention to the nature of thought and the endless chatter of our inner dialogue. If we truly just listen, it is as if we have this compulsive tour guide in our heads who is always there with an opinion, a judgment, a preference, a complaint, or a wish. Never content to just "be," it must always be in motion—the perpetual "mind grind." Many traditional spiritual practices are simply attempts to put this thinking mind to rest. When this is accomplished, the Peace that arises naturally is equated with words like "nirvana," "bliss," and "cosmic consciousness"—the expansiveness we find when we let our point of view dissolve.

If you are new to the idea that a mind can be quieted, and want to try a simple technique, here is a simple breath meditation that can take you far along the journey to Silence. Once there, the voice of Silence will speak to you of Peace, of Love, and of Joy, as these are simply aspects of your own true Self.

BREATH MEDITATION FOR CULTIVATING SILENCE

The purpose of this simple meditation is to help establish the experience of inner Peace. When we experience ourselves as the source of inner Peace, we become less anxious and feel more at home with ourselves. Happiness, we discover, is not something to pursue or gain, it is our natural state. By practicing this simple breath meditation once or twice daily, your inner Peace will begin to flow outward, spontaneously affecting the world around you without any other special effort on your part, as in the last image. Simply follow these suggestions. The mediation is a simple, foundational technique, to which you can later add other techniques as you progress on your inner path. This time is your gift to yourself—the value is in doing it. Find a quiet, comfortable place where you can sit undisturbed for fifteen or twenty minutes. You may (ironically!) want a watch or clock nearby so you check the time.

Begin simply to notice your easy, natural breath. There is no special effort required here, just watch your breathing and silently begin to label each breath cycle from 1 to 10.

When you notice your attention has wandered to a thought (which it will; the mind, we find, has a mind of its own!), simply label this experience as "thinking," and go back to the previous step. As simple as this seems, you are doing two profound things. First, you are experiencing yourself as the thinker of the thought—the Silent Observer—and you are choosing consciously to bring your attention back to the Now, where the breath will always bring you. You are the choice-maker or Higher Self. Second, whatever you can observe, you are not that thing. You've created a gap between the Observer and the thinking mind. This gap is your liberation from mental torture and psychological distress, which is the source of most human suffering. Thoughts, we discover, are based either in memory, which is the past, or planning, which is in the future. The past and future are mind-created, and don't really exist outside of our thinking. As you practice, you will begin to experience little patches of Silence that will expand as you continue to practice. This is where we experience ourselves as pure and peaceful Awareness, a peaceful state that tends to carry over into our daily lives.

That's all! Remember to keep a kind and easy attitude toward yourself. The meditation is not a challenge to master; it is simply a way to drink from the deep well of inner Peace within.

As you practice this daily—ideally morning and evening for ten to fifteen minutes—you will begin to take notice of your thoughts as they arise throughout the day from the perspective of the Silent Observer. You will begin to discriminate which thoughts deserve follow-up and which ones are just inconsequential chatter. It's like finding the station dial on a radio that you thought only had one station.

One my most profound personal breakthroughs occurred when I realized that my own thoughts were essentially meaningless. I remember I was walking on the beach with my wife and just blurted out: "I don't think I really know anything. I don't understand what anything is for—especially my own thoughts!" You may think that thoughts like this could easily become suicidal, but I also had a sense of having come to the end of a way of being that suddenly felt exhausting and obsolete—both an ending and a beginning. It was shortly after this that I began my study of *A Course in Miracles* and found, to my wonderment, that one of the first of 365 daily lessons said: "I do not understand anything I see—these thoughts do not mean anything."

I now call this insight my "beginning of wisdom." I had to realize (make real) what Truth is *not* before I could begin to see what it is.

CHAPTER 13

HOME—BEING BEYOND BOUNDARIES

Here is the final image in the series, in which the energy moving out from the center pushes back and dissolves the circle, expanding into infinity.

If you expand this from a flat 2-D to a 3-D image it evokes a further symbol of the torus—a donut-shaped field that, like the vortex, is one of the basic dynamics of creation. A torus can appear as an electro-magnetic field that is constantly moving energy from the center outward. The energy moves around the edge of the donut and then circulates back into the center at the bottom of the shape. Round and round the energy moves in perpetual renewal.

In the center is a transformational portal or standing scalar wave created by the intense juxtaposition of the moving lines of energy. The energy is thus constantly being refined and raised to higher and higher levels of purity as it circulates. Every living structure has a torus associated with it—from the individual cell to the galaxy and beyond. You could say the Tree of Life structure may be the standing scalar wave in the center of a toroidal process that repeats holographically in multiple dimensions and magnitudes from the macro to the micro.

In our model then, the previous stage of movement from the center of the circle may involve the beginning of a period of purification and circulation in preparation for the final phase—the total recognition and experience of oneself as the Divine, beyond all limits and concepts.

It is very difficult even to think about, much less describe what this would be like. It is the breaking down of the final barrier of separation—the belief in Oneness and something outside of Oneness, which, if you think about it, is impossible. It also can be said to represent the final collapse of duality in the mind—not only a state of Oneness with creation (still duality) but Oneness with Creator (non-dual, no separation).

The image also implies that eventually the whole game will be over. What happens when an illusion completely dissolves? Initially, there may be some *dis*illusionment. What we thought was real may just turn out to be a wisp of a dream quickly forgotten upon awakening. From within the dream, this prospect can appear threatening. The suggested *modus operandi* for those truly desiring to awaken is to Let It Go! Whatever you thought was valuable or independently real will eventually turn to empty space before you. So you can embrace this "freedom opportunity" now while you still are operating within the illusion we call time, or you can put it off until later. When you get there, you'll see that there was no "later" anyway, just the experience of unnecessary suffering until you got there.

Recall that the original True Cross of Creation resides symbolically at the galactic center. What this progression of images thus implies is a process involving the entire galaxy, if not the entire universe—a wave of No Time perhaps? We have no good reason to feel alone or isolated in the experience of the Collapse of Time. The non-dual principle states that the universe is simply a projection of the One Mind. Thus it should be no surprise that the universe will shift as we do, as easily as cause (us) and effect (the universe).

Realizing that nothing here is really of any value—only the value we give it in our quest for happiness—can help you let go effectively. Ask rich people "Are you happy?" They may say, "Yes, but not because of my riches!" More often and for many, there is a gnawing sense that riches can't bring happiness, nor can anything in this world for that matter. The value we put on anything in the dream is what keeps us in the dream. What we value here, we also fear to lose. You could say that our values are our fears. I am not suggesting you need to drift into a "who cares," numb existence. It is okay to have things and enjoy your experience, just don't count on it lasting, or be tempted to build an identity around it. "Anything Real cannot be threatened, anything unreal does not exist," says *A Course in Miracles*. When we value something, we fear the end of it. So allow your experiences to pass through you, but cling not! "Be passersby," advises Jeshua in the Gospel of Thomas. This is the same wisdom of non-attachment we find among the Buddhist teachings.

LOOKING WITHIN TO SEE BEYOND

Buddhism is a very psychologically astute philosophy. There is much we in the West can gain from this gentle but powerful thought system. Primarily, Buddhism encourages us to look within for the cause of our experiences. In this sense, it is more evolved than an outward-looking dualistic philosophy that posits us as victims of the past and circumstances beyond our control.

In a way, we can rehearse the eventuality of full Awakening on a small scale as we go along. Any time conflict arises from an attack on you or by you, or you feel the smallest disturbance of your peace, take the opportunity as soon as you can to become still. See the perception of duality behind the conflict (conflict is only possible within duality) as a circle of confinement constraining your true Being. Your true Self mistakenly and temporarily thinks it is limited and contained by this experience in the dream. Now see yourself expand beyond that circle and feel the freedom of transcending the need for conflict. Erase the circle in your mind if you like. Realize it was only drawn in chalk, and had no substance in reality.

You are Spirit—eternal, unlimited, invulnerable, and born to joyously Be, as are all the others in your dream of separation. We are all the same being having the same hallucination! This may be what John Lennon was trying to say in "I Am the Walrus"—"I am you and you are me and you are we and we are all together" (Northern Songs, 1967). This is true all the time, not just sometimes. Each time you realize this, you tell the ego, "I no longer subscribe to your little view of me. I go beyond your little circle of fear and look back and see it was nothing!" Now just sit in the Peace, and as you do this, you will bring more and more of this Peace back with you into the dream. People will begin to notice that you are not reacting as you used to do. Unknown to them, they are receiving the frequency of Peace in your presence. You have become the Light of the World.

What I have been describing here could also be called True Forgiveness. Not-so-true forgiveness, the dualistic kind, looks first at the offense, then out of moral superiority and the goodness of its heart, forgives. This kind of forgiveness never quite lets go of the offense, however, and will hold it in a secret place of vengeance, plotting eventually to balance the scales of justice. Sounds like ego again, doesn't it?

See the offense of the "other" as simply your Spirit trying to break free of its self-imposed circle of separation and show you how to do the same by reflecting an image of your secret guilt in the mirror world. Because we can't see, or are in denial of, the unforgiven areas in ourselves, we arrange for someone to stand in our place and hopefully take the heat. Forgiveness—that is, recognizing our total innocence in this charade—allows you to identify this behavior as something you have judged and tried to separate from in yourself by projecting it outward onto another, and to perceive it as entirely overlookable, just as the Divine overlooks it in you from the beginning. Your mistakes are not your identity, and are definitely not sins requiring sacrifice from you or anyone else. And no one but you holds you to a false identity. Your true will and desire is to have your own "circles" transcended and removed forever. True Forgiveness is how you do it.

Now you may be feeling an inner protest based on the seemingly impossible demand to forgive something that is just too big or painful in your life, or the seemingly intolerable injustices we see in the daily media. Here's the good part; *you* don't have to do the forgiving! The Divine messenger, Holy Spirit, or Presence does it on your behalf. This aspect of the Divine, which we *all* carry within, was charged with the job of being everywhere at once and knowing the perfect solution for every call for Love we make. All you are asked to do, like a telephone operator, is make the connection. This only takes *one percent willingness* on your part. You don't even have to feel forgiving to be willing.

Just do it! The only other choice is to hold on to the judgment, which is only hurting you. The Divine takes every little opportunity you give it, no matter how small, to heal the One Mind of needless suffering.

Once this pattern of total transcendence is embraced fully through practice, desire, and devotion to Truth, it will tend to become your experience more and more, until, as is entirely possible, you will walk through this dream of separation completely awake and aware of yourself as the Divine Dreamer. You will then be truly "in the world, but not of the world." Nothing that happens here will ever faze you. Not even death or the "end of the world," as for you, there is no death and the world never was. Not because you'll be some kind of blandly blissed-out drooler, but because your true nature as Joy, Freedom, and Love will naturally arise to meet each situation with fresh, playful, creative delight as it did when you were a child.

The Collapse of Time is part and parcel of the transcendence of the planet and of you to a higher dimensional state, that of the fifth dimension. We call this "ascension," itself an effect of the healing of the One Mind. Of course a dimension is simply an arbitrarily assigned description of a range of vibrational light frequency that does not exist in reality as a separate thing in itself. Can you see how enmeshed in duality we are here? No matter where we look, we project this hidden assumption of the separation of forms. Even our anatomically split brains reflect this entrenched belief.

With all of these suggestions and exercises I have been putting forward, you may be feeling a little overwhelmed or even discouraged if you know you'll never actually get around to doing all or any of these things. The beauty of all this is that you do not have to accomplish any of these things yourself. Your Divine Self has already done so. Just by hanging out with your Divine Self, by turning your mind in its direction, you will find that many blessings or gifts just show up in your life. We call this Grace. Even though your rational mind may be challenged by some of these ideas, a part of your mind already knows all of this and more, and so you experience glimpses of recognition—literally "knowing again" what was forgotten. I can confidently say that you know what I am talking about if you have come this far in reading this book. The words and ideas you read here are just carriers of something deeper—an energy that filters through the rational mind and stirs the sleeping one within. Pssst...it's time to wake up.

Part of you, even in the darkest depths of dreaming, knows that there must be a better way to live, to be. Even the experience of suffering must be held in contrast to not suffering. From the perspective of No Time, the time of your Awakening has already been scripted. The fact that you are reading this book indicates that it is much nearer than you suspect. You are pulling the experience of Awakening to you by putting your attention on it. This is quantum physics in action. Grace means that all is freely given you with no cost, no sacrifice or martyrdom required on your part. You are simply asked to give up what is not real. Just recognize Light when it shines, and welcome the dawn of your Awakening.

Be patient with yourself. Be kind to yourself. You and I have thousands of years of dualistic memory and conditioning to release. We now have the resources on the planet as never before to change our minds about all of it, however. If you devote yourself to these new ideas about your Self, you will find opportunities to learn popping up as you draw to yourself what you need for the next step in your Awakening. Maybe this little book is one of those resources. I certainly hope so!

CHAPTER 14

SOME NON-DUAL THOUGHTS ABOUT TIME—IT'S ABOUT TIME!

The following are quotations from *A Course In Miracles*.*
The *Course* will ultimately take its place among the great books of all time, if time is even a factor by then! There are other non-dual thought systems out there. This one is especially accessible to the Western mind, but you may also want to look at the Chinese Tao and/or Hindu Vedanta.

When I first looked into the *Course*, I found it dense and confusing. I did not feel comfortable with what looked to me like old-time religious language and terminology. However, I felt led at one point to read *The Disappearance of the Universe* by Gary Renard. This was both exhilarating and upsetting. The book upset many of my assumptions about myself, God, and the world. I had to put it down for a few days at a time while I allowed new thoughts to settle in place of the old illusions it was uncovering. But I suspected that if my assumptions could be rattled, maybe they weren't all that solid, and I respected the challenge. Reading Renard's book made the *Course* accessible to me.

---

* All quotes are from *A Course in Miracles*, Foundation for Inner Peace, Mill Valley, CA., 3rd ed., 2005. Notation follows the format *chapter: section. paragraph: sentence.* WL indicates workbook lesson. Words in italics are mine.

If you are at all interested in learning a new thought system to replace the old dualistic, time-bound beliefs we all inherited by our mutual choice, please read this book. If we sincerely want to help collapse time, we can speed things up tremendously by devoting ourselves to non-dual thinking—that is, the Thoughts of God—daily. Open yourself to the return of sanity.

Hold these thoughts in your mind. Allow yourself to go beyond the intellect and *feel* the freedom in the thought. You may not agree with a non-dual thought, but you cannot meaningfully argue either. After the Collapse of Time, it will be the *feeling* of these thoughts that will survive. The *feeling* will become your *experience*, and the experience will be of your *Self*—the All That Is.

> *The purpose of time is to allow you to use time constructively...time will cease when it is no longer useful in facilitating learning. (1:1.15:4)*

> *Atonement (the undoing of the dream) works all the time, and in all dimensions of time. (1:1.25:2)*

> *The Miracle (joining of Minds in recognizing their Oneness as Spirit) entails a sudden shift from horizontal to vertical perception. This introduces an interval from which the giver and receiver both emerge farther along in time than they otherwise have been. The Miracle thus has the unique property of abolishing time...the Miracle substitutes for learning that might have taken thousands of years. (1:2.6:3)*

> *The basic decision of the Miracle-minded is not to wait on time any longer than is necessary. Time can waste as well as be wasted...he recognizes that every collapse of time brings everyone closer to the ultimate release from time. (1:5.2:4)*

You do not belong in time. Your place is only in eternity where God (itself) placed you forever. (5:6.1:6)

Guilt Feelings are the preservers of time...You are not guiltless in time, but in eternity...the world you see is the delusional system of those made mad by guilt. If this were the real world, God would be cruel. (13: intro.3:1)

Always has no direction. Time seems to go in one direction, but when you reach its end it will roll up like a long carpet spread along the past behind you, and will disappear. (13:1.3:5)

The Holy Spirit (Divine messenger, memory of God) stands at the end of time, where you must be because He is with you...he has already undone everything unworthy of You... (13:1.4:5)

The ego invests heavily in the past, and in the end believes that the past is the only aspect of time that is meaningful...its emphasis on guilt enables it to ensure its continuity by making the future like the past, and thus avoiding the present. "Now" has no meaning to the ego. The present merely reminds it of past hurts, and it reacts to the present as if it were the past. (13:4.4:3)

Now is the closest approximation of eternity that this world offers. (13:4.7:5)

Healing cannot be accomplished in the past. It must be accomplished in the present to release the future. This interpretation ties the future to the present, and extends the present rather than the past...time will be as you interpret it, for of itself it is nothing. (13:4.9:3)

The belief in guilt must lead to the belief in hell, and always does. The only way in which the ego allows the fear of hell to be experienced is to bring hell here, but always as a foretaste of the future...the Holy Spirit teaches thus: There is no hell. Hell is only what the ego has made of the present. (15:1.6:5)

Start now to practice your little part in separating out the Holy Instant. To learn to separate out this single second, and to experience it as timeless, is to begin to experience yourself as not separate. (15:2.6:1)

The revelation that the Father and the Son (the Creator and the Created) are one will come in time to every mind...the time is set already. It appears to be quite arbitrary. Yet there is no step along the road that anyone takes but by chance. It has already been taken by him (in Spirit) although he has not yet embarked on it (in form). For time but seems to go in one direction. We but undertake a journey that is over. Yet it seems to have a future still unknown to us. Time is a trick, a sleight of hand, a vast illusion in which figures come and go as if by magic. Yet there is a plan behind appearances that does not change. The script is written...for we but see the journey from the point at which it ended, looking back on it, imagining we make it once again; reviewing mentally what has gone by. (WL 158.4:3)

Yet you have come far enough along the way to alter time sufficiently to rise above its laws, and walk into eternity a while. This you will learn to do increasingly...as this experience increases and all goals but this become of little worth, the world to which you will return becomes a little closer to the end of time; a little more like Heaven in its ways. (WL 157.3:2)

If you have come this far in this story of the Collapse of Time you are already beginning to experience all that has been discussed here. Otherwise your time-bound egoic mind would have had you toss this book in the trash long ago, or give it away to someone you want to torture! I am entirely confident, however, that each and every reader has within his or her Self the memory of the Divine and that we all share the same one Will to become conscious of Love again. If you are open and ready, you will also hear this voice whispering in the Silence. It is much like hearing a wisp of a long-forgotten song—that is, a vague familiarity wrapped up in a good feeling. You want to hear more.

I am also confident that you will experience some inner conflict around these ideas. How do I know this? Well, if you are here in a body, you are still subject to duality and the experience of a split mind. This is how we got here and what keeps us coming back for more. The split is between the ego and Spirit, or your "wrong mind" and your "right mind." The beauty is that only one of these is real, enduring, and meaningful. Nonetheless, the ego-mind is persistent, suspicious, doubtful, devious, and even treacherous. As long as we are here in bodies we seem to walk the line between these two selves. One thing we can do while here is to devote ourselves to being immersed in thoughts that correct the errors of the ego-mind. As the old conditioned patterns are systematically replaced with thoughts that point to Truth or Oneness, the dead thoughts will no longer weigh us down. Degree by degree, we will become lighter. This is the most appropriate use of time. The *Course* says, "We use time to undo time."

Finally, the mark of Truth is the Peace it brings. If your thoughts are not bringing you Peace, exchange them for ones that do. May the Peace within you be born into your Awareness daily. May you awaken to who you already are.

BIBLIOGRAPHY

A Course in Miracles. Mill Valley, CA: Foundation for Inner Peace, 3rd edition, 2005.

Ashley-Farrand, T. *Healing Mantras.* New York: Ballantine Wellspring, 1999.

Bauval, R. & A. Gilbert. *The Orion Mystery: Unlocking the Secrets of The Pyramids.* New York: Three Rivers Press, 1994.

Becker, R. *The Body Electric.* New York: W. Morrow & Co., 1985.

Braden, G. *Awakening to Zero Point.* Bellevue, WA: Radio Bookstore Press, 1993.

Burr, H. S. *Blueprint for Immortality: the Electric Patterns of Life.* London: Neville Spearman, 1972.

Calleman, C. J. *The Mayan Calendar.* London: Garev Pub. Intl., 2001.

————. *The Purposeful Universe.* Rochester, VT: Bear & Co., 2009.

Carey, K. *The Third Millennium, Living in the Post Historic World.* San Francisco: Harper Collins, 1991.

Clow, B. *The Pleiadian Agenda.* Santa Fe, NM: Bear & Co., 1996.

————. *Catastrophobia: the Truth Behind Earth Changes and the Coming Age of Light.* Santa Fe, NM: Bear & Co., 2001.

—————. *Alchemy of the Nine Dimensions*. Charlottes-ville, VA: Hampton Roads, 2010.

—————. *The Mayan Code*. Rochester, VT: Bear & Co., 2007.

Cohen. J. *What You Must Know about Statin Drugs and Their Natural Alternatives*. New York: Square One Pub-lishers, 2005.

Cori, P. *Atlantis Rising: The Struggle of Darkness and Light*. Berkeley, CA. North Atlantic Books, 2001, 2008.

Cruttenden, W. *The Lost Star of Myth and Time*. Pitts-burg, PA: St. Lynn's Press, 2006.

D'Adamo, P. J. *Eat Right 4 Your Type*. New York: G. P. Put-nam & Sons, 1996.

Dinshah, D. *Let There be Light, Sixth Ed*. Malaga, NJ: Din-shah Health Society, 1985.

Dufty, W. *Sugar Blues*. New York: Warner Books, 1975.

Free, W. and D. Wilcock. *The Reincarnation of Edgar Cayce?* Berkeley, CA: Frog Ltd., 2004.

Freer, N. *God Games: What Do You Do Forever?* Escon-dido, CA. The Book Tree, 1999.

Freke, T. and P. Gandy. *Jesus and the Lost Goddess*. New York: Three Rivers Press, 2001.

Fromm, E. *Escape from Freedom*. New York: Henry Holt & Co., 1941.

Gerber, R. *Vibrational Medicine*. Rochester, VT: Bear & Co., 2001.

Grabhorn, L. *Dear God, What Is Happening to Us?* Char-lottesville, VA: Hampton Roads, 2003.

Hancock, G. and S. Faiia. *Heavens' Mirror: Quest for the Lost Civilization*. Toronto, Ont.: Doubleday Canada, 1998.

Hawkins, D. *Power vs Force*. Carlsbad, CA: Hay House, 2002.

Hoffer, E. *The True Believer*. New York: Harper & Row, 1951.

Horowitz, L. *DNA: Pirates of the Sacred Spiral*. Rockport, MA: Tetrahedron Press, 2004.

Horowitz, L. *Emerging Viruses: AIDS and Ebola*. Rockport, MA. Tetrahedron Inc., 1996.

Howard, V. *The Mystic Path to Cosmic Power*. Pine, AZ: New Life Foundation, 1995.

Hunt, V. *Infinite Mind*. Malibu, CA: Malibu, 1989.

Huxley, A. *The Perennial Philosophy*. New York: Harper Collins, 1944.

Kervan, C. L. *Biological Transmutations*. Woodstock, NY: Beekman Publishers, Inc., 1998.

LaViolette, P. *Galactic Superwaves and Their Impact on Earth*. CD Rom. Alexandria, VA: Starlane Productions, 2001.

Marciniak, B. *Bringers of the Dawn*. Santa Fe, NM: Bear & Co., 1992.

Mercola, Dr. J., *No Grain Diet: Conquer Carbohydrate Addiction and Stay Slim for Life*. New York. Penguin Group, 2003

Oschman, J. *Energy Medicine: The Scientific Basis*. Edinburgh: Churchill Livingston, 2002.

Proctor, R. and A. *Healing Sick Homes*. Dublin: Gateway, 2000.

Renard, G. *The Disappearance of the Universe*. Carlsbad, CA: Hay House, 2003.

Rodale, J. I. *Natural Health, Sugar and the Criminal Mind*. New York: Pyramid Books, 1968.

Ruiz, D. M. *The Four Agreements*. San Raphael, CA: Amber-Allen Publishing, 1997.

Russell, P. *The Global Brain Awakens: Our Next Evolutionary Leap*. Palo Alto, Ca: Global Brain Inc., 1983.

Satprem. *Sri Aurobindo or the Adventure of Consciousness*. New York: The Institute for Evolutionary Research, 1984.

Sheldrake, R. *A New Science of Life: The Hypothesis of Morphic Resonance*. Rochester, VT: Park Street Press, 1981.

Silva, F. *Secrets in the Fields*. Charlottesville, VA: Hampton Roads, 2002.

Sitchin, Z. *The Twelfth Planet*. New York: Avon, 1976.

—————. *Genesis Revisited*. New York: Avon, 1990.

—————. *Earth Chronicles. Book 1: The 12th Planet; Book 2: The Stairway to Heaven; Book 3: The Wars of Gods and Men; Book 4: The Lost Realms; Book 5: When Time Began*. New York: Avon, 1976–1998.

Stray, G. *Beyond 2012: Catastrophe or Awakening?* Rochester, VT: Bear & Co., 2005.

Tolle, E. *The Power of Now*. Vancouver, BC: Namaste Publishing, 1999.

—————. *The New Earth*. New York: Penguin, 2005.

Tompkins, P. and C. Bird. *The Secret Life of Plants*. New York: Harper & Row, 1972.

Velikovsky, E. *Worlds in Collision*. Garden City, NY: Doubleday and Co., 1950.

Vitale, J. and I. H. Len. *Zero Limits*. New Jersey: Wiley, 2007.

Webre, A. O. *Exopolitics: Politics, Government and Law in the Universe*. Vancouver, BC: Universe Books, 2005.

Yukteswar, S. *The Holy Science*. Los Angeles: Self-Realization Fellowship, 1949.

WEB RESOURCES

www.youtube.com Find videos on any topic you can imagine, incuding the 2012 discussion. Search on "David Wilcock" for first-rate information on the Shift.

www.divinecosmos.com David Wilcock's home site.

www.meru.org Home for Stan Tenan's research into the scared geometries of light and language.

www.onenessuniversity.org Home of Sri Ammabaghavan (known as Sri Kalki in India) and the Oneness Movement, teachers of enlightenment and the Oneness Blessing.

www.calleman.com Home page of Carl Calleman, author of three books on the Mayan calendar; good source of up-to-date articles.

www.mercola.com An all-in-one source for alternative and natural healing information.

www.rolfgordon.co.uk Good source for information on geopathic stress, a hidden cause of disease.

www.bluesunenergetics.net David Ian Cowan and his wife Erina's home site. Take classes and join the newsletter.

www.heartmath.org Home of the Heart Math Institute; stellar research on heart-rate variability biofeedback with documented benefits.

ABOUT THE AUTHOR

STEPHEN Z PHOTOGRAPHY

DAVID IAN COWAN is a licensed Spiritual Health Coach who lives in Boulder, Colorado with his wife, Erina. He has morphed from a professional musician, counselor, alternative-health practitioner, and bio-feedback trainer into an author of and speaker on modern Spirituality. Together, the Cowans created *Blue Sun Energetics* in order to share some of the things you have read here through classes, webinars, and other publications, and to introduce cutting edge futuristic technologies. Currently, they offer classes in Spiritual Communication and Relationship Healing, and a certification program in Spiritual Dowsing. David invites your questions and comments, and also invites you to sign up for the newsletter on the website to stay updated on events, products, and other writings on topics of timely esoteric interest.

For more information or to email the author, please contact him at:

info@bluesunenergetics.net

or visit the website at:

www.bluesunenergetics.net

TO OUR READERS